The Student's Ovid

Selections from the *Metamorphoses*

With Introduction and Commentary by
Margaret Worsham Musgrove

University of Oklahoma Press : Norman

Library of Congress Cataloging-in-Publication Data

Ovid, 43 B.C.–17 or 18 A.D.
    [Metamorphoses. Selections]
    The student's Ovid : selections from the Metamorphoses / with an introduction
and commentary by Margaret Worsham Musgrove.
        p.   cm. — (Oklahoma series in classical culture; v. 26)
    Latin texts with English commentary.
    Includes bibliographical references.
    ISBN 0-8061-3219-1 (cloth)
    ISBN 0-8061-3220-5 (paper)
    1. Metamorphosis—Mythology—Poetry.   2. Mythology, Classical—Poetry.
3. Latin language—Readers.   4. Fables, Latin.   I. Title.   II. Series.
III. Musgrove, Margaret Worsham, 1962–

PA6519. M5 M87 2000
873′.01 21—dc21

                                                                        99-04581

The Student's Ovid: Selections from the "Metamorphoses" is Volume 26 in the
Oklahoma Series in Classical Culture.

The paper in this book meets the guidelines for permanence and durability of the
Committee on Production Guidelines for Book Longevity of the Council on
Library Resources. ∞

    2   3   4   5   6   7   8   9   10

Contents

Preface

This book grew out of my perception of the need for a text that would be useful for college Latin courses ranging from first reading courses (third and fourth semesters) to upper-division courses for Latin majors. In my experience, more advanced undergraduates may be able to read more lines of text per class session, but they still need some of the same kinds of help in their reading; their main needs, like those of their less experienced comrades, remain grammatical explanations, lexical hints, and clarification of Latin diction—not extensive literary or historical comments. Hence, the notes in the commentary focus upon problems that may be encountered by the relatively inexperienced reader of Latin poetry.

At the same time, college students deserve a Latin reading course that goes beyond the mere translation of a certain number of lines. Because most of our students today will not take more than three or four semesters of Latin, we may have to provide them with a meaningful experience of Latin literature during a stage when their reading skills are still rather uncertain. Hence, this book was designed so that teachers can help their students gain literary insight into an important work while their reading skills continue to improve.

This text is designed to be used in a variety of courses. Less experienced students may complete only a few of the stories, while more advanced students may be able to read many more. In either case, two problems will arise. First, the student's experience of the poem will be fragmentary or "choppy," as the stories that are read in the course may lack context. Second, the teacher may wish to read different stories from one term to the next, to serve students who take more than one Ovid course, or to prevent the course from becoming monotonous or stale (from the point of view of either the students or the teacher).

To remedy the problem of choppiness, it is desirable for students to read as much of the poem as possible in English beyond what is read in Latin. (A list of modern English translations of the *Metamorphoses* is provided in the bibliography.) But merely reading a translation of the entire *Metamorphoses,* with all its 250 stories, may not provide meaningful context for a handful of Latin stories; on the first reading, the poem in its entirety is somewhat overwhelming. Therefore, the teacher may wish to focus the course on a particular theme or a subset of stories from the complete poem. To assist the teacher in assembling thematic courses or units, **thematic lists** are provided. Six themes are suggested, with two kinds of story on each list: (1) stories included in this Latin text and (2) other stories not in this book, on the same theme, for reading in English.

The lists may be used in at least two ways. First, as suggested above, the teacher may choose to focus an entire course exclusively on **one theme.** It is understood that such an approach may give students a view of only one aspect of the poem, but at least that aspect can be treated in some depth, without the superficiality that comes from skipping around at random. Different themes may be chosen in different semesters, in accordance with the interests of the students or teacher. Alternatively, the teacher may select one or two Latin stories from each category, in order to introduce a **variety of themes,** and then assign other stories from each category to be read in English, to fill out each theme.

These lists are offered as **suggestions** or starting points. The themes presented here may strike the reader as conservative, even conventional, but I have intentionally chosen such themes in order that the connections between the stories on each list should be self-evident to most readers. I have avoided esoteric or idiosyncratic connections that might require extensive commentary or justification. All users of the book are free, are indeed encouraged, to compile alternative or personal lists that appeal to their own students' needs and their own interpretations of the poem. To avoid making the lists appear prescriptive, they have been placed in the introduction, and Latin passages in the book have not been arranged by theme but in the order in which they occur in the *Metamorphoses.*

Following one of the themes on the lists may thus entail skipping around in the textbook, so the commentaries on individual stories have been designed to be free-standing; notes on a story from Book 14, for example, do not assume knowledge of information that was conveyed in a note on a story from Book 1.

Finally, a note on the selection of the **Latin passages** included in the book. Only complete story units have been included; no ellipses skip over difficult or problematic portions of a story. Thus, students get a clear feel for the varying tones and paces of Ovid's narrative within a story. However, extremely long stories (those over about 150 lines) have been excluded, so that less experienced readers of Latin may complete at least several stories in the course of a term. The stories range from just over forty lines (Europa) to about 170 lines (Echo and Narcissus). Unfortunately, this limitation on length has resulted in the exclusion of some very important and entertaining stories. (Who could discuss the theme of "Mortal Daring" without the story of Phaethon? But his story is well over 300 lines long.) Thus, it is even more imperative that the teacher who wants to convey the real scope of the *Metamorphoses* supplement the Latin readings with readings in English translation. Almost any Latin passages will help improve students' Latin-reading skills, but careful planning is needed to improve skills such as synthesis, literary interpretation, and critical thinking.

Acknowledgments

This book would not have been possible without the support and asssistance of my friends and students at the University of Oklahoma and elsewhere. Special thanks are due to Cheryl Walker-Esbaugh, Richard Beck, and Melanie Rich, who read portions of the commentary, and to the many undergraduate Latin students who have served as guinea pigs. I am also extremely grateful for the support and encouragement of Kimberly Wiar, senior editor at the University of Oklahoma Press, of Susan Ford Wiltshire, editor of the Oklahoma Series in Classical Culture, and of the two readers for the Press.

Over the years, many people, either in person or in writing, have taught me about Latin literature and its interpretation. Outstanding among these are Sara Mack, Kenneth Reckford, Douglass Parker, W. S. Anderson, Denis Feeney, Betty Rose Nagle, and Stephen Hinds; without their writing and teaching I suspect I would have practically nothing to say about Ovid.

As I wrote the commentary, I discovered, however, that another line of influence was also directing me. While those scholars have taught me about the interpretation of literature, most of my commentary involved explaining the complexities of Latin grammar and syntax. As I searched for the best ways to explain troublesome words, phrases, and constructions, I realized that the words I was using came almost entirely from two sources, the two people who first taught me about Latin: Susan J. Fugate, my original Latin teacher in Austin, and the late Professor Gareth Morgan of the University of Texas, our mutual friend and mentor who died suddenly in 1996. Between them, they taught me almost everything I have ever really needed to know about the mechanics and linguistics of Latin, and it was not until I wrote this commentary that I fully realized the depth of my dependence on the foundations

xii *Acknowledgments*

provided by their talents, patience, expertise, and labors. It is to Susan and to the memory of Gareth that this book is dedicated, with affection and gratitude. *Sunt hic etiam sua praemia laudi.*

The Student's Ovid

Introduction

OVID: LIFE AND WORKS

LIFE

Ovid tells us a good deal about his life in his own works, especially in one poem, *Tristia* 4.10. He was born on March 20 in 43 B.C. Educated, like all privileged Romans of his day, with an emphasis on rhetoric and law, he was trained first in Rome and then in Greece by prominent rhetoricians and scholars. Ovid probably could have had a successful public career as a lawyer, judge, and speaker; Seneca the Elder writes that he himself heard the young Ovid declaim with great skill. Although Ovid served in a few minor judicial positions, he eventually abandoned this career path in favor of poetry—to the dismay of his father, as Ovid tells us.

During the next twenty years, Ovid became one of the most successful poets in Rome and moved in the literary circle of the patron Messala Corvinus. At the height of his success and literary powers, a mysterious disaster occurred, and the wrath of the Emperor Augustus fell upon the poet's head. For reasons still not fully understood, Ovid was sent into exile in the remote Black Sea town of Tomis. (Technically, Ovid's sentence was "relegation," not exile, for he was allowed to keep his citizenship and property, but the emperor specified the location to which he was sent; the barbaric region of Tomis was especially uncomfortable to the urbane poet.) Ovid himself is remarkably tight-lipped about the reasons for his banishment; his famous phrase of explanation, *carmen et error,* is almost as far as he goes. The *carmen* has long been thought to be his *Ars Amatoria,* which certainly did not fit into the emperor's campaign to restore traditional moral values, but this work had been published several years earlier. Over the centuries, the nature of Ovid's *error* has drawn wide speculation, ranging from the historically plausible to the ludicrous; a common theory makes the *error* something political, and perhaps something involved with the adultery case of the emperor's granddaughter Julia, also exiled in the same year. Despite years of pleading, Ovid never obtained a pardon and was forced to remain in exile even after Augustus' death in A.D. 14. Ovid himself died in Tomis in the A.D. 17 or 18.

MAJOR WORKS

Ovid made his reputation as a writer of love poetry in elegiac couplets. His first published collection, the *Amores,* continues the tradition of the previous generation of love elegists, especially Propertius and Tibullus. The poet writes in the voice of a man involved with an apparently manipulative woman, although the poetic lover of the *Amores* manipulates the conventions of the genre and the depictions of his woman in a most flagrant way. The three-book version of the *Amores* that we have is a second edition, published sometime after 16 B.C.

Ovid also experimented with a variety of uses of the elegiac couplet. Among the boldest experiments is his *Epistulae Heroidum,* "Letters from Heroines," a collection of poetic letters from mythological heroines to their absent or departed lovers. In these letters, Ovid attempts to write in a feminine voice, weaving together "lives" based on the whole corpus of earlier literature for characters such as Penelope, Medea, Aridane, and Dido.

Another experiment was Ovid's mock didactic poem, the *Ars Amatoria,* "The Art of Love," and its sequel, the *Remedia Amoris,* "The Cure for Love." Purporting to be a handbook on catching and keeping a lover, the *Ars* is notable for its irreverent attitude toward love, toward Roman institutions (triumphs are recommended as good places to meet potential lovers), and toward its dignified literary predecessors (the didactic poems of Hesiod and Vergil).

At the time his exile was decreed, Ovid was essentially finished with the *Metamorphoses* (discussed below) and was halfway through the *Fasti*. The latter is a poetic calendar of Roman holidays, with explanations of the folklore and mythology behind them; Ovid completed six books, covering the first six months of the year. In these books, we can see him wrestling with ways of approaching the politically delicate subject of the state religion, which had been revived and reformed by Augustus. The *Fasti* also shows Ovid's interest in Alexandrian Greek poetic style, especially the *Aetia* ("Causes") of Callimachus, another poem explaining why things are as they are.

After his exile Ovid wrote two collections of poetry, the *Tristia* ("Sorrows") and the *Epistulae ex Ponto* ("Letters from the Black Sea"). These works, most written in the form of letters to Ovid's wife and friends, attempt to defend or excuse his past writings and plead with his friends in Rome to lobby for the poet's recall. But even in his recantations of earlier works and in his addresses to the Emperor, Ovid maintains something of the same irreverence and cleverness that must have gotten him into trouble in the first place. Gloomy though his subject matter and mood may have been in Tomis, the exiled Ovid is still the same brilliant and imaginative poet we see in the earlier works.

Ovid also wrote, at some point in his career, a tragedy, *Medea,* which has not survived. It seems to have been quite successful and was admired by ancient critics.

THE *METAMORPHOSES*

THE *METAMORPHOSES* AND OVID'S EARLIER WORKS

Some of the themes and techniques we find in the *Metamorphoses* are prefigured in Ovid's earlier works; all reveal a tension between the traditions of his literary predecessors and his own innovations. The first poem of the *Amores* begins with an image of the poet forced to abandon serious epic poetry in favor of light elegiac writing. Ovid works patently in the tradition of the previous generation of Latin love elegists, but he also meditates constantly on the balance of genres in his own poetry, a topic that will be addressed in the opening lines of the *Metamorphoses* and through-out the whole poem. In the *Epistulae Heroidum,* Ovid first displays the incredibly bold combination of genres that will be seen in the *Metamorphoses.* Poetic epistles may have had a history, as did solil-oquies by mythological heroines, mainly in tragedy, but combining the written form of the letter with the psychological monologue of drama is Ovid's innovation. The *Epistulae Heroidum* also shows Ovid's interest in reworking some of the best-known mythological stories from different perspectives, filling in gaps in the stories and presenting them from the viewpoint of characters not usually heard from (for example, letting Penelope recount her own thoughts during Ulysses' absence). This emphasis on new versions of old stories, as well as on feminine psychology, persists in the *Meta-morphoses.* In the *Ars Amatoria* and the *Fasti,* Ovid experiments with the creation of a narrative voice that can, on its own, unify the poem. The *Ars* presents a so-called unreliable narrator, in this case a Love Doctor whose learning is put to bad use and whose advice is dubious. The *Fasti* is narrated by an antiquarian investigator, whose voice, explaining how he came upon the information, intrudes repeatedly into the narrative to illustrate his control of the poem. The *Metamorphoses* contain both kinds of narrators, the internal ones of doubtful reliability, and the primary narrator, whose voice controls the poem as well as the reader's response to it.

STYLE OF THE POEM

A major difference between Ovid's earlier works and the *Meta-morphoses* is in the meter. Prior to the *Metamorphoses* (and also afterwards), all of Ovid's poetry is written in elegiac couplets, a meter thought appropriate to lighter, less serious subjects such as love poetry. The *Metamorphoses,* however, is written in dactylic hexameter, the meter of epic, the most serious and prestigious of genres. (On the form of this meter, see the appendix.) While this switch from elegiac couplet to dactylic hexameter may seem to us a purely technical decision, it has a dramatic effect on the position of Ovid's poem. The poet seems to be setting himself a great challenge, to write in a loftier meter and style and on a vaster scale, while not abandoning the features that made him successful in elegy.

In fact, epic, both in Ovid's hands and in its previous manifestations, turns out to be a much more flexible genre than we might imagine. While the most prominent authors of epic poetry in the Greek and Latin traditions are Homer and Vergil, and the standard topics of epic are wars, heroic journeys, and Roman history, other levels and styles of epic exist in both Greek and Latin. Didactic (instructive) epic had a history going back to Hesiod, a Greek poet probably only slightly younger than Homer, and continued most prominently in Latin by Lucretius' philosophical poem *De Rerum Natura* (*On the Nature of Things*), and Vergil's *Georgics,* on farming. Dactylic hexameter per se had not been rejected by the anti-epic Alexandrian Greek poets, such as Callimachus, and was also the meter of even less serious poetry, such as the Latin satire. Ovid attempts to subsume all these traditions of dactylic poetry into his *Metamorphoses.* At various times, the poem treats epic battles, heroic journeys, and historical topics, but it also presents philosophy, satirical invective, and Alexandrian mini-epic. The traditional length of epic gave Ovid the opportunity to experiment with mingling all these genres and styles into one continuous work, made unique by his own process of interweaving.

As the synopsis below shows, the *Metamorphoses* flows in a meandering path from beginning to end. While the current text removes stories from their narrative settings, the reader should be alert for the **connections between stories.** The reader should always be aware of which stories precede and follow a given story, and whether a story fits into an ongoing sequence of similar tales. For instance, the story of Io should be compared with other tales of divine rapes, such as the immediately preceding tale of Daphne and the later stories of Callisto and Europa. Only by comparing Ovid's different variations on a theme can we understand what he is doing with that theme.

Another notable feature of Ovid's narrative is the variety of his **transitions** from one story to another. When the stories are separated in a text such as this one, this variety among his transitions may cause the beginning of each selection to seem somewhat obscure; the notes attempt to explain the context in which each story is begun, but sometimes it may be helpful to read a translation of the preceding story before beginning the Latin passage.

One of Ovid's great talents is his ability to present stories from different **points of view.** Sometimes he uses internal narrators to give a particular perspective to a story; the woman-hating Orpheus of Book 10 and the self-interested Cephalus of Book 7 are examples of narrators whose perspectives should always be remembered as their tales are read. Sometimes Ovid retells a familiar story from a novel point of view; for example, the Homeric story of how Circe turned Ulysses' men into pigs—told by the hero himself in Homer—is retold in the *Metamorphoses* by one of the men who actually became a pig. Sometimes Ovid even switches from one perspective to another and back within a single story; the divine rape stories are masterpieces of this technique, showing now the god's perspective, now the victim's, and now the jealous Juno's or an external observer's. This inconsistency has been criticized for creating an unevenness of tone, but these variations should not be seen as mere caprice, but rather examined for the insight that they may provide into the characters, their stories, or their literary histories.

Finally, the reader should remember that most of Ovid's stories have been told before, usually in very famous works. Almost every story in the *Metamorphoses* can be illuminated by a reading of one of its **literary ancestors,** whether Greek or Latin (except those stories for which Ovid's version is the only one that has survived). Some of Ovid's funniest jokes and some of his deepest statements about literature can be appreciated only by comparing his version with its model; a comparison of Ovid's story of Orpheus in *Metamorphoses* 10 with the version in Vergil's fourth *Georgic* provides examples of both jokes and literary commentary. Whenever possible, the reader should seek to learn something about other works that treat the story being read in Ovid.

STRUCTURE OF THE POEM

The *Metamorphoses* consists of fifteen books, a total of about twelve thousand verses. In the course of the poem, about 250 stories are recounted, most (but not all) of which end with a transformation of some kind. The most common is the aetiological metamorphosis, which tells how a certain species or natural feature came to be. The stories are almost all known from previous literary sources, but are of varying familiarity, some as traditional as Medea, others as obscure as Canens; a few seem to have been made up by Ovid. The arrangement of the stories is generally chronological, from the creation of the world to the deification of Julius Caesar, although during the long mythical generations the chronological arrangement is not dominant or consistent. Many other features serve to unite various sections of the poem: themes (such as the jealousy of the gods), characters (Orpheus, narrator of most of the stories in Book 10), genealogy (the Theban royal family, subject of most of the stories in Books 3–4), or even literary models (the running story of Aeneas' travels in Books 13–14, following the outline of Vergil's narrative). In general, attempts to find one dominant theme in the whole of the *Metamorphoses* have been thwarted, probably by the poet's own design.

A general outline of the poem inevitably becomes mired in specifics. The scheme that follows covers broad themes and cycles of stories, without detailing all the individual stories.

After a brief introduction, Book 1 begins with a somewhat vague and condensed narrative of the creation of the universe, its subsequent arrangement, and the development of human civilization. When humans become too sinful, as evidenced by the behavior of the king Lycaon, Jupiter sends a great flood to wipe out all humans except the virtuous couple Deucalion and Pyrrha. These two repopulate the earth with stones that change into humans, ancestors of the earth's current inhabitants.

The rest of Book 1 and all of Book 2 concern relations between gods and mortals. Bridging the division between Books 1 and 2 is the story of the Sun-god's child Phaethon, who attempts to do the job of a god, driving his father's chariot across the sky, and fails tragically. Especially prominent in Books 1 and 2 are stories that recount sexual liaisons between male gods and female humans or nymphs; Apollo, Jupiter, and Mercury are all depicted as rapists, potential rapists, or lovers in less than dignified situations.

Books 3 and 4 are organized around a human dynasty, the royal family of Thebes, but relations between humans and gods are still a major issue. The Theban royals Actaeon and Semele suffer at the hands of gods, and the king Pentheus is killed as punishment for his denial of the divinity of Bacchus. Set into these family tragedies are the stories of Echo and Narcissus and the exotic-erotic stories told for amusement by the Minyeides, who also scorn Bacchus and are eventually punished.

Late in Book 4 and throughout Book 5, Ovid recounts his first stories of a major heroic figure, Perseus. All the adventures of Perseus *except* his best-known one, the killing of Medusa, are narrated at length, especially his rescue of the princess Andromeda and his marriage to her. At their wedding feast, a battle breaks out between Perseus and a former suitor of Andromeda's; this battle is one of the goriest episodes in the poem.

In the remainder of Book 5, several themes come together: punishment of human daring, divine sexuality, and storytelling. Minerva visits the Muses, who tell her of a recent singing competition between themselves and a group of nine human sisters (changed into magpies for their hybristic challenge). The Muses' entry, which is repeated for Minerva, told of the rape of Proserpina (Persephone) by Pluto.

Stories of human daring and evil continue in Book 6 with the stories of two women, Arachne and Niobe, who challenge goddesses and are punished, although perhaps excessively. Again, sex and violence are prominent: Arachne's tale includes several small inset stories of gods' liaisons with mortal women, while Niobe's tale depicts the various gory deaths of her fourteen children. The rest of Book 6 continues in this vein, recounting the story of Tereus, Procne, and Philomela, an exclusively human tale of rape, jealousy, and murderous vengeance.

Book 7 continues the focus on human affairs. Another heroic tale emerges, the story of Jason and Medea, but, as in the case of Perseus, the most famous of their exploits—the voyage of the *Argo,* the Golden Fleece, Medea's infanticide—receive little or no mention. Instead, Ovid depicts the beginning of their love affair, Medea's magical trick on the daughters of Pelias, and her flying-chariot journey to Athens. This journey transfers the narrative to Athens; this city's war with King Minos of Crete provides the context for the next several stories. These include the tale of the plague of Aegina and the troubled marriage of Cephalus, king of Athens, and his wife, Procris.

Book 8 opens with another episode from Minos' war, in which the princess Scylla falls in love with Minos, betrays her father for him, and is then rejected by him. (Scylla's story recapitulates some of the untold portion of Medea's story; a sequence of lovestruck heroines appears in Books 7–10: Medea, Scylla, Byblis, and Myrrha.) The Crete-Athens connection continues with the story of Daedalus, an Athenian who builds wings to escape from Crete, but loses his son on the way. The story again returns to Athens and its national hero Theseus, who goes off to join in the Calydonian Boar Hunt, a cooperative project of numerous mythological heroes. (Like Perseus, Theseus is depicted only on his less famous adventures.) Returning from the Hunt, Theseus' company is blocked by the flooded river Achelous; while waiting, the river god and his guests entertain themselves with various stories.

Achelous' narrative continues into Book 9 and introduces the adventures of another hero, Hercules. Several episodes of Hercules' life are recounted (but not, of course, his Twelve Labors), ending with the story of his death and then of his birth. The rest of Book 9 is concerned with stories of unusual erotic situations: first, Byblis, a girl in love with her brother, and then Iphis, a girl raised as a boy and granted a sex change on the eve of her wedding.

Book 10 is devoted to Orpheus and his songs. After failing to recover his wife from the underworld, Orpheus proceeds to sing a variety of songs, which focus, as did the last stories of Book 9, on unusual erotic adventures, both of humans and of gods: Apollo's tragic loss of his lover Hyacinthus; Pygmalion's love for his statue woman; Myrrha's incestuous affair with her father; and Venus' relationship with Adonis.

Book 11 finishes the story of Orpheus, with his death at the hands of Maenads. Then come two stories of the foolish King Midas, whom both Bacchus and Apollo punish. As Ovid begins his approach to the Trojan War, Ovid tells how Apollo traveled to the site of Troy and built walls for the treacherous king Laomedon. The prehistory of the Trojan War continues with the courtship of Peleus and Thetis, parents of Achilles. Peleus encounters King Ceyx, about whom several stories are told, including his tragic death at sea and his faithful wife's mourning. Finally, a story is told of Aesacus, Priam's son, who became a bird.

Book 12 begins the story of the Trojan War and its aftermath, which will include the voyages of Aeneas and Ulysses, continuing into Book 14. Following an outline of the prewar and pre-Homeric events, such as the sacrifice of Iphigenia at Aulis, Ovid recounts an early battle of Achilles against a supposedly invulnerable man, Cygnus. After this victory, Achilles listens to Nestor tell the story of an earlier battle, that between the Centaurs and the Lapiths, where another invulnerable man, Caeneus, fought. This Centaur battle (another of Ovid's long and gory showpieces, outdoing even the Perseus episode of Book 4) is followed by the account of the death of Achilles, whose Homeric exploits are omitted.

Like Book 12, Book 13 is dominated by an extremely long piece, the two speeches by Ajax and Ulysses, who vie to inherit the weapons of Achilles. During their speeches, they recall numerous Iliadic episodes. Ulysses wins the debate, and Ajax commits suicide. After various postwar episodes (mainly the tragedy of Hecuba), Ovid begins his version of the journey of Aeneas, who escapes from Troy's ruin. Various minor episodes or allusions from Vergil's *Aeneid* are expanded into major episodes (e.g., the story of King Anius of Delos), while major Vergilian episodes (e.g., Dido) are given only the briefest of mentions.

A major digression from the Aeneas story bridges the division between Books 13 and 14: the story of the nymph Scylla, before she became a monster, and of her friend Galatea, who was once courted by the Cyclops Polyphemus. These stories introduce characters otherwise known from Homer's *Odyssey*, such as the Cyclops, Ulysses, and Circe.

Book 14 continues the story of Aeneas, which blends into the story of the *Odyssey,* as Aeneas and his men are told about Ulysses' adventures with the Cyclops and with Circe. As in Vergil, Aeneas lands in Italy and fights a war with Turnus and the natives. Another Vergilian episode, in which the Italians ask the Greek hero Diomedes for aid, is expanded by Ovid so that Diomedes can tell the story of his own wanderings. Aeneas' war in Italy then concludes. Later, Aeneas himself dies and becomes a god. Ovid has thus moved from Greek mythology to the world of Roman historical legend, represented by a list of the kings of Alba Longa and by the story of two Italian deities, Pomona and Vertumnus. Finally, Book 14 ends with the reign, death, and deification of Romulus.

In Book 15, the second king of Rome, Numa, travels in search of wisdom and is told of the extensive teachings of the philosopher Pythagoras, who expounded upon reincarnation, vegetarianism, and the rise and fall of empires (including Rome). More legends of early Rome follow: Virbius (who is really the Greek Hippolytus reborn), Cipus (a man who refused to become king), and the journey of the god Aesculapius from Greece to Rome. Finally, having made the transition to his own times, Ovid can describe the deification of Julius Caesar and anticipate the deification of Augustus. The poem then ends with a prophecy of Ovid's own immortality, through the immortality of his poetry. Thus, the sequence of mortals who become immortal is completed: Hercules (Book 9), Aeneas and Romulus (Book 14), Caesar, Augustus, and . . . Ovid (Book 15).

THEMATIC LISTS

See the preface for notes on use of these lists. Some stories appear under more than one theme.

Latin Stories in This Text   *Other Stories*

GODS IN LOVE

Latin Stories in This Text	Other Stories
Daphne	Callisto
Io	Aglauros
Europa	Clytie
Semele	Proserpina
Boreas and Orithyia	Hyacinthus
The Sibyl	Acis and Galatea
	Scylla and Glaucus
	Pomona and Vertumnus

DIVINE ANGER

The Flood	Lycaon
Io	Callisto
Semele	Raven and Crow
Lycian Farmers	Battus
Boreas and Orithyia	Tiresias
Midas	Actaeon
Diomedes	Pentheus
	Athamas and Ino
	Arachne
	Niobe
	Marsyas
	Birth of Herculer

MORTAL DARING

Cadmus	Phaethon
Perseus and Andromeda	Calydonian Boar Hunt
Medea's Magic	Achelous and Hercules
Daedalus and Icarus	Achilles and Cygnus
Orpheus	Lapiths and Centaurs
	Archaemenides

HUMAN LOVE

Deucalion and Pyrrha	Cephalus and Procris
Echo and Narcissus	Scylla and Minos
Pyramus and Thisbe	Baucis and Philomon

Orpheus	Byblis
Pygmalion	Myrrha
	Atalanta and Hippomenes
	Ceyx and Alcyone
	Picus and Canens
	Iphis and Anaxarete

HUMAN INIQUITY

Lycian Farmers	Aglauros
Medea's Magic	Pentheus
Daedalus and Perdix	Tereus, Procne, and Philomela
Midas	Erysichthon
Diomedes	Byblis
	Myrrha
	Hecuba

COSMIC EVENTS

Creation	Deification of Hercules
The Flood	Deification of Aeneas
Deucalion and Pyrrha	Deification of Romulus
Deification of Caesar	

GRAMMATICAL INTRODUCTION

POETIC FORMS AND USAGE

Note should be made of several Latin forms and usages that are more common in poetry than in prose and that may not have been encountered in introductory courses; likewise, students whose reading experience is limited to Latin prose may not be familiar with these poetic conventions. **The following six categories of forms and usage should be learned and recognized.** The poetic forms do not replace the more common forms but are alternatives to them.

1. The third-declension accusative plural, masculine and feminine, in -*īs* instead of -*ēs*. Vowel quantity is particularly

important in this form, so that it can be distinguished from the
-is of the genitive singular. Notes attempt to point out the
quantity of the vowel when the form may cause problems.

2. Second-declension genitive plural in *-um* instead of *-ōrum.*
This form is especially common in words such as *deum* (for
deōrum) and *superum* (for *superōrum*).

3. Syncopated verb forms, in which the syllable *-vi-* or *-ve-* drops
out of the middle of a form, usually a perfect-stem form: e.g.,
optasse for *optavisse*, or *formarat* for *formaverat*. Notes point
out this form when it occurs.

4. Third-person-plural, perfect active indicative, ending in *-ēre*
instead of *-ērunt.* This form should *not* be mistaken for an
infinitive; the ending is affixed to the *perfect* stem and can
occur in all conjugations, not just those that might have
infinitives in *-ēre*. For example, notice the difference between
the present infinitive *habēre* and the third-plural perfect form
habuēre, a variant of *habuērunt.* Notes point out this form
when it occurs.

5. Omission of forms of *sum.* This omission can take place when
the form of *sum* is the main verb or an infinitive, or when *sum*
is the auxiliary in a compound verb form (as in the perfect
passive). For example, *visum* may be short for *visum est.*
When a sentence lacks a verb, it is usually a good idea to try
supplying an appropriate form of *sum.*

6. Use of plural nouns to express a singular idea and singular
nouns to express a plural idea; for example, *colla dabat retro:*
"he drew back his neck(s)." Notes point this out.

**These additional habits of poetry should also be studied for
familiarity.**

1. Use of the dative to complete the meaning of compound verbs
(where prose may prefer a prepositional phrase). Example:
circumdat vincula collo ("he puts chains around her neck").

2. Omission of prepositions in expressions of place: accusative
without preposition, to express "place to which," used with

common as well as proper nouns (limited to some proper nouns in prose); ablative without preposition to show "place where"; ablative without preposition to show "place from which."

3. Accusative of specification or respect, especially with a part of body: *tectus caligine vultum* "covered by fog *with respect to his face*" ("with his face covered by fog"); *nuda pedem* "naked with respect to her foot" ("barefooted").

4. Ablative of source to show parentage, with words such as *satus, natus, editus, creatus, ortus.* Examples: *satus Iapeto* ("the one fathered by Iapetus" = Prometheus); *Agenore natus* ("the one born from Agenor" = Cadmus).

5. Negative commands: where prose normally uses *noli(te)* + infinitive, poetry may also use a variety of other constructions: *ne* + present subjunctive; *ne* + imperative; or some synonym of *noli* (such as *mitte*) + infinitive. Examples: *ne . . . patiare* ("don't allow"); *ne fuge me* ("don't run away from me"); *mitte precari* ("cease to pray" = "don't pray").

6. Use of the passive voice in a reflexive sense, sometimes called "middle voice," after Greek usage. Example: *volvuntur in aequora* ("they roll themselves down to the sea"). Often, these verb forms are associated with an accusative of respect (see above): *induitur pallam* ("she girds herself in a cloak").

7. Periphrasis of names, usually for poetic effect. Ovid often calls people by patronymics (names based on their father's name: *Pelides,* "son of Peleus" = Achilles), or by adjectives describing their parentage or geographical origin (*Sidonius heros,* "the Sidonian [Phoenician] hero" = Cadmus; *Cythereius heros,* "the Cytherean hero" = son of Venus = Aeneas).

8. Occasional archaic forms, such as *ausim* for *ausus sim* or *faxo* for *fecero.*

POETIC WORD ORDER

Word order is generally much freer in poetry than in prose. Arrangement of the words is part of the poet's artistry. In reading

Latin poetry, it is even more necessary than in prose to rely on case endings to determine a word's syntactical function. Also, some word order in poetry separates or reverses words that are always seen together or in a certain order in prose. The following habits of poetry should be noted:

1. Separation of nouns and their modifiers, often by some distance; poetry especially tends to place the adjective before the noun.
2. Chiastic and interlocked word arrangement: adjective a, adjective b, noun b, noun a; or adjective a, adjective b, noun a, noun b. Examples: non bene **iunctarum** *discordia semina* **rerum**; *mollia* **securae** peragebant *otia* **gentes**.
3. Placement of prepositions *after* their objects: *umbras . . . recentes inter* ("among the fresh ghosts").
4. Postponing of words introducing a clause, often to second position, sometimes later. Such words include relative pronouns, subordinating conjunctions (such as *ut* or *cum*), and coordinating conjunctions (*et*): *peregrinum ut viseret orbem* ("in order to visit foreign lands"); *geminas qui separat Arctos* ("which separates the twin Bears").
5. A relative clause preceding its antecedent: *et, quae deciderant arbore, glandes* ("and acorns, which had fallen from the tree").
6. *Tmesis* ("cutting"): the separation of elements of a compound word normally seen together. Example: *postquam* and *antequam* may appear as *post . . . quam* and *ante . . . quam*.

DECLENSION OF GREEK PROPER NOUNS

Because most of Ovid's stories come from Greek sources, he was obliged to include many Greek names of people and places in his poetry. (All educated Romans of his day read Greek.) This text does not assume that students will learn to decline Greek nouns; therefore, the notes identify Greek forms when they occur.

The following examples of representative Greek proper nouns are provided as a guide. Students may want to become accustomed to some Greek forms in order to read more quickly. One useful rule to remember for the recognition of Greek nouns is the -*n* or -*a* as the symbol of the accusative singular. Many forms of Greek nouns are Latinized (as they must be when they appear in the ablative case, which is lacking in Greek). Most Greek proper nouns encountered in Ovid are singular.

First-declension nouns: These include both masculines (generally in -*ēs* and -*as*) and feminines (in -*ē*); note especially the patronymics in -*idēs*.

nom.	Cyllenē (f.)	Aeneas (m.)	Promethidēs (m.)
gen.	Cyllenēs	Aeneae	Promethidae
dat.	Cyllenae	Aeneae	Promethidae
acc.	Cyllenēn	Aenean	Promethidēn
abl.	Cyllenē	Aeneā	Promethidē

Second-declension nouns: These almost all have regular Latin endings, except for the -*n* in the accusative singular. Greek nouns in -*os* may be masculine or, sometimes, feminine; neuters end in -*n*.

nom.	Delos (m.)	Lesbos (f.)	Ilion (n.)
gen.	Deli	Lesbi	Ilii
dat.	Delo	Lesbo	Ilio
acc.	Delon (-um)	Lesbon	Ilion
abl.	Delo	Lesbo	Ilio

Third-declension nouns: These nouns are notable for their stem changes and for the -*a* in their accusative singular. Genitive singular forms sometimes have the Latin -*is* and sometimes the Greek -*os*. When these nouns appear in the plural, the nominative -*es* and the accusative -*as* have short vowels. Other forms have regular Latin endings.

nom.	Atlas (m.)	Naïs (f. sing.)	Naïdes (f. pl.)
gen.	Atlantis	Naïdos	Naïdum
dat.	Atlanti	Naïdi	Naïdibus

acc.	Atlanta	Naïda	Naïdas
abl.	Atlante	Naïde	Naïdibus

Third-declension common nouns, seen frequently with Greek accusatives: *aer* (acc. *aera*) and *aether* (acc. *aethera*).

SELECT BIBLIOGRAPHY

TRANSLATIONS

A number of new English translations of Ovid's works have been published in the last several years. The most recent translations of the *Metamorphoses* are those of David Slavitt (Baltimore, 1994) and Allen Mandelbaum (New York, 1993). Also available are the verse translations of A. D. Melville (Oxford, 1986), Horace Gregory (New York, 1958), and Rolfe Humphries (Bloomington, Ind., 1955), and the Penguin series' prose translation by Mary Innes (1955). The choice of a particular translation is a matter of individual taste. Any of these will serve the purpose of familiarizing students with the complete poem or with the gist of individual stories; none captures the tone of Ovid's poetic voice or the music of the Latin.

Because students may want to compare the *Metamorphoses* with Ovid's other works, here is a list of modern translations of each of his other major works.

Ars Amatoria, Remedia Amoris, and *Amores: The Love Poems,* translated by A. D. Melville (Oxford, 1990).
Heroides: Ovid's Heroines, translated by Daryl Hine (New Haven, 1991).
Tristia: Sorrows of an Exile, translated by A. D. Melville (Oxford, 1992).
Fasti: Ovid's Fasti: Roman Holidays, translated by Betty Rose Nagle (Bloomington, Ind., 1995).

All of Ovid's works are available in Harvard's Loeb series, with Latin text and facing English translation.

SECONDARY STUDIES

General books in English on the *Metamorphoses* are few. Listed below are three that are notable for their comprehensive and accessible treatment of the entire poem.

Otis, Brooks. *Ovid as an Epic Poet,* 2d edition. Cambridge, 1970.
Galinsky, Karl. *Ovid's Metamorphoses: An Introduction to the Basic Aspects.* Berkeley, 1975.
Solodow, Joseph B. *The World of Ovid's Metamorphoses.* Chapel Hill, N.C., 1988.

A few other books may also be recommended to provide background on Ovid and the *Metamorphoses.* Gian Biagio Conte's excellent survey of Latin literary history is available in English as *Latin Literature: A History,* translated by Joseph B. Solodow (Baltimore, 1994). The Latin Literature volume of the *Cambridge History of Classical Literature* (1982) contains a chapter on Ovid by E. J. Kenney. Sara Mack's *Ovid* in the Hermes series from Yale (New Haven, 1988) is a general introduction to all the poet's works and to his influence on later literature. Some topics related to the *Metamorphoses* are discussed in D. C. Feeney, *The Gods in Epic* (Oxford, 1991), and in P. M. C. Forbes Irving, *Metamorphosis in Greek Myths* (Oxford, 1990).

Finally, three books may be consulted for information on Ovid's immense influence on later literature: the classic E. K. Rand, *Ovid and His Influence* (New York, 1963); a more recent collection of essays, edited by W. S. Anderson, *Ovid: The Classical Heritage* (New York, 1995); and another collection edited by Charles Martindale, *Ovid Renewed* (Cambridge, 1988), which treats Ovid's influence on both literature and art.

A NOTE ON THE TEXT

This book, being a collection only of portions of the *Metamorphoses*, has not attempted to create a new critical edition. The text printed here is the Loeb edition of F. J. Miller (Books I–VIII: 2d edition, 1921; Books IX–XV: 1st edition, 1916). In general, I have attempted not to make changes in the Loeb's readings. In a few passages, where Miller's text seems obviously erroneous and where other, more recent, editions provide a better reading, I have made small changes in single words or in punctuation. In very troubled or notorious passages (e.g., 1.2 or 1.543–547), I have left the Loeb text as it stands and have discussed the problem briefly in the note; the chief aim of such notes has been to provide a text *that the student can read* and not necessarily to introduce the student to the complications of Ovidian textual criticism or to make a complete, scholarly case for the reading presented. In choosing solutions to textual problems, I have been guided primarily by the revised Loeb of G. P. Goold, by the Teubner edition of W. S. Anderson, and by the commentaries of Franz Bömer. (The Latin text printed here retains the Loeb's convention of using lowercase letters to begin sentences, except at the beginning of paragraphs.)

The notes in the commentary mark vowels with a macron where it is most likely to clarify form or vocabulary. Not all vowels are marked in the notes, but I have made a special effort to mark vowels and adjective endings where quantity can often help identify case. Students are encouraged to learn quantities of vowels, especially in these endings, to take advantage of these notes.

Latin Texts

1

Introduction and Creation: 1.1–150

In nova fert animus mutatas dicere formas
corpora; di, coeptis (nam vos mutastis et illas)
adspirate meis primaque ab origine mundi
ad mea perpetuum deducite tempora carmen!
Ante mare et terras et quod tegit omnia caelum   5
unus erat toto naturae vultus in orbe,
quem dixere chaos: rudis indigestaque moles
nec quicquam nisi pondus iners congestaque eodem
non bene iunctarum discordia semina rerum.
nullus adhuc mundo praebebat lumina Titan,   10
nec nova crescendo reparabat cornua Phoebe,
nec circumfuso pendebat in aere tellus
ponderibus librata suis, nec bracchia longo
margine terrarum porrexerat Amphitrite;
utque erat et tellus illic et pontus et aer,   15
sic erat instabilis tellus, innabilis unda,
lucis egens aer; nulli sua forma manebat,
obstabatque aliis aliud, quia corpore in uno
frigida pugnabant calidis, umentia siccis,
mollia cum duris, sine pondere, habentia pondus.   20
  Hanc deus et melior litem natura diremit.
nam caelo terras et terris abscidit undas
et liquidum spisso secrevit ab aere caelum.
quae postquam evolvit caecoque exemit acervo,
dissociata locis concordi pace ligavit: 25
ignea convexi vis et sine pondere caeli
emicuit summaque locum sibi fecit in arce;
proximus est aer illi levitate locoque;
densior his tellus elementaque grandia traxit

25

et pressa est gravitate sua; circumfluus umor   30
ultima possedit solidumque coercuit orbem.
   Sic ubi dispositam quisquis fuit ille deorum
congeriem secuit sectamque in membra coegit,
principio terram, ne non aequalis ab omni
parte foret, magni speciem glomeravit in orbis.   35
tum freta diffundi rapidisque tumescere ventis
iussit et ambitae circumdare litora terrae;
addidit et fontes et stagna inmensa lacusque
fluminaque obliquis cinxit declivia ripis,
quae, diversa locis, partim sorbentur ab ipsa,   40
in mare perveniunt partim campoque recepta
liberioris aquae pro ripis litora pulsant.
iussit et extendi campos, subsidere valles,
fronde tegi silvas, lapidosos surgere montes,
utque duae dextra caelum totidemque sinistra   45
parte secant zonae, quinta est ardentior illis,
sic onus inclusum numero distinxit eodem
cura dei, totidemque plagae tellure premuntur.
quarum quae media est, non est habitabilis aestu;
nix tegit alta duas; totidem inter utramque locavit   50
temperiemque dedit mixta cum frigore flamma.
   Inminet his aer, qui quanto est pondere terrae,
pondere aquae levior, tanto est onerosior igni.
illic et nebulas, illic consistere nubes
iussit et humanas motura tonitrua mentes   55
et cum fulminibus facientes frigora ventos.
   His quoque non passim mundi fabricator habendum
aera permisit; vix nunc obsistitur illis,
cum sua quisque regat diverso flamina tractu,
quin lanient mundum; tanta est discordia fratrum.   60
Eurus ad Auroram Nabataeaque regna recessit
Persidaque et radiis iuga subdita matutinis;
vesper et occiduo quae litora sole tepescunt,
proxima sunt Zephyro; Scythiam septemque triones
horrifer invasit Boreas; contraria tellus   65

nubibus adsiduis pluviaque madescit ab Austro.
haec super inposuit liquidum et gravitate carentem
aethera nec quicquam terrenae faecis habentem.
   Vix ita limitibus dissaepserat omnia certis,
cum, quae pressa diu fuerant caligine caeca,   70
sidera coeperunt toto effervescere caelo;
neu regio foret ulla suis animalibus orba,
astra tenent caeleste solum formaeque deorum,
cesserunt nitidis habitandae piscibus undae,
terra feras cepit, volucres agitabilis aer.   75
   Sanctius his animal mentisque capacius altae
deerat adhuc et quod dominari in cetera posset:
natus homo est, sive hunc divino semine fecit
ille opifex rerum, mundi melioris origo,
sive recens tellus seductaque nuper ab alto   80
aethere cognati retinebat semina caeli.
quam satus Iapeto, mixtam pluvialibus undis,
finxit in effigiem moderantum cuncta deorum,
pronaque cum spectent animalia cetera terram,
os homini sublime dedit caelumque videre   85
iussit et erectos ad sidera tollere vultus:
sic, modo quae fuerat rudis et sine imagine, tellus
induit ignotas hominum conversa figuras.
   Aurea prima sata est aetas, quae vindice nullo,
sponte sua, sine lege fidem rectumque colebat.   90
poena metusque aberant, nec verba minantia fixo
aere legebantur, nec supplex turba timebat
iudicis ora sui, sed erant sine iudice tuti.
nondum caesa suis, peregrinum ut viseret orbem,
montibus in liquidas pinus descenderat undas,   95
nullaque mortales praeter sua litora norant;
nondum praecipites cingebant oppida fossae;
non tuba directi, non aeris cornua flexi,
non galeae, non ensis erant: sine militis usu
mollia securae peragebant otia gentes.   100
ipsa quoque inmunis rastroque intacta nec ullis

saucia vomeribus per se dabat omnia tellus,
contentique cibis nullo cogente creatis
arbuteos fetus montanaque fraga legebant
cornaque et in duris haerentia mora rubetis   105
et quae deciderant patula Iovis arbore glandes.
ver erat aeternum, placidique tepentibus auris
mulcebant zephyri natos sine semine flores;
mox etiam fruges tellus inarata ferebat,
nec renovatus ager gravidis canebat aristis;   110
flumina iam lactis, iam flumina nectaris ibant,
flavaque de viridi stillabant ilice mella.
  Postquam Saturno tenebrosa in Tartara misso
sub Iove mundus erat, subiit argentea proles,
auro deterior, fulvo pretiosior aere.   115
Iuppiter antiqui contraxit tempora veris
perque hiemes aestusque et inaequalis autumnos
et breve ver spatiis exegit quattuor annum.
tum primum siccis aer fervoribus ustus
canduit, et ventis glacies adstricta pependit;   120
tum primum subiere domos; domus antra fuerunt
et densi frutices et vinctae cortice virgae.
semina tum primum longis Cerealia sulcis
obruta sunt, pressique iugo gemuere iuvenci.
  Tertia post illam successit aenea proles,   125
saevior ingeniis et ad horrida promptior arma,
non scelerata tamen; de duro est ultima ferro.
protinus inrupit venae peioris in aevum
omne nefas fugitque pudor verumque fidesque;
in quorum subiere locum fraudesque dolusque   130
insidiaeque et vis et amor sceleratus habendi.
vela dabant ventis nec adhuc bene noverat illos
navita, quaeque prius steterant in montibus altis,
fluctibus ignotis exsultavere carinae,
communemque prius ceu lumina solis et auras   135
cautus humum longo signavit limite mensor.
nec tantum segetes alimentaque debita dives

poscebatur humus, sed itum est in viscera terrae,
quasque recondiderat Stygiisque admoverat umbris,
effodiuntur opes, inritamenta malorum. 140
iamque nocens ferrum ferroque nocentius aurum
prodierat, prodit bellum, quod pugnat utroque,
sanguineaque manu crepitantia concutit arma.
vivitur ex rapto: non hospes ab hospite tutus,
non socer a genero, fratrum quoque gratia rara est; 145
inminet exitio vir coniugis, illa mariti,
lurida terribiles miscent aconita novercae,
filius ante diem patrios inquirit in annos:
victa iacet pietas, et virgo caede madentis
ultima caelestum terras Astraea reliquit. 150

2

The Flood: 1.262–312

Protinus Aeoliis Aquilonem claudit in antris
et quaecumque fugant inductas flamina nubes
emittitque Notum. madidis Notus evolat alis,
terribilem picea tectus caligine vultum: 265
barba gravis nimbis, canis fluit unda capillis;
fronte sedent nebulae, rorant pennaeque sinusque.
utque manu lata pendentia nubila pressit,
fit fragor: hinc densi funduntur ab aethere nimbi;
nuntia Iunonis varios induta colores   270
concipit Iris aquas alimentaque nubibus adfert.
sternuntur segetes et deplorata coloni
vota iacent, longique perit labor inritus anni.
Nec caelo contenta suo est Iovis ira, sed illum
caeruleus frater iuvat auxiliaribus undis.   275
convocat hic amnes: qui postquam tecta tyranni
intravere sui, "non est hortamine longo
nunc" ait "utendum; vires effundite vestras:
sic opus est! aperite domos ac mole remota
fluminibus vestris totas inmittite habenas!"   280
iusserat; hi redeunt ac fontibus ora relaxant
et defrenato volvuntur in aequora cursu.
Ipse tridente suo terram percussit, at illa
intremuit motuque vias patefecit aquarum.
exspatiata ruunt per apertos flumina campos   285
cumque satis arbusta simul pecudesque virosque
tectaque cumque suis rapiunt penetralia sacris.
si qua domus mansit potuitque resistere tanto
indeiecta malo, culmen tamen altior huius
unda tegit, pressaeque latent sub gurgite turres.   290

iamque mare et tellus nullum discrimen habebant:
omnia pontus erant, deerant quoque litora ponto.
Occupat hic collem, cumba sedet alter adunca
et ducit remos illic, ubi nuper arabat:
ille supra segetes aut mersae culmina villae   295
navigat, hic summa piscem deprendit in ulmo.
figitur in viridi, si fors tulit, ancora prato,
aut subiecta terunt curvae vineta carinae;
et, modo qua graciles gramen carpsere capellae,
nunc ibi deformes ponunt sua corpora phocae.   300
mirantur sub aqua lucos urbesque domosque
Nereides, silvasque tenent delphines et altis
incursant ramis agitataque robora pulsant.
nat lupus inter oves, fulvos vehit unda leones,
unda vehit tigres; nec vires fulminis apro,   305
crura nec ablato prosunt velocia cervo,
quaesitisque diu terris, ubi sistere possit,
in mare lassatis volucris vaga decidit alis.
obruerat tumulos inmensa licentia ponti,
pulsabantque novi montana cacumina fluctus.   310
maxima pars unda rapitur; quibus unda pepercit,
illos longa domant inopi ieiunia victu.

3

Deucalion and Pyrrha: 1.313–415

Separat Aonios Oetaeis Phocis ab arvis,
terra ferax, dum terra fuit, sed tempore in illo
pars maris et latus subitarum campus aquarum.   315
mons ibi verticibus petit arduus astra duobus,
nomine Parnasus, superantque cacumina nubes.
hic ubi Deucalion (nam cetera texerat aequor)
cum consorte tori parva rate vectus adhaesit,
Corycidas nymphas et numina montis adorant   320
fatidicamque Themin, quae tunc oracla tenebat:
non illo melior quisquam nec amantior aequi
vir fuit aut illa metuentior ulla deorum.
Iuppiter ut liquidis stagnare paludibus orbem
et superesse virum de tot modo milibus unum,   325
et superesse vidit de tot modo milibus unam,
innocuos ambo, cultores numinis ambo,
nubila disiecit nimbisque aquilone remotis
et caelo terras ostendit et aethera terris.
nec maris ira manet, positoque tricuspide telo   330
mulcet aquas rector pelagi supraque profundum
exstantem atque umeros innato murice tectum
caeruleum Tritona vocat conchaeque sonanti
inspirare iubet fluctusque et flumina signo
iam revocare dato: cava bucina sumitur illi,   335
tortilis, in latum quae turbine crescit ab imo,
bucina, quae medio concepit ubi aera ponto,
litora voce replet sub utroque iacentia Phoebo;
tum quoque, ut ora dei madida rorantia barba
contigit et cecinit iussos inflata receptus,   340
omnibus audita est telluris et aequoris undis,

et quibus est undis audita, coercuit omnes.
iam mare litus habet, plenos capit alveus amnes,
flumina subsidunt collesque exire videntur;
surgit humus, crescunt loca decrescentibus undis,   345
postque diem longam nudata cacumina silvae
ostendunt limumque tenent in fronde relictum.
Redditus orbis erat; quem postquam vidit inanem
et desolatas agere alta silentia terras,
Deucalion lacrimis ita Pyrrham adfatur obortis: 350
"o soror, o coniunx, o femina sola superstes,
quam commune mihi genus et patruelis origo,
deinde torus iunxit, nunc ipsa pericula iungunt,
terrarum, quascumque vident occasus et ortus,
nos duo turba sumus; possedit cetera pontus.   355
haec quoque adhuc vitae non est fiducia nostrae
certa satis; terrent etiamnum nubila mentem.
quis tibi, si sine me fatis erepta fuisses,
nunc animus, miseranda, foret? quo sola timorem
ferre modo posses? quo consolante doleres?   360
namque ego (crede mihi), si te quoque pontus haberet,
te sequerer, coniunx, et me quoque pontus haberet.
o utinam possim populos reparare paternis
artibus atque animas formatae infundere terrae!
nunc genus in nobis restat mortale duobus.   365
sic visum superis: hominumque exempla manemus."
dixerat, et flebant: placuit caeleste precari
numen et auxilium per sacras quaerere sortes.
nulla mora est: adeunt pariter Cephesidas undas,
ut nondum liquidas, sic iam vada nota secantes.   370
inde ubi libatos inroravere liquores
vestibus et capiti, flectunt vestigia sanctae
ad delubra deae, quorum fastigia turpi
pallebant musco stabantque sine ignibus arae.
ut templi tetigere gradus, procumbit uterque   375
pronus humi gelidoque pavens dedit oscula saxo
atque ita "si precibus" dixerunt "numina iustis

victa remollescunt, si flectitur ira deorum,
dic, Themi, qua generis damnum reparabile nostri
arte sit, et mersis fer opem, mitissima, rebus!"   380
Mota dea est sortemque dedit: "discedite templo
et velate caput cinctasque resolvite vestes
ossaque post tergum magnae iactate parentis!"
obstipuere diu: rumpitque silentia voce
Pyrrha prior iussisque deae parere recusat,   385
detque sibi veniam pavido rogat ore pavetque
laedere iactatis maternas ossibus umbras.
interea repetunt caecis obscura latebris
verba datae sortis secum inter seque volutant.
inde Promethides placidis Epimethida dictis   390
mulcet et "aut fallax" ait "est sollertia nobis,
aut (pia sunt nullumque nefas oracula suadent!)
magna parens terra est: lapides in corpore terrae
ossa reor dici; iacere hos post terga iubemur."
Coniugis augurio quamquam Titania mota est,   395
spes tamen in dubio est: adeo caelestibus ambo
diffidunt monitis; sed quid temptare nocebit?
descendunt: velantque caput tunicasque recingunt
et iussos lapides sua post vestigia mittunt.
saxa (quis hoc credat, nisi sit pro teste vetustas?)   400
ponere duritiem coepere suumque rigorem
mollirique mora mollitaque ducere formam.
mox ubi creverunt naturaque mitior illis
contigit, ut quaedam, sic non manifesta videri
forma potest hominis, sed uti de marmore coepta   405
non exacta satis rudibusque simillima signis,
quae tamen ex illis aliquo pars umida suco
et terrena fuit, versa est in corporis usum;
quod solidum est flectique nequit, mutatur in ossa,
quae modo vena fuit, sub eodem nomine mansit,   410
inque brevi spatio superorum numine saxa
missa viri manibus faciem traxere virorum
et de femineo reparata est femina iactu.

inde genus durum sumus experiensque laborum
et documenta damus qua simus origine nati.   415

4

Daphne and Apollo: 1.452–567

Primus amor Phoebi Daphne Peneia, quem non
fors ignara dedit, sed saeva Cupidinis ira.
Delius hunc nuper, victa serpente superbus,
viderat adducto flectentem cornua nervo   455
"quid"que "tibi, lascive puer, cum fortibus armis?"
dixerat: "ista decent umeros gestamina nostros,
qui dare certa ferae, dare vulnera possumus hosti,
qui modo pestifero tot iugera ventre prementem
stravimus innumeris tumidum Pythona sagittis.   460
tu face nescio quos esto contentus amores
inritare tua, nec laudes adsere nostras!"
filius huic Veneris "figat tuus omnia, Phoebe,
te meus arcus" ait; "quantoque animalia cedunt
cuncta deo, tanto minor est tua gloria nostra."   465
dixit et eliso percussis aere pennis
inpiger umbrosa Parnasi constitit arce
eque sagittifera prompsit duo tela pharetra
diversorum operum: fugat hoc, facit illud amorem;
quod facit, auratum est et cuspide fulget acuta,   470
quod fugat, obtusum est et habet sub harundine plumbum.
hoc deus in nympha Peneide fixit, at illo
laesit Apollineas traiecta per ossa medullas;
protinus alter amat, fugit altera nomen amantis
silvarum latebris capitavarumque ferarum   475
exuviis gaudens innuptaeque aemula Phoebes:
vitta coercebat positos sine lege capillos.
multi illam petiere, illa aversata petentes
inpatiens expersque viri nemora avia lustrat
nec, quid Hymen, quid Amor, quid sint conubia curat.   480

saepe pater dixit: "generum mihi, filia, debes,"
saepe pater dixit: "debes mihi, nata, nepotes";
illa velut crimen taedas exosa iugales
pulchra verecundo suffunditur ora rubore
inque patris blandis haerens cervice lacertis   485
"da mihi perpetua, genitor carissime," dixit
"virginitate frui! dedit hoc pater ante Dianae."
ille quidem obsequitur, sed te decor iste quod optas
esse vetat, votoque tuo tua forma repugnat:
Phoebus amat visaeque cupit conubia Daphnes,   490
quodque cupit, sperat, suaque illum oracula fallunt,
utque leves stipulae demptis adolentur aristis,
ut facibus saepes ardent, quas forte viator
vel nimis admovit vel iam sub luce reliquit,
sic deus in flammas abiit, sic pectore toto   495
uritur et sterilem sperando nutrit amorem.
spectat inornatos collo pendere capillos
et "quid, si comantur?" ait. videt igne micantes
sideribus similes oculos, videt oscula, quae non
est vidisse satis; laudat digitosque manusque   500
bracchiaque et nudos media plus parte lacertos;
si qua latent, meliora putat. fugit ocior aura
illa levi neque ad haec revocantis verba resistit:
"nympha, precor, Penei, mane! non insequor hostis;
nympha, mane! sic agna lupum, sic cerva leonem,   505
sic aquilam penna fugiunt trepidante columbae,
hostes quaeque suos: amor est mihi causa sequendi!
me miserum! ne prona cadas indignave laedi
crura notent sentes et sim tibi causa doloris!
aspera, qua properas, loca sunt: moderatius, oro,   510
curre fugamque inhibe, moderatius insequar ipse.
cui placeas, inquire tamen: non incola montis,
non ego sum pastor, non hic armenta gregesque
horridus observo. nescis, temeraria, nescis,
quem fugias, ideoque fugis: mihi Delphica tellus   515
et Claros et Tenedos Patareaque regia servit;

Iuppiter est genitor; per me, quod eritque fuitque
estque, patet; per me concordant carmina nervis.
certa quidem nostra est, nostra tamen una sagitta
certior, in vacuo quae vulnera pectore fecit!   520
inventum medicina meum est, opiferque per orbem
dicor, et herbarum subiecta potentia nobis.
ei mihi, quod nullis amor est sanabilis herbis
nec prosunt domino, quae prosunt omnibus, artes!"
    Plura locuturum timido Peneia cursu   525
fugit cumque ipso verba inperfecta reliquit,
tum quoque visa decens; nudabant corpora venti,
obviaque adversas vibrabant flamina vestes,
et levis inpulsos retro dabat aura capillos,
auctaque forma fuga est. sed enim non sustinet ultra   530
perdere blanditias iuvenis deus, utque movebat
ipse amor, admisso sequitur vestigia passu.
ut canis in vacuo leporem cum Gallicus arvo
vidit, et hic praedam pedibus petit, ille salutem;
alter inhaesuro similis iam iamque tenere   535
sperat et extento stringit vestigia rostro,
alter in ambiguo est, an sit conprensus, et ipsis
morsibus eripitur tangentiaque ora relinquit:
sic deus et virgo est hic spe celer, illa timore.
qui tamen insequitur pennis adiutus Amoris,   540
ocior est requiemque negat tergoque fugacis
inminet et crinem sparsum cervicibus adflat.
viribus absumptis expalluit illa citaeque
victa labore fugae spectans Peneidas undas   544
"fer, pater," inquit "opem! si flumina numen habetis,
qua nimium placui, mutando perde figuram!"   547
vix prece finita torpor gravis occupat artus,
mollia cinguntur tenui praecordia libro,
in frondem crines, in ramos bracchia crescunt,   550
pes modo tam velox pigris radicibus haeret,
ora cacumen habet: remanet nitor unus in illa.
    Hanc quoque Phoebus amat positaque in stipite dextra

sentit adhuc trepidare novo sub cortice pectus
conplexusque suis ramos ut membra lacertis   555
oscula dat ligno; refugit tamen oscula lignum.
cui deus "at, quoniam coniunx mea non potes esse,
arbor eris certe" dixit "mea! semper habebunt
te coma, te citharae, te nostrae, laure, pharetrae;
tu ducibus Latiis aderis, cum laeta Triumphum   560
vox canet et visent longas Capitolia pompas;
postibus Augustis eadem fidissima custos
ante fores stabis mediamque tuebere quercum,
utque meum intonsis caput est iuvenale capillis,
tu quoque perpetuos semper gere frondis honores!"   565
finierat Paean: factis modo laurea ramis
adnuit utque caput visa est agitasse cacumen.

5

Io: 1.588-667

Viderat a patrio redeuntem Iuppiter illam
flumine et "o virgo Iove digna tuoque beatum
nescio quem factura toro, pete" dixerat "umbras   590
altorum nemorum" (et nemorum monstraverat umbras)
"dum calet, et medio sol est altissimus orbe!
quodsi sola times latebras intrare ferarum,
praeside tuta deo nemorum secreta subibis,
nec de plebe deo, sed qui caelestia magna   595
sceptra manu teneo, sed qui vaga fulmina mitto.
ne fuge me!" fugiebat enim. iam pascua Lernae
consitaque arboribus Lyrcea reliquerat arva,
cum deus inducta latas caligine terras
occuluit tenuitque fugam rapuitque pudorem.   600
   Interea medios Iuno dispexit in Argos
et noctis faciem nebulas fecisse volucres
sub nitido mirata die, non fluminis illas
esse, nec umenti sensit tellure remitti;
atque suus coniunx ubi sit circumspicit, ut quae   605
deprensi totiens iam nosset furta mariti.
quem postquam caelo non repperit, "aut ego fallor
aut ego laedor" ait delapsaque ab aethere summo
constitit in terris nebulasque recedere iussit.
coniugis adventum praesenserat inque nitentem   610
Inachidos vultus mutaverat ille iuvencam
(bos quoque formosa est): speciem Saturnia vaccae,
quamquam invita, probat nec non, et cuius et unde
quove sit armento, veri quasi nescia quaerit.
Iuppiter e terra genitam mentitur, ut auctor   615
desinat inquiri: petit hanc Saturnia munus.

40

quid faciat? crudele suos addicere amores,
non dare suspectum est: Pudor est, qui suadeat illinc,
hinc dissuadet Amor. victus Pudor esset Amore,
sed leve si munus sociae generisque torique   620
vacca negaretur, poterat non vacca videri!
   Paelice donata non protinus exuit omnem
diva metum timuitque Iovem et fuit anxia furti,
donec Arestoridae servandam tradidit Argo.
centum luminibus cinctum caput Argus habebat   625
inde suis vicibus capiebant bina quietem,
cetera servabant atque in statione manebant.
constiterat quocumque modo, spectabat ad Io,
ante oculos Io, quamvis aversus, habebat.
luce sinit pasci; cum sol tellure sub alta est,   630
claudit et indigno circumdat vincula collo.
frondibus arboreis et amara pascitur herba.
proque toro terrae non semper gramen habenti
incubat infelix limosaque flumina potat.
illa etiam supplex Argo cum bracchia vellet   635
tendere, non habuit, quae bracchia tenderet Argo,
et conata queri mugitus edidit ore
pertimuitque sonos propriaque exterrita voce est.
venit ad ripas, ubi ludere saepe solebat,
Inachidas: rictus novaque ut conspexit in unda   640
cornua, pertimuit seque exsternata refugit.
naides ignorant, ignorat et Inachus ipse,
quae sit; at illa patrem sequitur sequiturque sorores
et patitur tangi seque admirantibus offert.
decerptas senior porrexerat Inachus herbas: 645
illa manus lambit patriisque dat oscula palmis
nec retinet lacrimas, et si modo verba sequantur,
oret opem nomenque suum casusque loquatur;
littera pro verbis, quam pes in pulvere duxit,
corporis indicium mutati triste peregit.   650
"me miserum!" exclamat pater Inachus inque gementis
cornibus et niveae pendens cervice iuvencae

"me miserum!" ingeminat; "tune es quaesita per omnes
nata mihi terras? tu non inventa reperta
luctus eras levior! retices nec mutua nostris   655
dicta refers, alto tantum suspiria ducis
pectore, quodque unum potes, ad mea verba remugis!
at tibi ego ignarus thalamos taedasque parabam,
spesque fuit generi mihi prima, secunda nepotum.
de grege nunc tibi vir, nunc de grege natus habendus.   660
nec finire licet tantos mihi morte dolores;
sed nocet esse deum, praeclusaque ianua leti
aeternum nostros luctus extendit in aevum."
talia maerentes stellatus submovet Argus
ereptamque patri diversa in pascua natam   665
abstrahit. ipse procul montis sublime cacumen
occupat, unde sedens partes speculatur in omnes.

6

Europa: 2.833–875

Has ubi verborum poenas mentisque profanae
cepit Atlantiades, dictas a Pallade terras
linquit et ingreditur iactatis aethera pennis.   835
sevocat hunc genitor nec causam fassus amoris
"fide minister" ait "iussorum, nate, meorum,
pelle moram solitoque celer delabere cursu,
quaeque tuam matrem tellus a parte sinistra
suspicit (indigenae Sidonida nomine dicunt),   840
hanc pete, quodque procul montano gramine pasci
armentum regale vides, ad litora verte!"
dixit, et expulsi iamdudum monte iuvenci
litora iussa petunt, ubi magni filia regis
ludere virginibus Tyriis comitata solebat.   845
non bene conveniunt nec in una sede morantur
maiestas et amor; sceptri gravitate relicta
ille pater rectorque deum, cui dextra trisulcis
ignibus armata est, qui nutu concutit orbem,
induitur faciem tauri mixtusque iuvencis   850
mugit et in teneris formosus obambulat herbis.
quippe color nivis est, quam nec vestigia duri
calcavere pedis nec solvit aquaticus auster.
colla toris exstant, armis palearia pendent,
cornua parva quidem, sed quae contendere possis   855
facta manu, puraque magis perlucida gemma.
nullae in fronte minae, nec formidabile lumen:
pacem vultus habet. miratur Agenore nata,
quod tam formosus, quod proelia nulla minetur;
sed quamvis mitem metuit contingere primo,   860
mox adit et flores ad candida porrigit ora.

43

gaudet amans et, dum veniat sperata voluptas,
oscula dat manibus; vix iam, vix cetera differt;
et nunc adludit viridique exsultat in herba,
nunc latus in fulvis niveum deponit harenis;   865
paullatimque metu dempto modo pectora praebet
virginea plaudenda manu, modo cornua sertis
inpedienda novis; ausa est quoque regia virgo
nescia, quem premeret, tergo considere tauri,
cum deus a terra siccoque a litore sensim   870
falsa pedum primo vestigia ponit in undis;
inde abit ulterius mediique per aequora ponti
fert praedam: pavet haec litusque ablata relictum
respicit et dextra cornum tenet, altera dorso
inposita est; tremulae sinuantur flamine vestes.   875

7

Cadmus: 3.1–130

Iamque deus posita fallacis imagine tauri
se confessus erat Dictaeaque rura tenebat,
cum pater ignarus Cadmo perquirere raptam
imperat et poenam, si non invenerit, addit
exilium, facto pius et sceleratus eodem.   5
orbe pererrato (quis enim deprendere possit
furta Iovis?) profugus patriamque iramque parentis
vitat Agenorides Phoebique oracula supplex
consulit et, quae sit tellus habitanda, requirit.
"bos tibi" Phoebus ait "solis occurret in arvis,   10
nullum passa iugum curvique inmunis aratri.
hac duce carpe vias et, qua requieverit herba,
moenia fac condas Boeotiaque illa vocato."
vix bene Castalio Cadmus descenderat antro,
incustoditam lente videt ire iuvencam   15
nullum servitii signum cervice gerentem.
subsequitur pressoque legit vestigia passu
auctoremque viae Phoebum taciturnus adorat.
iam vada Cephisi Panopesque evaserat arva:
bos stetit et tollens speciosam cornibus altis   20
ad caelum frontem mugitibus inpulit auras
atque ita respiciens comites sua terga sequentis
procubuit teneraque latus submisit in herba.
Cadmus agit grates peregrinaeque oscula terrae
figit et ignotos montes agrosque salutat.   25
    Sacra Iovi facturus erat: iubet ire ministros
et petere e vivis libandas fontibus undas.
silva vetus stabat nulla violata securi,
et specus in media virgis ac vimine densus

efficiens humilem lapidum conpagibus arcum   30
uberibus fecundus aquis; ubi conditus antro
Martius anguis erat, cristis praesignis et auro;
igne micant oculi, corpus tumet omne venenis,
tres vibrant linguae, triplici stant ordine dentes.
quem postquam Tyria lucum de gente profecti   35
infausto tetigere gradu, demissaque in undas
urna dedit sonitum, longo caput extulit antro
caeruleus serpens horrendaque sibila misit.
effluxere urnae manibus sanguisque reliquit
corpus et attonitos subitus tremor occupat artus.   40
ille volubilibus squamosos nexibus orbes
torquet et inmensos saltu sinuatur in arcus
ac media plus parte leves erectus in auras
despicit omne nemus tantoque est corpore, quanto,
si totum spectes, geminas qui separat arctos.   45
nec mora, Phoenicas, sive illi tela parabant
sive fugam, sive ipse timor prohibebat utrumque,
occupat: hos morsu, longis conplexibus illos,
hos necat adflatu funesti tabe veneni.
   Fecerat exiguas iam sol altissimus umbras: 50
quae mora sit sociis, miratur Agenore natus
vestigatque viros. tegumen derepta leoni
pellis erat, telum splendenti lancea ferro
et iaculum teloque animus praestantior omni.
ut nemus intravit letataque corpora vidit   55
victoremque supra spatiosi corporis hostem
tristia sanguinea lambentem vulnera lingua,
"aut ultor vestrae, fidissima corpora, mortis,
aut comes" inquit "ero." dixit dextraque molarem
sustulit et magnum magno conamine misit.   60
illius inpulsu cum turribus ardua celsis
moenia mota forent, serpens sine vulnere mansit
loricaeque modo squamis defensus et atrae
duritia pellis validos cute reppulit ictus;
at non duritia iaculum quoque vicit eadem,   65

quod medio lentae spinae curvamine fixum
constitit et totum descendit in ilia ferrum.
ille dolore ferox caput in sua terga retorsit
vulneraque adspexit fixumque hastile momordit,
idque ubi vi multa partem labefecit in omnem,   70
vix tergo eripuit; ferrum tamen ossibus haesit.
tum vero postquam solitas accessit ad iras
causa recens, plenis tumuerunt guttura venis,
spumaque pestiferos circumfluit albida rictus,
terraque rasa sonat squamis, quique halitus exit   75
ore niger Stygio, vitiatas inficit auras.
ipse modo inmensum spiris facientibus orbem
cingitur, interdum longa trabe rectior exstat,
inpete nunc vasto ceu concitus imbribus amnis
fertur et obstantis proturbat pectore silvas.   80
cedit Agenorides paullum spolioque leonis
sustinet incursus instantiaque ora retardat
cuspide praetenta: furit ille et inania duro
vulnera dat ferro figitque in acumine dentes.
iamque venenifero sanguis manare palato   85
coeperat et virides adspergine tinxerat herbas;
sed leve vulnus erat, quia se retrahebat ab ictu
laesaque colla dabat retro plagamque sedere
cedendo arcebat nec longius ire sinebat,
donec Agenorides coniectum in gutture ferrum   90
usque sequens pressit, dum retro quercus eunti
obstitit et fixa est pariter cum robore cervix.
pondere serpentis curvata est arbor et ima
parte flagellari gemuit sua robora caudae.
    Dum spatium victor victi considerat hostis,   95
vox subito audita est; neque erat cognoscere promptum,
unde, sed audita est: "quid, Agenore nate, peremptum
serpentem spectas? et tu spectabere serpens."
ille diu pavidus pariter cum mente colorem
perdiderat, gelidoque comae terrore rigebant: 100
ecce viri fautrix superas delapsa per auras

Pallas adest motaeque iubet supponere terrae
vipereos dentes, populi incrementa futuri.
paret et, ut presso sulcum patefecit aratro,
spargit humi iussos, mortalia semina, dentes.   105
inde (fide maius) glaebae coepere moveri,
primaque de sulcis acies adparuit hastae,
tegmina mox capitum picto nutantia cono,
mox umeri pectusque onerataque bracchia telis
exsistunt, crescitque seges clipeata virorum: 110
sic, ubi tolluntur festis aulaea theatris,
surgere signa solent primumque ostendere vultus,
cetera paullatim, placidoque educta tenore
tota patent imoque pedes in margine ponunt.
    Territus hoste novo Cadmus capere arma parabat: 115
"ne cape!" de populo, quem terra creaverat, unus
exclamat "ne te civilibus insere bellis!"
atque ita terrigenis rigido de fratribus unum
comminus ense ferit, iaculo cadit eminus ipse;
hunc quoque qui leto dederat, non longius illo   120
vivit et exspirat modo quas acceperat auras,
exemploque pari furit omnis turba, suoque
Marte cadunt subiti per mutua vulnera fratres,
iamque brevis vitae spatium sortita iuventus
sanguineam tepido plangebat pectore matrem,   125
quinque superstitibus, quorum fuit unus Echion.
is sua iecit humo monitu Tritonidis arma
fraternaeque fidem pacis petiitque deditque:
hos operis comites habuit Sidonius hospes,
cum posuit iussus Phoebeis sortibus urbem.   130

8

Semele: 3.253–315

Rumor in ambiguo est; aliis violentior aequo
visa dea est, alii laudant dignamque severa
virginitate vocant: pars invenit utraque causas.   255
sola Iovis coniunx non tam, culpetne probetne,
eloquitur, quam clade domus ab Agenore ductae
gaudet et a Tyria collectum paelice transfert
in generis socios odium; subit ecce priori
causa recens, gravidamque dolet de semine magni   260
esse Iovis Semelen; dum linguam ad iurgia solvit,
"profeci quid enim totiens per iurgia?" dixit,
"ipsa petenda mihi est; ipsam, si maxima Iuno
rite vocor, perdam, si me gemmantia dextra
sceptra tenere decet, si sum regina Iovisque   265
et soror et coniunx, certe soror. at, puto, furto est
contenta, et thalami brevis est iniuria nostri.
concipit: id deerat; manifestaque crimina pleno
fert utero et mater, quod vix mihi contigit, uno
de Iove vult fieri: tanta est fiducia formae.   270
fallat eam faxo; nec sum Saturnia, si non
ab Iove mersa suo Stygias penetrabit in undas."
 Surgit ab his solio fulvaque recondita nube
limen adit Semeles nec nubes ante removit
quam simulavit anum posuitque ad tempora canos   275
sulcavitque cutem rugis et curva trementi
membra tulit passu; vocem quoque fecit anilem,
ipsaque erat Beroe, Semeles Epidauria nutrix.
ergo ubi captato sermone diuque loquendo
ad nomen venere Iovis, suspirat et "opto,   280
Iuppiter ut sit" ait; "metuo tamen omnia: multi

nomine divorum thalamos iniere pudicos.
nec tamen esse Iovem satis est: det pignus amoris,
si modo verus is est; quantusque et qualis ab alta
Iunone excipitur, tantus talisque, rogato,   285
det tibi conplexus suaque ante insignia sumat!"
    Talibus ignaram Iuno Cadmeida dictis
formarat: rogat illa Iovem sine nomine munus.
cui deus "elige!" ait "nullam patiere repulsam,
quoque magis credas, Stygii quoque conscia sunto   290
numina torrentis: timor et deus ille deorum est."
laeta malo nimiumque potens perituraque amantis
obsequio Semele "qualem Saturnia" dixit
"te solet amplecti, Veneris cum foedus initis,
da mihi te talem!" voluit deus ora loquentis   295
opprimere: exierat iam vox properata sub auras.
ingemuit; neque enim non haec optasse, neque ille
non iurasse potest. ergo maestissimus altum
aethera conscendit vultuque sequentia traxit
nubila, quis nimbos inmixtaque fulgura ventis   300
addidit et tonitrus et inevitabile fulmen;
qua tamen usque potest, vires sibi demere temptat
nec, quo centimanum deiecerat igne Typhoea,
nunc armatur eo: nimium feritatis in illo est.
est aliud levius fulmen, cui dextra cyclopum   305
saevitiae flammaeque minus, minus addidit irae:
tela secunda vocant superi; capit illa domumque
intrat Agenoream. corpus mortale tumultus
non tulit aetherios donisque iugalibus arsit.
inperfectus adhuc infans genetricis ab alvo   310
eripitur patrioque tener (si credere dignum est)
insuitur femori maternaque tempora conplet.
furtim illum primis Ino matertera cunis
educat, inde datum nymphae Nyseides antris
occuluere suis lactisque alimenta dedere.   315

9

Echo and Narcissus: 3.339–510

Ille per Aonias fama celeberrimus urbes
inreprehensa dabat populo responsa petenti;   340
prima fide vocisque ratae temptamina sumpsit
caerula Liriope, quam quondam flumine curvo
inplicuit clausaeque suis Cephisos in undis
vim tulit: enixa est utero pulcherrima pleno
infantem nymphe, iam tunc qui posset amari,   345
Narcissumque vocat. de quo consultus, an esset
tempora maturae visurus longa senectae,
fatidicus vates "si se non noverit" inquit.
vana diu visa est vox auguris: exitus illam
resque probat letique genus novitasque furoris.   350
namque ter ad quinos unum Cephisius annum
addiderat poteratque puer iuvenisque videri:
multi illum iuvenes, multae cupiere puellae;
sed fuit in tenera tam dura superbia forma,
nulli illum iuvenes, nullae tetigere puellae.   355
adspicit hunc trepidos agitantem in retia cervos
vocalis nymphe, quae nec reticere loquenti
nec prior ipsa loqui didicit, resonabilis Echo.
     Corpus adhuc Echo, non vox erat et tamen usum
garrula non alium, quam nunc habet, oris habebat,   360
reddere de multis ut verba novissima posset.
fecerat hoc Iuno, quia, cum deprendere posset
sub Iove saepe suo nymphas in monte iacentis,
illa deam longo prudens sermone tenebat,
dum fugerent nymphae. postquam hoc Saturnia sensit,   365
"huius" ait "linguae, qua sum delusa, potestas
parva tibi dabitur vocisque brevissimus usus,"

reque minas firmat. tamen haec in fine loquendi
ingeminat voces auditaque verba reportat.
ergo ubi Narcissum per devia rura vagantem   370
vidit et incaluit, sequitur vestigia furtim,
quoque magis sequitur, flamma propiore calescit,
non aliter quam cum summis circumlita taedis
admotas rapiunt vivacia sulphura flammas.
o quotiens voluit blandis accedere dictis   375
et mollis adhibere preces! natura repugnat
nec sinit, incipiat, sed, quod sinit, illa parata est
exspectare sonos, ad quos sua verba remittat.
forte puer comitum seductus ab agmine fido
dixerat: "ecquis adest?" et "adest" responderat Echo.   380
hic stupet, utque aciem partes dimittit in omnis,
voce "veni!" magna clamat: vocat illa vocantem.
respicit et rursus nullo veniente "quid" inquit
"me fugis?" et totidem, quot dixit, verba recepit.
perstat et alternae deceptus imagine vocis   385
"huc coeamus" ait, nullique libentius umquam
responsura sono "coeamus" rettulit Echo
et verbis favet ipsa suis egressaque silva
ibat, ut iniceret sperato bracchia collo;
ille fugit fugiensque "manus conplexibus aufer!   390
ante" ait "emoriar, quam sit tibi copia nostri";
rettulit illa nihil nisi "sit tibi copia nostri!"
spreta latet silvis pudibundaque frondibus ora
protegit et solis ex illo vivit in antris;
sed tamen haeret amor crescitque dolore repulsae;   395
et tenuant vigiles corpus miserabile curae
adducitque cutem macies et in aera sucus
corporis omnis abit; vox tantum atque ossa supersunt:
vox manet, ossa ferunt lapidis traxisse figuram.
inde latet silvis nulloque in monte videtur,   400
omnibus auditur: sonus est, qui vivit in illa.
    Sic hanc, sic alias undis aut montibus ortas
luserat hic nymphas, sic coetus ante viriles;

inde manus aliquis despectus ad aethera tollens
"sic amet ipse licet, sic non potiatur amato!"   405
dixerat: adsensit precibus Rhamnusia iustis.
fons erat inlimis, nitidis argenteus undis,
quem neque pastores neque pastae monte capellae
contigerant aliudve pecus, quem nulla volucris
nec fera turbarat nec lapsus ab arbore ramus;   410
gramen erat circa, quod proximus umor alebat,
silvaque sole locum passura tepescere nullo.
hic puer et studio venandi lassus et aestu
procubuit faciemque loci fontemque secutus,
dumque sitim sedare cupit, sitis altera crevit,   415
dumque bibit, visae correptus imagine formae
spem sine corpore amat, corpus putat esse, quod umbra est.
adstupet ipse sibi vultuque inmotus eodem
haeret, ut e Pario formatum marmore signum;
spectat humi positus geminum, sua lumina, sidus   420
et dignos Baccho, dignos et Apolline crines
inpubesque genas et eburnea colla decusque
oris et in niveo mixtum candore ruborem,
cunctaque miratur, quibus est mirabilis ipse:
se cupit inprudens et, qui probat, ipse probatur,   425
dumque petit, petitur, pariterque accendit et ardet.
inrita fallaci quotiens dedit oscula fonti,
in medias quotiens visum captantia collum
bracchia mersit aquas nec se deprendit in illis!
quid videat, nescit; sed quod videt, uritur illo,   430
atque oculos idem, qui decipit, incitat error.
credule, quid frustra simulacra fugacia captas?
quod petis, est nusquam; quod amas, avertere, perdes!
ista repercussae, quam cernis, imaginis umbra est:
nil habet ista sui; tecum venitque manetque;   435
tecum discedet, si tu discedere possis!
    Non illum Cereris, non illum cura quietis
abstrahere inde potest, sed opaca fusus in herba
spectat inexpleto mendacem lumine formam

perque oculos perit ipse suos; paulumque levatus   440
ad circumstantes tendens sua bracchia silvas
"ecquis, io silvae, crudelius" inquit "amavit?
scitis enim et multis latebra opportuna fuistis.
ecquem, cum vestrae tot agantur saecula vitae,
qui sic tabuerit, longo meministis in aevo?   445
et placet et video; sed quod videoque placetque,
non tamen invenio: tantus tenet error amantem.
quoque magis doleam, nec nos mare separat ingens
nec via nec montes nec clausis moenia portis;
exigua prohibemur aqua! cupit ipse teneri: 450
nam quotiens liquidis porreximus oscula lymphis,
hic totiens ad me resupino nititur ore.
posse putes tangi: minimum est, quod amantibus obstat.
quisquis es, huc exi! quid me, puer unice, fallis
quove petitus abis? certe nec forma nec aetas   455
est mea, quam fugias, et amarunt me quoque nymphae!
spem mihi nescio quam vultu promittis amico,
cumque ego porrexi tibi bracchia, porrigis ultro,
cum risi, adrides; lacrimas quoque saepe notavi
me lacrimante tuas; nutu quoque signa remittis   460
et, quantum motu formosi suspicor oris,
verba refers aures non pervenientia nostras!
iste ego sum: sensi, nec me mea fallit imago:
uror amore mei: flammas moveoque feroque.
quid faciam? roger anne rogem? quid deinde rogabo?   465
quod cupio mecum est: inopem me copia fecit.
o utinam a nostro secedere corpore possem!
votum in amante novum, vellem, quod amamus, abesset.
iamque dolor vires adimit, nec tempora vitae
longa meae superant, primoque exstinguor in aevo.   470
nec mihi mors gravis est posituro morte dolores,
hic, qui diligitur, vellem diuturnior esset;
nunc duo concordes anima moriemur in una."
       Dixit et ad faciem rediit male sanus eandem
et lacrimis turbavit aquas, obscuraque moto   475

reddita forma lacu est; quam cum vidisset abire,
"quo refugis? remane nec me, crudelis, amantem
desere!" clamavit; "liceat, quod tangere non est,
adspicere et misero praebere alimenta furori!"
dumque dolet, summa vestem deduxit ab ora   480
nudaque marmoreis percussit pectora palmis.
pectora traxerunt roseum percussa ruborem,
non aliter quam poma solent, quae candida parte,
parte rubent, aut ut variis solet uva racemis
ducere purpureum nondum matura colorem.   485
quae simul adspexit liquefacta rursus in unda,
non tulit ulterius, sed ut intabescere flavae
igne levi cerae matutinaeque pruinae
sole tepente solent, sic attenuatus amore
liquitur et tecto paulatim carpitur igni;   490
et neque iam color est mixto candore rubori,
nec vigor et vires et quae modo visa placebant,
nec corpus remanet, quondam quod amaverat Echo.
quae tamen ut vidit quamvis irata memorque
indoluit, quotiensque puer miserabilis "eheu"   495
dixerat, haec resonis iterabat vocibus "eheu";
cumque suos manibus percusserat ille lacertos,
haec quoque reddebat sonitum plangoris eundem.
ultima vox solitam fuit haec spectantis in undam:
"heu frustra dilecte puer!" totidemque remisit   500
verba locus, dictoque vale "vale" inquit et Echo.
ille caput viridi fessum submisit in herba,
lumina mors clausit domini mirantia formam:
tum quoque se, postquam est inferna sede receptus,
in Stygia spectabat aqua. planxere sorores   505
naides et sectos fratri posuere capillos,
planxerunt dryades; plangentibus adsonat Echo.
iamque rogum quassasque faces feretrumque parabant:
nusquam corpus erat; croceum pro corpore florem
inveniunt foliis medium cingentibus albis.   510

10

Pyramus and Thisbe: 4.55–166

Pyramus et Thisbe, iuvenum pulcherrimus alter,　　　　55
altera, quas Oriens habuit, praelata puellis,
contiguas tenuere domos, ubi dicitur altam
coctilibus muris cinxisse Semiramis urbem.
notitiam primosque gradus vicinia fecit,
tempore crevit amor; taedae quoque iure coissent,　　　60
sed vetuere patres: quod non potuere vetare,
ex aequo captis ardebant mentibus ambo.
conscius omnis abest; nutu signisque loquuntur,
quoque magis tegitur, tectus magis aestuat ignis.
fissus erat tenui rima, quam duxerat olim,　　　　　65
cum fieret, paries domui communis utrique.
id vitium nulli per saecula longa notatum—
quid non sentit amor?—primi vidistis amantes
et vocis fecistis iter, tutaeque per illud
murmure blanditiae minimo transire solebant.　　　　70
saepe, ubi constiterant hinc Thisbe, Pyramus illinc,
inque vices fuerat captatus anhelitus oris,
"invide" dicebant "paries, quid amantibus obstas?
quantum erat, ut sineres toto nos corpore iungi
aut, hoc si nimium est, vel ad oscula danda pateres?　75
nec sumus ingrati: tibi nos debere fatemur,
quod datus est verbis ad amicas transitus auris."
talia diversa nequiquam sede locuti
sub noctem dixere "vale" partique dedere
oscula quisque suae non pervenientia contra.　　　　80
postera nocturnos Aurora removerat ignes,
solque pruinosas radiis siccaverat herbas:
ad solitum coiere locum. tum murmure parvo

multa prius questi statuunt, ut nocte silenti
fallere custodes foribusque excedere temptent,   85
cumque domo exierint, urbis quoque tecta relinquant,
neve sit errandum lato spatiantibus arvo,
conveniant ad busta Nini lateantque sub umbra
arboris: arbor ibi niveis uberrima pomis
(ardua morus erat) gelido contermina fonti.   90
pacta placent; et lux, tarde discedere visa,
praecipitatur aquis, et aquis nox exit ab isdem.
    Callida per tenebras versato cardine Thisbe
egreditur fallitque suos adopertaque vultum
pervenit ad tumulum dictaque sub arbore sedit.   95
audacem faciebat amor. venit ecce recenti
caede leaena boum spumantis oblita rictus
depositura sitim vicini fontis in unda;
quam procul ad lunae radios Babylonia Thisbe
vidit et obscurum timido pede fugit in antrum,   100
dumque fugit, tergo velamina lapsa reliquit.
ut lea saeva sitim multa conpescuit unda,
dum redit in silvas, inventos forte sine ipsa
ore cruentato tenues laniavit amictus.
serius egressus vestigia vidit in alto   105
pulvere certa ferae totoque expalluit ore
Pyramus; ut vero vestem quoque sanguine tinctam
repperit, "una duos" inquit "nox perdet amantes,
e quibus illa fuit longa dignissima vita;
nostra nocens anima est. ego te, miseranda, peremi,   110
in loca plena metus qui iussi nocte venires
nec prior huc veni. nostrum divellite corpus
et scelerata fero consumite viscera morsu,
o quicumque sub hac habitatis rupe leones!
sed timidi est optare necem." velamina Thisbes   115
tollit et ad pactae secum fert arboris umbram,
utque dedit notae lacrimas, dedit oscula vesti,
"accipe nunc" inquit "nostri quoque sanguinis haustus!"
quoque erat accinctus, demisit in ilia ferrum,

nec mora, ferventi moriens e vulnere traxit.   120
ut iacuit resupinus humo, cruor emicat alte,
non aliter quam cum vitiato fistula plumbo
scinditur et tenui stridente foramine longas
eiaculatur aquas atque ictibus aera rumpit.
arborei fetus adspergine caedis in atram   125
vertuntur faciem, madefactaque sanguine radix
purpureo tinguit pendentia mora colore.
    Ecce metu nondum posito, ne fallat amantem,
illa redit iuvenemque oculis animoque requirit,
quantaque vitarit narrare pericula gestit;   130
utque locum et visa cognoscit in arbore formam,
sic facit incertam pomi color: haeret, an haec sit.
dum dubitat, tremebunda videt pulsare cruentum
membra solum, retroque pedem tulit, oraque buxo
pallidiora gerens exhorruit aequoris instar,   135
quod tremit, exigua cum summum stringitur aura.
sed postquam remorata suos cognovit amores,
percutit indignos claro plangore lacertos
et laniata comas amplexaque corpus amatum
vulnera supplevit lacrimis fletumque cruori   140
miscuit et gelidis in vultibus oscula figens
"Pyrame," clamavit, "quis te mihi casus ademit?
Pyrame, responde! tua te carissima Thisbe
nominat; exaudi vultusque attolle iacentes!"
ad nomen Thisbes oculos a morte gravatos   145
Pyramus erexit visaque recondidit illa.
    Quae postquam vestemque suam cognovit et ense
vidit ebur vacuum, "tua te manus" inquit "amorque
perdidit, infelix! est et mihi fortis in unum
hoc manus, est et amor: dabit hic in vulnera vires.   150
persequar extinctum letique miserrima dicar
causa comesque tui: quique a me morte revelli
heu sola poteras, poteris nec morte revelli.
hoc tamen amborum verbis estote rogati,
o multum miseri meus illiusque parentes,   155

ut, quos certus amor, quos hora novissima iunxit,
conponi tumulo non invideatis eodem;
at tu quae ramis arbor miserabile corpus
nunc tegis unius, mox es tectura duorum,
signa tene caedis pullosque et luctibus aptos   160
semper habe fetus, gemini monimenta cruoris."
dixit et aptato pectus mucrone sub imum
incubuit ferro, quod adhuc a caede tepebat.
vota tamen tetigere deos, tetigere parentes;
nam color in pomo est, ubi permaturuit, ater,   165
quodque rogis superest, una requiescit in urna.

11

Perseus and Andromeda: 4.663–752

Clauserat Hippotades aeterno carcere ventos,
admonitorque operum caelo clarissimus alto
Lucifer ortus erat: pennis ligat ille resumptis   665
parte ab utraque pedes teloque accingitur unco
et liquidum motis talaribus aera findit.
gentibus innumeris circumque infraque relictis
Aethiopum populos Cepheaque conspicit arva.
illic inmeritam maternae pendere linguae   670
Andromedan poenas iniustus iusserat Ammon;
quam simul ad duras religatam bracchia cautes
vidit Abantiades (nisi quod levis aura capillos
moverat et tepido manabant lumina fletu,
marmoreum ratus esset opus), trahit inscius ignes   675
et stupet eximiae correptus imagine formae
paene suas quatere est oblitus in aere pennas.
ut stetit, "o" dixit "non istis digna catenis,
sed quibus inter se cupidi iunguntur amantes,
pande requirenti nomen terraeque tuumque,   680
et cur vincla geras." primo silet illa nec audet
adpellare virum virgo, manibusque modestos
celasset vultus, si non religata fuisset;
lumina, quod potuit, lacrimis inplevit obortis.
saepius instanti, sua ne delicta fateri   685
nolle videretur, nomen terraeque suumque,
quantaque maternae fuerit fiducia formae,
indicat, et nondum memoratis omnibus unda
insonuit, veniensque inmenso belua ponto
inminet et latum sub pectore possidet aequor.   690
conclamat virgo: genitor lugubris et una

mater adest, ambo miseri, sed iustius illa,
nec secum auxilium, sed dignos tempore fletus
plangoremque ferunt vinctoque in corpore adhaerent,
cum sic hospes ait "lacrimarum longa manere   695
tempora vos poterunt, ad opem brevis hora ferendam est.
hanc ego si peterem Perseus Iove natus et illa,
quam clausam inplevit fecundo Iuppiter auro,
Gorgonis anguicomae Perseus superator et alis
aerias ausus iactatis ire per auras,   700
praeferrer cunctis certe gener; addere tantis
dotibus et meritum, faveant modo numina, tempto:
ut mea sit servata mea virtute, paciscor."
accipiunt legem (quis enim dubitaret?) et orant
promittuntque super regnum dotale parentes.   705
    Ecce, velut navis praefixo concita rostro
sulcat aquas iuvenum sudantibus acta lacertis,
sic fera dimotis inpulsu pectoris undis;
tantum aberat scopulis, quantum Balearica torto
funda potest plumbo medii transmittere caeli,   710
cum subito iuvenis pedibus tellure repulsa
arduus in nubes abiit: ut in aequore summo
umbra viri visa est, visa fera saevit in umbra,
utque Iovis praepes, vacuo cum vidit in arvo
praebentem Phoebo liventia terga draconem,   715
occupat aversum, neu saeva retorqueat ora,
squamigeris avidos figit cervicibus ungues,
sic celeri missus praeceps per inane volatu
terga ferae pressit dextroque frementis in armo
Inachides ferrum curvo tenus abdidit hamo.   720
vulnere laesa gravi modo se sublimis in auras
attollit, modo subdit aquis, modo more ferocis
versat apri, quem turba canum circumsona terret.
ille avidos morsus velocibus effugit alis
quaque patet, nunc terga cavis super obsita conchis, 725
nunc laterum costas, nunc qua tenuissima cauda
desinit in piscem, falcato verberat ense;

belua puniceo mixtos cum sanguine fluctus
ore vomit: maduere graves adspergine pennae.
nec bibulis ultra Perseus talaribus ausus   730
credere conspexit scopulum, qui vertice summo
stantibus exstat aquis, operitur ab aequore moto.
nixus eo rupisque tenens iuga prima sinistra
ter quater exegit repetita per ilia ferrum.
litora cum plausu clamor superasque deorum   735
inplevere domos: gaudent generumque salutant
auxiliumque domus servatoremque fatentur
Cassiope Cepheusque pater; resoluta catenis
incedit virgo, pretiumque et causa laboris.
ipse manus hausta victrices abluit unda,   740
anguiferumque caput dura ne laedat harena,
mollit humum foliis natasque sub aequore virgas
sternit et inponit Phorcynidos ora Medusae.
virga recens bibulaque etiamnum viva medulla
vim rapuit monstri tactuqe induruit huius   745
percepitque novum ramis et fronde rigorem.
at pelagi nymphae factum mirabile temptant
pluribus in virgis et idem contingere gaudent
seminaque ex illis iterant iactata per undas:
nunc quoque curaliis eadem natura remansit,   750
duritiam tacto capiant ut ab aere quodque
vimen in aequore erat, fiat super aequora saxum.

12

Lycian Farmers: 6.313–381

Tum vero cuncti manifestam numinis iram
femina virque timent cultuque inpensius omnes
magna gemelliparae venerantur numina divae;   315
utque fit, a facto propiore priora renarrant.
e quibus unus ait: "Lyciae quoque fertilis agris
non inpune deam veteres sprevere coloni.
res obscura quidem est ignobilitate virorum,
mira tamen: vidi praesens stagnumque locumque   320
prodigio notum. nam me iam grandior aevo
inpatiensque viae genitor deducere lectos
iusserat inde boves gentisque illius eunti
ipse ducem dederat, cum quo dum pascua lustro,
ecce lacu medio sacrorum nigra favilla   325
ara vetus stabat tremulis circumdata cannis.
restitit et pavido 'faveas mihi!' murmure dixit
dux meus, et simili 'faveas!' ego murmure dixi.
Naiadum Faunine foret tamen ara rogabam
indigenaene dei, cum talia rettulit hospes: 330
'non hac, o iuvenis, montanum numen in ara est;
illa suam vocat hanc, cui quondam regia coniunx
orbem interdixit, quam vix erratica Delos
orantem accepit tum, cum levis insula nabat;
illic incumbens cum Palladis arbore palmae   335
edidit invita geminos Latona noverca.
hinc quoque Iunonem fugisse puerpera fertur
inque suo portasse sinu, duo numina, natos.
iamque Chimaeriferae, cum sol gravis ureret arva,
finibus in Lyciae longo dea fessa labore   340
sidereo siccata sitim collegit ab aestu,

63

uberaque ebiberant avidi lactantia nati.
forte lacum mediocris aquae prospexit in imis
vallibus; agrestes illic fruticosa legebant
vimina cum iuncis gratamque paludibus ulvam;   345
accessit positoque genu Titania terram
pressit, ut hauriret gelidos potura liquores.
rustica turba vetat; dea sic adfata vetantis:
"quid prohibetis aquis? usus communis aquarum est.
nec solem proprium natura nec aera fecit   350
nec tenues undas: ad publica munera veni;
quae tamen ut detis, supplex peto. non ego nostros
abluere hic artus lassataque membra parabam,
sed relevare sitim. caret os umore loquentis,
et fauces arent, vixque est via vocis in illis.   355
hautus aquae mihi nectar erit, vitamque fatebor
accepisse simul: vitam dederitis in unda.
hi quoque vos moveant, qui nostro bracchia tendunt
parva sinu," et casu tendebant bracchia nati.
quem non blanda deae potuissent verba movere?   360
hi tamen orantem perstant prohibere minasque,
ni procul abscedat, conviciaque insuper addunt.
nec satis est, ipsos etiam pedibusque manuque
turbavere lacus imoque e gurgite mollem
huc illuc limum saltu movere maligno.   365
distulit ira sitim; neque enim iam filia Coei
supplicat indignis nec dicere sustinet ultra
verba minora dea tollensque ad sidera palmas
"aeternum stagno" dixit "vivatis in isto!"
eveniunt optata deae: iuvat esse sub undis   370
et modo tota cava submergere membra palude,
nunc proferre caput, summo modo gurgite nare,
saepe super ripam stagni consistere, saepe
in gelidos resilire lacus, sed nunc quoque turpes
litibus exercent linguas pulsoque pudore,   375
quamvis sint sub aqua, sub aqua maledicere temptant.
vox quoque iam rauca est, inflataque colla tumescunt,

ipsaque dilatant patulos convicia rictus;
turpe caput tendunt, colla intercepta videntur,
spina viret, venter, pars maxima corporis, albet,   380
limosoque novae saliunt in gurgite ranae.'"

13

Boreas and Orithyia: 6.675–721

Hic dolor ante diem longaeque extrema senectae 675
tempora Tartareas Pandiona misit ad umbras.
sceptra loci rerumque capit moderamen Erechtheus,
iustitia dubium validisne potentior armis.
quattuor ille quidem iuvenes totidemque crearat
femineae sortis, sed erat par forma duarum. 680
e quibus Aeolides Cephalus te coniuge felix,
Procri, fuit; Boreae Tereus Thracesque nocebant,
dilectaque diu caruit deus Orithyia,
dum rogat et precibus mavult quam viribus uti;
ast ubi blanditiis agitur nil, horridus ira, 685
quae solita est illi nimiumque domestica vento,
"et merito!" dixit; "quid enim mea tela reliqui,
saevitiam et vires iramque animosque minaces,
admovique preces, quarum me dedecet usus?
apta mihi vis est: vi tristia nubila pello, 690
vi freta concutio nodosaque robora verto
induroque nives et terras grandine pulso;
idem ego, cum fratres caelo sum nactus aperto
(nam mihi campus is est), tanto molimine luctor,
ut medius nostris concursibus insonet aether 695
exsiliantque cavis elisi nubibus ignes;
idem ego, cum subii convexa foramina terrae
supposuique ferox imis mea terga cavernis,
sollicito manes totumque tremoribus orbem.
hac ope debueram thalamos petiisse, socerque 700
non orandus erat mihi sed faciendus Erechtheus."
   Haec Boreas aut his non inferiora locutus
excussit pennas, quarum iactatibus omnis

adflata est tellus latumque perhorruit aequor,
pulvereamque trahens per summa cacumina pallam   705
verrit humum pavidamque metu caligine tectus
Orithyian amans fulvis amplectitur alis.
dum volat, arserunt agitati fortius ignes,
nec prius aerii cursus suppressit habenas,
quam Ciconum tenuit populos et moenia raptor.   710
illic et gelidi coniunx Actaea tyranni
et genetrix facta est, partus enixa gemellos,
cetera qui matris, pennas genitoris haberent.
non tamen has una memorant cum corpore natas,
barbaque dum rutilis aberat subnixa capillis,   715
inplumes Calaisque puer Zetesque fuerunt;
mox pariter pennae ritu coepere volucrum
cingere utrumque latus, pariter flavescere malae.
ergo ubi concessit tempus puerile iuventae,
vellera cum Minyis nitido radiantia villo   720
per mare non notum prima petiere carina.

14

Medea's Magic: 7.251–349

Quos ubi placavit precibusque et murmure longo,
Aesonis effetum proferri corpus ad auras
iussit et in plenos resolutum carmine somnos
exanimi similem stratis porrexit in herbis.
hinc procul Aesoniden, procul hinc iubet ire ministros   255
et monet arcanis oculos removere profanos.
diffugiunt iussi; passis Medea capillis
bacchantum ritu flagrantis circuit aras
multifidasque faces in fossa sanguinis atra
tinguit et infectas geminis accendit in aris   260
terque senem flamma, ter aqua, ter sulphure lustrat.
  Interea validum posito medicamen aeno
fervet et exsultat spumisque tumentibus albet.
illic Haemonia radices valle resectas
seminaque floresque et sucos incoquit acres;   265
adicit extremo lapides Oriente petitos
et quas Oceani refluum mare lavit harenas;
addit et exceptas luna pernocte pruinas
et strigis infamis ipsis cum carnibus alas
inque virum soliti vultus mutare ferinos   270
ambigui prosecta lupi; nec defuit illis
squamea Cinyphii tenuis membrana chelydri
vivacisque iecur cervi; quibus insuper addit
ova caputque novem cornicis saecula passae.
his et mille aliis postquam sine nomine rebus   275
propositum instruxit mortali barbara maius,
arenti ramo iampridem mitis olivae
omnia confudit summisque inmiscuit ima.
ecce vetus calido versatus stipes aeno

fit viridis primo nec longo tempore frondes   280
induit et subito gravidis oneratur olivis:
at quacumque cavo spumas eiecit aeno
ignis et in terram guttae cecidere calentes,
vernat humus, floresque et mollia pabula surgunt.
quae simul ac vidit, stricto Medea recludit   285
ense senis iugulum veteremque exire cruorem
passa replet sucis; quos postquam conbibit Aeson
aut ore acceptos aut vulnere, barba comaeque
canitie posita nigrum rapuere colorem,
pulsa fugit macies, abeunt pallorque situsque,   290
adiectoque cavae supplentur corpore rugae,
membraque luxuriant: Aeson miratur et olim
ante quater denos hunc se reminiscitur annos.
   Viderat ex alto tanti miracula monstri
Liber et admonitus, iuvenes nutricibus annos   295
posse suis reddi, capit hoc a Colchide munus.
   Neve doli cessent, odium cum coniuge falsum
Phasias adsimulat Peliaeque ad limina supplex
confugit; atque illam, quoniam gravis ipse senecta est,
excipiunt natae; quas tempore callida parvo   300
Colchis amicitiae mendacis imagine cepit,
dumque refert inter meritorum maxima demptos
Aesonis esse situs atque hac in parte moratur,
spes est virginibus Pelia subiecta creatis,
arte suum parili revirescere posse parentem,   305
idque petunt pretiumque iubent sine fine pacisci.
illa brevi spatio silet et dubitare videtur
suspenditque animos ficta gravitate rogantes.
mox ubi pollicita est, "quo sit fiducia maior
muneris huius" ait, "qui vestri maximus aevo est   310
dux gregis inter oves, agnus medicamine fiet."
protinus innumeris effetus laniger annis
attrahitur flexo circum cava tempora cornu;
cuius ut Haemonio marcentia guttura cultro
fodit et exiguo maculavit sanguine ferrum,   315

membra simul pecudis validosque venefica sucos
mergit in aere cavo: minuunt ea corporis artus
cornuaque exurunt nec non cum cornibus annos,
et tener auditur medio balatus aeno:
nec mora, balatum mirantibus exsilit agnus   320
lascivitque fuga lactantiaque ubera quaerit.
   Obstipuere satae Pelia, promissaque postquam
exhibuere fidem, tum vero inpensius instant.
ter iuga Phoebus equis in Hibero flumine mersis
dempserat et quarta radiantia nocte micabant   325
sidera, cum rapido fallax Aeetias igni
imponit purum laticem et sine viribus herbas.
iamque neci similis resoluto corpore regem
et cum rege suo custodes somnus habebat,
quem dederant cantus magicaeque potentia linguae;   330
intrarant iussae cum Colchide limina natae
ambierantque torum: "quid nunc dubitatis inertes?
stringite" ait "gladios veteremque haurite cruorem,
ut repleam vacuas iuvenali sanguine venas!
in manibus vestris vita est aetasque parentis: 335
si pietas ulla est nec spes agitatis inanis,
officium praestate patri telisque senectam
exigite, et saniem coniecto emittite ferro!"
his, ut quaeque pia est, hortatibus inpia prima est
et, ne sit scelerata, facit scelus: haud tamen ictus   340
ulla suos spectare potest, oculosque reflectunt,
caecaque dant saevis aversae vulnera dextris.
ille cruore fluens, cubito tamen adlevat artus,
semilacerque toro temptat consurgere, et inter
tot medius gladios pallentia bracchia tendens   345
"quid facitis, gnatae? quid vos in fata parentis
armat?" ait: cecidere illis animique manusque;
plura locuturo cum verbis guttura Colchis
abstulit et calidis laniatum mersit in undis.

15

Daedalus: 8.183–259

Daedalus interea Creten longumque perosus
exilium tactusque loci natalis amore
clausus erat pelago. "terras licet" inquit "et undas   185
obstruat: et caelum certe patet; ibimus illac:
omnia possideat, non possidet aera Minos."
dixit et ignotas animum dimittit in artes
naturamque novat. nam ponit in ordine pennas
a minima coeptas, longam breviore sequenti,   190
ut clivo crevisse putes: sic rustica quondam
fistula disparibus paulatim surgit avenis;
tum lino medias et ceris alligat imas
atque ita conpositas parvo curvamine flectit,
ut veras imitetur aves. puer Icarus una   195
stabat et ignarus, sua se tractare pericla,
ore renidenti modo, quas vaga moverat aura,
captabat plumas, flavam modo pollice ceram
mollibat lusuque suo mirabile patris
impediebat opus. postquam manus ultima coepto   200
inposita est, geminas opifex libravit in alas
ipse suum corpus motaque pependit in aura;
instruit et natum "medio"que "ut limite curras,
Icare," ait "moneo, ne, si demissior ibis,
unda gravet pennas, si celsior, ignis adurat: 205
inter utrumque vola. nec te spectare Booten
aut Helicen iubeo strictumque Orionis ensem:
me duce carpe viam!" pariter praecepta volandi
tradit et ignotas umeris accommodat alas.
inter opus monitusque genae maduere seniles,   210
et patriae tremuere manus; dedit oscula nato

71

non iterum repetenda suo pennisque levatus
ante volat comitique timet, velut ales, ab alto
quae teneram prolem produxit in aera nido,
hortaturque sequi damnosasque erudit artes   215
et movet ipse suas et nati respicit alas.
hos aliquis tremula dum captat harundine pisces,
aut pastor baculo stivave innixus arator
vidit et obstipuit, quique aethera carpere possent,
credidit esse deos. et iam Iunonia laeva   220
parte Samos (fuerant Delosque Parosque relictae)
dextra Lebinthus erat fecundaque melle Calymne,
cum puer audaci coepit gaudere volatu
deseruitque ducem caelique cupidine tractus
altius egit iter. rapidi vicinia solis   225
mollit odoratas, pennarum vincula, ceras;
tabuerant cerae: nudos quatit ille lacertos,
remigioque carens non ullas percipit auras,
oraque caerulea patrium clamantia nomen
excipiuntur aqua, quae nomen traxit ab illo.   230
at pater infelix, nec iam pater, "Icare," dixit,
"Icare," dixit "ubi es? qua te regione requiram?"
"Icare" dicebat: pennas aspexit in undis
devovitque suas artes corpusque sepulcro
condidit, et tellus a nomine dicta sepulti.   235
    Hunc miseri tumulo ponentem corpora nati
garrula limoso prospexit ab elice perdix
et plausit pennis testataque gaudia cantu est,
unica tunc volucris nec visa prioribus annis,
factaque nuper avis longum tibi, Daedale, crimen.   240
namque huic tradiderat, fatorum ignara, docendam
progeniem germana suam, natalibus actis
bis puerum senis, animi ad praecepta capacis;
ille etiam medio spinas in pisce notatas
traxit in exemplum ferroque incidit acuto   245
perpetuos dentes et serrae repperit usum;
primus et ex uno duo ferrea bracchia nodo

vinxit, ut aequali spatio distantibus illis
altera pars staret, pars altera duceret orbem.
Daedalus invidit sacraque ex arce Minervae   250
praecipitem misit, lapsum mentitus; at illum,
quae favet ingeniis, excepit Pallas avemque
reddidit et medio velavit in aere pennis,
sed vigor ingenii quondam velocis in alas
inque pedes abiit; nomen, quod et ante, remansit.   255
non tamen haec alte volucris sua corpora tollit,
nec facit in ramis altoque cacumine nidos:
propter humum volitat ponitque in saepibus ova
antiquique memor metuit sublimia casus.

16

Orpheus: 10.1–85

Inde per inmensum croceo velatus amictu
aethera digreditur Ciconumque Hymenaeus ad oras
tendit et Orphea nequiquam voce vocatur.
adfuit ille quidem, sed nec sollemnia verba
nec laetos vultus nec felix attulit omen.   5
fax quoque, quam tenuit, lacrimoso stridula fumo
usque fuit nullosque invenit motibus ignes.
exitus auspicio gravior: nam nupta per herbas
dum nova naiadum turba comitata vagatur,
occidit in talum serpentis dente recepto.   10
quam satis ad superas postquam Rhodopeius auras
deflevit vates, ne non temptaret et umbras,
ad Styga Taenaria est ausus descendere porta
perque leves populos simulacraque functa sepulcro
Persephonen adiit inamoenaque regna tenentem   15
umbrarum dominum pulsisque ad carmina nervis
sic ait: "o positi sub terra numina mundi,
in quem reccidimus, quicquid mortale creamur,
si licet et falsi positis ambagibus oris
vera loqui sinitis, non huc, ut opaca viderem   20
Tartara, descendi, nec uti villosa colubris
terna Medusaei vincirem guttura monstri:
causa viae est coniunx, in quam calcata venenum
vipera diffudit crescentesque abstulit annos.
posse pati volui nec me temptasse negabo: 25
vicit Amor. supera deus hic bene notus in ora est;
an sit et hic, dubito: sed et hic tamen auguror esse,
famaque si veteris non est mentita rapinae,
vos quoque iunxit Amor. per ego haec loca plena timoris,

per Chaos hoc ingens vastique silentia regni,　　　　　　30
Eurydices, oro, properata retexite fata.
omnia debemur vobis, paulumque morati
serius aut citius sedem properamus ad unam.
tendimus huc omnes, haec est domus ultima, vosque
humani generis longissima regna tenetis.　　　　　　　35
haec quoque, cum iustos matura peregerit annos,
iuris erit vestri: pro munere poscimus usum;
quodsi fata negant veniam pro coniuge, certum est
nolle redire mihi: leto gaudete duorum."
　　Talia dicentem nervosque ad verba moventem　　　40
exsangues flebant animae; nec Tantalus undam
captavit refugam, stupuitque Ixionis orbis,
nec carpsere iecur volucres, urnisque vacarunt
Belides, inque tuo sedisti, Sisyphe, saxo.
tunc primum lacrimis victarum carmine fama est　　　45
Eumenidum maduisse genas, nec regia coniunx
sustinet oranti nec, qui regit ima, negare,
Eurydicenque vocant: umbras erat illa recentes
inter et incessit passu de vulnere tardo.
hanc simul et legem Rhodopeius accipit Orpheus,　　　50
ne flectat retro sua lumina, donec Avernas
exierit valles; aut inrita dona futura.
carpitur adclivis per muta silentia trames,
arduus, obscurus, caligine densus opaca,
nec procul afuerunt telluris margine summae:　　　　　55
hic, ne deficeret, metuens avidusque videndi
flexit amans oculos, et protinus illa relapsa est.
bracchiaque intendens prendique et prendere certans
nil nisi cedentes infelix arripit auras,
iamque iterum moriens non est de coniuge quicquam　60
questa suo (quid enim nisi se quereretur amatam?)
supremumque "vale," quod iam vix auribus ille
acciperet, dixit revolutaque rursus eodem est.
　　Non aliter stupuit gemina nece coniugis Orpheus,
quam tria qui timidus, medio portante catenas,　　　65

colla canis vidit, quem non pavor ante reliquit,
quam natura prior saxo per corpus oborto,
quique in se crimen traxit voluitque videri
Olenos esse nocens, tuque, o confisa figurae
infelix Lethaea tuae, iunctissima quondam   70
pectora, nunc lapides, quos umida sustinet Ide.
orantem frustraque iterum transire volentem
portitor arcuerat: septem tamen ille diebus
squalidus in ripa Cereris sine munere sedit;
cura dolorque animi lacrimaeque alimenta fuere.   75
esse deos Erebi crudeles questus, in altam
se recipit Rhodopen pulsumque aquilonibus Haemum.
    Tertius aequoreis inclusum Piscibus annum
finierat Titan, omnemque refugerat Orpheus
femineam Venerem, seu quod male cesserat illi,   80
sive fidem dederat; multas tamen ardor habebat
iungere se vati, multae doluere repulsae.
ille etiam Thracum populis fuit auctor amorem
in teneros transferre mares citraque iuventam
aetatis breve ver et primos carpere flores.   85

17

Pygmalion: 10.243–297

Quas quia Pygmalion aevum per crimen agentis
viderat, offensus vitiis, quae plurima menti
femineae natura dedit, sine coniuge caelebs   245
vivebat thalamique diu consorte carebat.
interea niveum mira feliciter arte
sculpsit ebur formamque dedit, qua femina nasci
nulla potest, operisque sui concepit amorem.
virginis est verae facies, quam vivere credas,   250
et, si non obstet reverentia, velle moveri:
ars adeo latet arte sua. miratur et haurit
pectore Pygmalion simulati corporis ignes.
saepe manus operi temptantes admovet, an sit
corpus an illud ebur, nec adhuc ebur esse fatetur.   255
oscula dat reddique putat loquiturque tenetque
et credit tactis digitos insidere membris
et metuit, pressos veniat ne livor in artus,
et modo blanditias adhibet, modo grata puellis
munera fert illi conchas teretesque lapillos   260
et parvas volucres et flores mille colorum
liliaque pictasque pilas et ab arbore lapsas
Heliadum lacrimas; ornat quoque vestibus artus,
dat digitis gemmas, dat longa monilia collo,
aure leves bacae, redimicula pectore pendent: 265
cuncta decent; nec nuda minus formosa videtur.
conlocat hanc stratis concha Sidonide tinctis
appellatque tori sociam adclinataque colla
mollibus in plumis, tamquam sensura, reponit.
    Festa dies Veneris tota celeberrima Cypro   270
venerat, et pandis inductae cornibus aurum

conciderant ictae nivea cervice iuvencae,
turaque fumabant, cum munere functus ad aras
constitit et timide "si di dare cuncta potestis,
sit coniunx, opto" non ausus "eburnea virgo"   275
dicere, Pygmalion "similis mea" dixit "eburnae."
sensit, ut ipsa suis aderat Venus aurea festis,
vota quid illa velint et, amici numinis omen,
flamma ter accensa est apicemque per aera duxit.
ut rediit, simulacra suae petit ille puellae   280
incumbensque toro dedit oscula: visa tepere est;
admovet os iterum, manibus quoque pectora temptat:
temptatum mollescit ebur positoque rigore
subsidit digitis ceditque, ut Hymettia sole
cera remollescit tractataque pollice multas   285
flectitur in facies ipsoque fit utilis usu.
dum stupet et dubie gaudet fallique veretur,
rursus amans rursusque manu sua vota retractat.
corpus erat! saliunt temptatae pollice venae.
tum vero Paphius plenissima concipit heros   290
verba, quibus Veneri grates agat, oraque tandem
ore suo non falsa premit, dataque oscula virgo
sensit et erubuit timidumque ad lumina lumen
attollens pariter cum caelo vidit amantem.
coniugio, quod fecit, adest dea, iamque coactis   295
cornibus in plenum noviens lunaribus orbem
illa Paphon genuit, de qua tenet insula nomen.

18

Midas: 11.100–145

Huic deus optandi gratum, sed inutile fecit 100
muneris arbitrium gaudens altore recepto.
ille male usurus donis ait "effice, quicquid
corpore contigero, fulvum vertatur in aurum."
adnuit optatis nocituraque munera solvit
Liber et indoluit, quod non meliora petisset. 105
laetus abit gaudetque malo Berecyntius heros
pollicitique fidem tangendo singula temptat
vixque sibi credens, non alta fronde virentem
ilice detraxit virgam: virga aurea facta est;
tollit humo saxum: saxum quoque palluit auro; 110
contigit et glaebam: contactu glaeba potenti
massa fit; arentis Cereris decerpsit aristas:
aurea messis erat; demptum tenet arbore pomum:
Hesperidas donasse putes; si postibus altis
admovit digitos, postes radiare videntur; 115
ille etiam liquidis palmas ubi laverat undis,
unda fluens palmis Danaen eludere posset;
vix spes ipse suas animo capit aurea fingens
omnia. gaudenti mensas posuere ministri
exstructas dapibus nec tostae frugis egentes: 120
tum vero, sive ille sua Cerealia dextra
munera contigerat, Cerealia dona rigebant,
sive dapes avido convellere dente parabat,
lammina fulva dapes admoto dente premebat;
miscuerat puris auctorem muneris undis: 125
fusile per rictus aurum fluitare videres.
    Attonitus novitate mali divesque miserque
effugere optat opes et quae modo voverat, odit.

copia nulla famem relevat; sitis arida guttur
urit, et inviso meritus torquetur ab auro   130
ad caelumque manus et splendida bracchia tollens
"da veniam, Lenaee pater! peccavimus" inquit,
"sed miserere, precor, speciosoque eripe damno!"
mite deum numen: Bacchus peccasse fatentem
restituit pactique fide data munera solvit   135
"neve male optato maneas circumlitus auro,
vade" ait "ad magnis vicinum Sardibus amnem
perque iugum Lydum labentibus obvius undis
carpe viam, donec venias ad fluminis ortus,
spumigeroque tuum fonti, qua plurimus exit,   140
subde caput corpusque simul, simul elue crimen."
rex iussae succedit aquae: vis aurea tinxit
flumen et humano de corpore cessit in amnem;
nunc quoque iam veteris percepto semine venae
arva rigent auro madidis pallentia glaebis.   145

19

Aeneas and the Sibyl: 14.101–153

Has ubi praeteriit et Parthenopeia dextra
moenia deseruit, laeva de parte canori
Aeolidae tumulum et, loca feta palustribus undis,
litora Cumarum vivacisque antra Sibyllae
intrat, et ad manes veniat per Averna paternos,   105
orat. at illa diu vultum tellure moratum
erexit tandemque deo furibunda recepto
"magna petis," dixit, "vir factis maxime, cuius
dextera per ferrum, pietas spectata per ignes.
pone tamen, Troiane, metum: potiere petitis   110
Elysiasque domos et regna novissima mundi
me duce cognosces simulacraque cara parentis.
invia virtuti nulla est via." dixit et auro
fulgentem ramum silva Iunonis Avernae
monstravit iussitque suo divellere trunco.   115
paruit Aeneas et formidabilis Orci
vidit opes atavosque suos umbramque senilem
magnanimi Anchisae; didicit quoque iura locorum,
quaeque novis essent adeunda pericula bellis.
inde ferens lassos adverso tramite passus   120
cum duce Cumaea mollit sermone laborem.
dumque iter horrendum per opaca crepuscula carpit,
"seu dea tu praesens, seu dis gratissima," dixit,
"numinis instar eris semper mihi, meque fatebor
muneris esse tui, quae me loca mortis adire,   125
quae loca me visae voluisti evadere mortis.
pro quibus aerias meritis evectus ad auras
templa tibi statuam, tribuam tibi turis honores."
respicit hunc vates et suspiratibus haustis

"nec dea sum," dixit "nec sacri turis honore   130
humanum dignare caput, neu nescius erres,
lux aeterna mihi carituraque fine dabatur,
si mea virginitas Phoebo patuisset amanti.
dum tamen hanc sperat, dum praecorrumpere donis
me cupit, "elige," ait "virgo Cumaea, quid optes: 135
optatis potiere tuis." ego pulveris hausti
ostendi cumulum: quot haberet corpora pulvis,
tot mihi natales contingere vana rogavi;
excidit, ut peterem iuvenes quoque protinus annos.
hos tamen ille mihi dabat aeternamque iuventam,   140
si Venerem paterer: contempto munere Phoebi
innuba permaneo; sed iam felicior aetas
terga dedit, tremuloque gradu venit aegra senectus,
quae patienda diu est. nam iam mihi saecula septem
acta vides: superest, numeros ut pulveris aequem,   145
ter centum messes, ter centum musta videre.
tempus erit, cum de tanto me corpore parvam
longa dies faciet, consumptaque membra senecta
ad minimum redigentur onus: nec amata videbor
nec placuisse deo, Phoebus quoque forsitan ipse   150
vel non cognoscet, vel dilexisse negabit:
usque adeo mutata ferar nullique videnda,
voce tamen noscar; vocem mihi fata relinquent."

20

Diomedes: 14.454–511

Auget uterque suas externo robore vires,
et multi Rutulos, multi Troiana tuentur   455
castra, neque Aeneas Evandri ad moenia frustra,
at Venulus frustra profugi Diomedis ad urbem
venerat: ille quidem sub Iapyge maxima Dauno
moenia condiderat dotaliaque arva tenebat;
sed Venulus Turni postquam mandata peregit   460
auxiliumque petit, vires Aetolius heros
excusat: nec se aut soceri committere pugnae
velle sui populos, aut quos e gente suorum
armet habere ullos, "neve haec commenta putetis,
admonitu quamquam luctus renoventur amari,   465
perpetiar memorare tamen. postquam alta cremata est
Ilios, et Danaas paverunt Pergama flammas,
Naryciusque heros, a virgine virgine rapta,
quam meruit poenam solus, digessit in omnes,
spargimur et ventis inimica per aequora rapti   470
fulmina, noctem, imbres, iram caelique marisque
perpetimur Danai cumulumque Capherea cladis,
neve morer referens tristes ex ordine casus,
Graecia tum potuit Priamo quoque flenda videri.
me tamen armiferae servatum cura Minervae   475
fluctibus eripuit, patriis sed rursus ab Argis
pellor, et antiquo memores de vulnere poenas
exigit alma Venus, tantosque per alta labores
aequora sustinui, tantos terrestribus armis,
ut mihi felices sint illi saepe vocati,   480
quos communis hiems inportunusque Caphereus
mersit aquis, vellemque horum pars una fuissem.

"Ultima iam passi comites belloque fretoque
deficiunt finemque rogant erroris, at Acmon
fervidus ingenio, tum vero et cladibus asper,   485
'quid superest, quod iam patientia vestra recuset
ferre, viri?' dixit 'quid habet Cytherea, quod ultra,
velle puta, faciat? nam dum peiora timentur,
est locus in vulnus: sors autem ubi pessima rerum,
sub pedibus timor est securaque summa malorum.   490
audiat ipsa licet et, quod facit, oderit omnes
sub Diomede viros, odium tamen illius omnes
spernimus, et magno stat magna potentia nobis.'
talibus inritans Venerem Pleuronius Acmon
instimulat verbis veteremque resuscitat iram.   495
dicta placent paucis, numeri maioris amici
Acmona conripimus; cui respondere volenti
vox pariter vocisque via est tenuata, comaeque
in plumas abeunt, plumis nova colla teguntur
pectoraque et tergum, maiores bracchia pennas   500
accipiunt, cubitique leves sinuantur in alas;
magna pedis digitos pars occupat, oraque cornu
indurata rigent finemque in acumine ponunt.
hunc Lycus, hunc Idas et cum Rhexenore Nycteus,
hunc miratur Abas, et dum mirantur, eandem   505
accipiunt faciem, numerusque ex agmine maior
subvolat et remos plausis circumvolat alis:
si volucrum quae sit dubiarum forma requiris,
ut non cygnorum, sic albis proxima cygnis.
vix equidem has sedes et Iapygis arida Dauni   510
arva gener teneo minima cum parte meorum."

21

Caesar's Deification and the Epilogue:
15.843–879

Vix ea fatus erat, media cum sede senatus
constitit alma Venus nulli cernenda suique
Caesaris eripuit membris nec in aera solvi   845
passa recentem animam caelestibus intulit astris
dumque tulit, lumen capere atque ignescere sensit
emisitque sinu: luna volat altius illa
flammiferumque trahens spatioso limite crinem
stella micat natique videns bene facta fatetur   850
esse suis maiora et vinci gaudet ab illo.
hic sua praeferri quamquam vetat acta paternis,
libera fama tamen nullisque obnoxia iussis
invitum praefert unaque in parte repugnat:
sic magnus cedit titulis Agamemnonis Atreus,   855
Aegea sic Theseus, sic Pelea vicit Achilles;
denique, ut exemplis ipsos aequantibus utar,
sic et Saturnus minor est Iove: Iuppiter arces
temperat aetherias et mundi regna triformis,
terra sub Augusto est; pater est et rector uterque.   860
di, precor, Aeneae comites, quibus ensis et ignis
cesserunt, dique Indigetes genitorque Quirine
urbis et invicti genitor Gradive Quirini
Vestaque Caesareos inter sacrata penates,
et cum Caesarea tu, Phoebe domestice, Vesta,   865
quique tenes altus Tarpeias Iuppiter arces,
quosque alios vati fas appellare piumque est:
tarda sit illa dies et nostro serior aevo,
qua caput Augustum, quem temperat, orbe relicto
accedat caelo faveatque precantibus absens!   870
    Iamque opus exegi, quid nec Iovis ira nec ignis

nec poterit ferrum nec edax abolere vetustas.
cum volet, illa dies, quae nil nisi corporis huius
ius habet, incerti spatium mihi finiat aevi:
parte tamen meliore mei super alta perennis   875
astra ferar, nomenque erit indelebile nostrum,
quaque patet domitis Romana potentia terris,
ore legar populi, perque omnia saecula fama,
siquid habent veri vatum praesagia, vivam.

Notes

1. Introduction and Creation: 1.1–150

Ovid's creation story is modeled on a number of Greek and Latin creation accounts, going back to Hesiod's *Theogony* and to the natural science writings of the pre-Socratic philosophers; from Hesiod, Ovid takes the story of the successive Ages, and from the pre-Socratics he takes the theory of the four elements (fire, air, water, earth). In Latin, Ovid's most important model is the Epicurean poet Lucretius, whose *De Rerum Natura* provides Ovid with a model of Latin poetic language and phrasing in the description of scientific matters. Ovid's own creation story does not follow any particular philosophical school but is a pastiche of details found in his various predecessors. Therefore, we should probably read this passage as a statement of Ovid's literary interests and loyalties, rather than of his philosophical or religious beliefs.

1 *fert [me] animus [meus]:* "my mind moves me" or "inspires me." *dicere:* "tell of" or "tell about."

2 *coeptīs:* the neuter plural participle *coeptum* (from *coepi*), used as a noun: "beginnings" or "undertakings"; dative with the compound verb *adspirate* (3). *mutastis = mutavistis. et =* "also." *illās:* Our various manuscripts of the *Metamorphoses* give both *illās* and *illa,* either of which makes some sense. If we read *illās,* the pronoun must refer to the feminine plural *formās;* if we read *illa,* the pronoun refers to the neuter plural *coeptīs.* Depending on which reading we choose, the gods have changed either the bodies (*formās*) which underwent metamorphosis, *or* the poet's own poetry (*coeptīs . . . meīs*). In the *Metamorphoses,* Ovid's poetry, previously all in the elegiac meter, has undergone a change to the epic dactylic hexameter.

4 *perpetuum . . . carmen:* a technical Latin term for an epic poem, a long, "continuous" (*perpetuum*) song. Some readers question the degree to which the *Metamorphoses* should be considered "epic," especially if *deducite* ("spin out thinly") in this same line is a reference to the Hellenistic ideal of finely crafted, small-scale poetry, which is traditionally opposed to epic. Ovid would then be announcing his perhaps paradoxical intention to write a poem in both the grand epic tradition and the Hellenistic tradition.

5 *ante:* preposition + acc.

6 *orbe [terrārum]* = the world (a Latin idiom, literally meaning "the circle of the lands").

7 *dixēre: -ēre* for *-ērunt.* The subject is an unspecified "they." Here the verb has the meaning "call"; compare its meaning "tell of" in line 1. Chaos is the first subject in the description of Creation in Hesiod's *Theogony.*

8 *quicquam:* neuter of *quisquam. eōdem:* "in (or to) the same place."

9 *semina rērum:* Lucretius' term for the smallest elements of matter, from which all things are made. *non bene iunctārum: Non bene = male;* to be understood

89

closely with the participle *iunctārum*. Latin poetry frequently expresses a concept by negating its opposite.

10 *Tītan = Sōl*.

11 *Phoebe = Lūna*. The points of the crescent moon are often called "horns" in Latin; each month the moon seems to grow new horns (hence *crescendo reparabat*).

14 *Amphitrite* = ocean, which is often depicted as a kind of river that encircles the edge of the earth. Amphitrite is properly the wife of Neptune.

15–16 *ut...sic:* "although ... yet (or nevertheless)..."

17 *lucis egens: egeo* here takes a genitive; often it takes an ablative. *nullī sua forma manēbat: nullī* is a dative of possession. Like most sentences with a dative of possession, this sentence works better if turned around: "Its own form remained to nothing," or better, "Nothing kept its own form."

18 *aliīs aliud:* when two forms of *alius* are used together, they mean "one ... the other." *aliīs* is dative after the compound *obstabat*.

19–20 *frigida, umentia, mollia, habentia:* neuter plural adjectives used as nouns ("things"). The corresponding adjectives in each pair (*calidīs, siccīs, durīs*) are also neuter plurals. Supply *cum* with *calidīs* and *siccīs*, by analogy with *cum durīs*. *sine pondere habentia pondus:* Ovid now varies the formula a bit: *habentia pondus [pugnabant cum illīs quae erant] sine pondere.*

21 *deus et melior ... natura:* Not two separate entities, but alternatives (*Oxford Latin Dictionary*, s.v. *et* 3: "or rather"); *melior natura* renames *deus*, because Ovid ascribes creation to no particular deity.

22 *caelō terrās et terrīs abscidit undās:* The compound verb *abscindo* means "divide one thing (acc.) from another (dat. or abl.)"; here are two accusative nouns, each with a dative noun.

24 *quae postquam = postquam quae. quae = illa* (neuter pl. acc.), a general reference to the elements that the god had separated.

25 *dissociata [elementa] locīs [in] concordī pace ligavit:* The action in the participle *dissociata* must be imagined to have taken place before the action indicated by *ligavit*. To paraphrase: "When the elements had been separated in their (proper) places, he bound them in a harmonious peace."

26 *vis* is modified by the adjective *ignea* and by the prepositional phrase *sine pondere. et* should be seen as joining these two modifiers, and not as separating *convexī ... caelī.*

26–31 Of the four elements, fire is considered the "lightest," so it naturally rises to the highest level of the universe (where it feeds its light to the stars that shine in the heavens). Below the level of heavenly fire is the *āēr,* which we might call the "atmosphere," the air that surrounds us near the earth. Next comes earth, which is kept down by its own *gravitas* (which, for once, we might legitimately translate as "gravity"!). Finally, the water of the sea is imagined to be in some way heavier than the land, because the land is surrounded and held in the grasp of the sea.

28 *proximus . . . illī [ignī]. levitate locōque:* ablative of respect.

29 *hīs = igne et āere. densior hīs tellus [est] elementaque grandia traxit:* two clauses, separated by *-que.*

30 *umor = aqua.*

31 *ultima [loca].*

32 *quisquis fuit ille deōrum:* subject of *secuit* and *coegit;* the unspecified creating *deus* of line 21. Ovid's refusal to name this god (or even to investigate his identity) is becoming almost defiant. (Compare *mundī fabricator* in line 57, below.)

32–33 *Sic . . . dispositam . . . congeriem secuit:* as in line 25, the perfect participle indicates the first of two actions and really deserves to be translated first, in its own clause: "When the *congeries* had been thus arranged, he cut it. . . ." The same technique should also be used for the next clause: *sectamque [congeriem] in membra coegit.* Note the juxtaposition of two forms of *seco* in this line: *secuit sectamque.*

34–35 *ab omnī / parte = in omnī parte.*

35 *magnī speciem . . . in orbis = in speciem magnī orbis;* note the placement of the preposition next to the genitive (*orbis*), which depends on the preposition's object (*speciem*), rather than next to the object itself.

36–37 The god is ordering the waters to arrange themselves into the seas. *iussit* is followed by the noun *freta* (= *aquās*) and three infinitives: *diffundī, tumescere,* and *circumdāre. (Iubeo* is the only verb of ordering that can be followed by an infinitive instead of an *ut*-clause.)

38–39 The three objects of *addidit,* in line 38, are joined by *et . . . et . . . -que.* The next *-que (fluminaque)* at the beginning of line 39 joins the two clauses ("*addidit . . .*" and "*cinxit . . .*").

40 *quae = flumina. ab ipsā [terrā].*

40–42 With the two clauses containing *partim,* Ovid describes the different fates of rivers: the waters of some rivers soak into the earth, while the waters of other rivers eventually reach the sea. Note the difference between *ripa* (the bank of a river) and *litora* (the shores of the seas); translating both as "shore" will not always do.

41–42 *campō . . . liberioris aquae = aequore; campus,* which usually denotes a flat expanse of land, here indicates the flat open surface of the sea.

42 *pro =* "instead of."

43 Here, as in lines 36–37, the Creator seems to speak to the geographical elements (*iussit*), which arrange themselves according to his instructions.

45 *utque: ut* here, with the indicative, means "as" and begins a comparison that is completed by the *sic* clause in 47–48. Just as (*ut*) there are five zones in the sky, as marked off by Roman augury, so (*sic*) there are five zones on the earth. *dextrā [parte], sinistrā [parte].*

47–48 With the Arctic and Antarctic Circles, and the Tropics of Cancer and Capricorn, the earth can be divided into five "zones" or regions (which correspond to the augurs' five "zones" of the sky). The Mediterranean Romans and Greeks considered the equatorial and polar regions to be uninhabitable; only those regions in the Northern Hemisphere between the Arctic Circle and the Tropic of Cancer and in the Southern Hemisphere (only a theoretical place to most ancient Europeans) between the Antarctic Circle and the Tropic of Capricorn were considered fit for human habitation.

48 *premuntur:* "are stamped," as if the lines demarcating the regions were physically drawn on the earth.

49 *quārum = hārum zonārum. [ea] quae media est, non est habitabilis:* the equatorial region. *aestū:* ablative of cause

50 *duās:* the polar regions. *totidem [zonās]:* "the same number," i.e., two, the number both of the polar regions and of the temperate regions. *inter utramque:* between each polar region.

51 *mixtā . . . flammā:* ablative absolute.

52–68 God now arranges the air, or atmosphere, which contains the weather and the winds.

52 *āēr:* In this Greek word for "air," both vowels are long and separate, not a diphthong (single syllable) as *ae* usually is in Latin.

52–53 The text is difficult as it stands here, although it makes sense if we accept the suggested reading: *quī quantō est pondere terrae / pondus aquae levius, tantō est onerosior ignī.* Then we can understand the sentence as: *[aer] est onerosior ignī [abl. of comparison] tantō quantō pondus aquae est levius pondere terrae. tantō . . . quantō:* "by as much as . . ."; ablative degree of difference.

54 *illīc:* in the *aer.*

54–56 The god orders four items to "take up residence" (*consistere*) in the *aer: nebulās, nubēs, tonitrua,* and *ventōs.*

55 *humanās . . . mentēs:* object of *motura.*

56 *frigora:* object of *facientēs. cum fulminibus . . . frigora = fulmina et frigora* (both were considered to be caused by winds).

57–66 The creating deity does not give free run of the air to all the winds; he separates them into their own provinces.

57 *hīs [ventīs]. habendum:* "to be held" or "for the purpose of holding"; compare *habitandae* in line 74, below.

58 *āera:* accusative singular, Greek form. *obsistitur:* used impersonally (producing the nonsensical translation: "it is scarcely hindered or impeded to them"); can be translated actively, if you supply a subject (the deity?): "he scarcely hinders them"; or passively, "they are scarcely impeded." *illīs [ventīs]:* dative after the compound verb *obsisto.*

59 *cum:* "although." *cum . . . tractū:* "although each [wind-god] rules his own winds in a different district (*tractus*)."

60 *quin lanient mundum:* depends on the main verb *obsistitur.* When verbs of hindering or preventing, such as *obsisto,* are negated (as *vix* in line 58 effectively negates *obsistitur*), the subjunctive clause that completes their meaning

begins with *quīn.* English will usually use "from" plus a gerund to translate this clause: "they were scarcely impeded *from tearing up* the world." *" fratrum:* the wind-gods are seen as brothers.

61–66 Note the variety of sentence structures Ovid uses to describe the locations of the various major winds (East, West, North, and South).

63 *occiduō quae litora sole tepescunt: litora* belongs outside the relative clause, while *occiduo* belongs inside it. *litora* is a subject of *sunt,* in line 64.

64 *septemque trionēs = et septemtriōnēs:* The Septemtriones are the seven stars of the Great Bear or Little Bear constellations, which appear in the northern sky and are thus representative of the entire region of the North. The breaking up of a compound word with another word, as is done here with *-que,* is called *tmesis* (Greek for "cutting").

66 *pluviāque:* From *pluvia, ae* (f.), "rain."

67 *haec super = super haec.*

68 *aethera:* Greek accusative form, modified by the adjective *liquidum* (67) and by the participial phrases *gravitate carentem* (67) and *nec quicquam terrenae faecis habentem* (68). *quicquam = quidquam. terrenae faecis:* partitive genitive with *quicquam;* Latin literally says "any(thing) *of* earthly dregs," where English usually omits the "of."

70 *quae:* refers to *sidera* (71).

72 *neu = nēve,* here equivalent to *et nē* (introducing a negative purpose clause); *nēve* is used in this same way at 1.151 and 1.445. *foret = esset. suīs animalibus orba: orbus* can take an ablative of separation, although English demands the translation "deprived *of . . .*"

74 *habitandae:* "to be inhabited" (gerundive to express purpose; see *habendum* in line 57, above).

75 *volucrēs [cēpit] agitabilis āēr.*

76–77 *animal* is modified by the phrases *sanctius hīs, mentisque capacius altae,* and the relative clause *quod dominārī in cetera posset.*

79 *ille opifex rērum, mundī melioris origo:* two more of Ovid's nonspecific names for the creating divinity, if there was one; the alternative scientific explanation is given in the next two lines.

80–81 The earth was only recently separated from the *aether* (lines 21–31) and so may retain some of the "seeds" of the heavenly element, which can then give rise to new creations. In this quasi-scientific explanation Ovid still retains some of the language of a mythological version, in which Mother Earth is impregnated by Father Sky.

82 *[tellurem] quam. satus Iapetō =* Prometheus, the son of Iapetus; literally "the one begotten by Iapetus" (*satus* from *sero*). Iapetus was one of the Titans, a race of gods supposedly born before the Olympians, but Ovid makes no effort to explain the origins of any of these beings. For a more comprehensive account, see Hesiod's *Theogony.*

83 Prometheus makes humans in the image of the gods. *moderantum cuncta deōrum: cuncta* (neu. pl. acc.) is the object of the present participle.
84 *cum:* "although."
85 *os:* "face."
86 *iussit [hominem].*
87 *modo quae fuerat:* Note the pluperfect tense, modified by *modo* ("just recently"): the earth had, until just recently, been *rudis et sine imagine.*
89–113 Description of the Golden Age. Note the way this period is described primarily in negative terms, with long sequences of negative words such as *sine* and *nec* organizing Ovid's sentences: *nec . . . nec . . . sine* (91–93), *nondum . . . nondum* (94–97), *non* four times in 98–99, etc.
89–90 *vindice nullō, sponte suā:* ablative of manner; *sponte suā* is the usual Latin phrase for "of one's own accord."
91–92 *nec verba minantia fixō / aere legebantur:* The Laws of the Twelve Tables, Rome's earliest laws (*verba minantia*), were displayed in public on bronze tablets (*fixō aere*); in the Golden Age, humanity had no need for such things. Ovid describes the peace of the Golden Age through the absence of all the things Romans would have thought necessary to orderly life: laws, courts, deterrent punishments. *aere:* from *aes, aeris,* n.: "bronze"; in this word, the *ae*-combination *does* form a diphthong, so that the genitive singular is only a two-syllable word. Contrast the Greek noun *āēr, āeris* (m., "air"), in which the vowels are separate and the genitive has three syllables (e.g., lines 12, 15, 17, 23, above).
94–95 The cutting of trees to make ships is always seen by ancient authors as a landmark event in the development of human culture. See lines 132–134, below, on the development of sailing in the Iron Age. *nondum:* modifies the verbal actions in both the participle *caesa* and the main verb *descenderat:* the trees had "not yet" been cut *and* had "not yet" descended. *suīs . . . montibus:* ablative of separation, with *caesa. caesa . . . pinus: pinus,* like all names of trees, is feminine.
96 *nov[er]ant:* from the verb *nosco.*
97–100 The Golden Age is also characterized by the absence of war and military trappings, such as defensive constructions (*fossae*), war trumpets, armor, and weapons.
99 *militis:* usually *miles* refers to an individual soldier, but is sometimes used collectively as "the soldiery" or "the military."
99–100 The freedom from war and military service is described as *otia,* "leisure"; this leisure is then extended in the next lines to describe freedom from another sort of drudgery, farmwork.
101–102 *ipsa . . . tellus.*
103 *[homines] contentī. cibīs nullō cogente creatīs: cibīs . . . creatīs* is ablative depending on *contentī* ("content with . . ."); *nullō [homine] cogente* describes how the food was created ("with no one compelling [it to grow]").

104 *legēbant:* "they picked."

104–106 The diet of Golden Age people: *arbuteōs fetūs, montana fraga, corna, mora, glandēs.* Note how Ovid varies the amount and type of description he gives each item: the first two are nouns with adjectives; the third is a noun alone; the fourth is a noun with a participial phrase; and the fifth is a noun with a relative clause.

106 *decĭderant:* from *decĭdo* (*de* + *cado*); not from *decīdo* (*de* + *caedo*). *Iovis arbore:* the oak.

108 *natōs sine semine florēs:* "flowers born without a seed" must mean without a seed that any human had planted; the winds of course helped spread the wild seeds.

109 *frugēs:* "grain," an addition to the diet of fruits and berries described above. *inarata:* "unplowed": formed from *in* ("not") + the perfect participle of *aro, arare* ("to plow").

110 *nec renovatus ager:* "the farmland, not renewed"; "renewed" means made fertile again by being left fallow. In the Golden Age, land did not lose its fertility with repeated crop-bearing and thus did not have to be left fallow periodically to renew its productiveness. *canēbat:* from *caneo, canēre* ("to be white"); the field full of ripe grain would present a light-colored vista. Note the imperfect, which indicates repeated action, the point made by *nec renovatus:* over and over, the fields produced crops without being left fallow.

111–12 Without any work, people in the Golden Age can have milk and honey, substances that normally require the intensive labor of cattle raising and beekeeping.

113 *Saturnō tenebrosa in Tartara missō:* Saturn, father of Jupiter, is traditionally said to have ruled during the Golden Age, before his overthrow by Jupiter. Thus, Saturn's departure marks the end of the Golden Age. In some versions, Saturn is banished to Italy, where he continues to rule, but in this case, Ovid has Saturn banished to the Underworld (Tartarus).

115 *aurō, aere:* ablative of comparison after the two comparative adjectives (*deterior, pretiosior*). Since ancient texts did not have punctuation, we cannot tell with certainty which of the nouns *fulvō* is meant to modify; it might have been read with both or either.

116–20 The chief innovation of the Silver Age is the institution of seasons, which cause humans to build houses for shelter and to invent seasonal agriculture.

118 *exegit . . . annum:* "completed the year." *spatiīs . . . quattuor:* ablative of the time within which. Remember that Latin words for numbers higher than 3 do not decline; the form *quattuor* can therefore be any case.

120 *ventīs glacies adstricta:* icicles are imagined to be formed by the action of the wind on the ice.

121 *[homines] subiēre:* *-ēre* for *-ērunt. fuērunt:* previously, during the Golden Age, people's "homes" were caves, bushes, etc.

123   *Cerealia:* "relating to Ceres." Since Ceres is the goddess of grain, "seeds related to Ceres" is a poetic expression for "grain."

124   *gemuēre: -ēre* for *-ērunt.*

125–27   The Bronze Age gets a scant three lines. The innovation of this age seems to have been warfare (*arma,* 126), but war had not yet become criminal or sinful (*scelerata*). The Bronze Age serves mainly as a transition to the Iron Age.

125   *tertia . . . aenea proles:* in English, the two adjectives must be separated from one another: "the third generation, the bronze," or "the third and bronze generation," rather than "the third bronze generation."

127–50   Ovid describes the Iron Age as the age in which all evils now known to humanity broke forth and spread through the world: virtues were replaced by vices; human daring manifested itself in seafaring (traditionally seen as a hybristic activity); private property became the norm; precious metals were mined, and wars broke out over their possession; greed and jealousy led humans to all other sorts of crimes. Finally, Justice (*Astraea*) fled the earth.

127   *ultima [aetas].*

128   *venae peioris in aevum:* Since all the Ages are named after metals, they are said to be of a certain "vein." Iron is cheaper or "worse" (*peior*) than bronze, silver, or gold.

129   *fugitque pudor verumque fidesque:* each of the three is individually the subject of *fugit. verum = veritas.* Occasionally, the neuter form of an adjective is used in place of an abstraction.

130   *subiēre = subiērunt. fraudēsque dolusque:* polysyndeton (excessive use of connectives); the first *-que* does not join anything.

131   *amor sceleratus habendī:* "criminal love of Having (i.e., possession)"

132–34   Sailing is often mentioned in ancient literature as evidence of humans' excessive daring: man, a land creature, tries to travel on the water, while trees are uprooted from the land to form boats and travel far from their native lands. See the opening lines of Euripides' *Medea;* Horace, *Ode* 1.3; and Catullus, *Carmen* 64.

132–33   *nec adhuc bene noverat illōs [ventōs] / navita:* Sailing is still such a new skill that sailors do not yet understand how to interpret the winds.

133   *navita = nauta.*

133–34   *quaeque prius . . . , carinae: Carina* ("keel") is a frequent metonymy for "boat." Here, the boats are equated to the trees from whose wood they are made. Note the geographic contrast between *in montibus altīs* (where the trees grew) and *fluctibus ignotīs* (where the ships built from those trees now sail).

134   *exsultavēre = exsultavērunt.*

135   *communemque prius:* take *prius* adverbially with the adjective: "previously communal."

135–36   The land surveyor (*cautus . . . mensor,* 136) is another typically Roman feature of civilized life.

137–38   *nec tantum . . . sed:* "not only . . . , but (also) . . ." *Posco* takes the "double accusative" construction in the active: "I demand something (acc.) from something-or-someone (acc.)," or "I ask-for something (acc.) from something-or-someone (acc.)." When *posco* is used passively, one of these accusatives remains, that designating the thing asked for: "Something or someone (nom.) is asked for something (acc.)." Thus we find the unusual use of a sort of "object" after a passive verb: here, the nouns *segetes* and *alimenta* are accusatives.

138   *itum est:* impersonal passive: "it was gone," i.e., "people went."

139   The subject of *recondiderat* and *admoverat* is *terra.*

142   *prodierat, prodit:* subject is *terra. bellum, quod pugnat utroque:* War itself is here treated as an agent which "fights." *pugnat* might be translated as if it were *geritur. utrōque:* ablative of means; i.e., by means of either iron (weapons) or gold (bribery).

143   *sanguineāque manū crepitantia concutit arma:* continuing the personification of *bellum* (the subject again of *concutit*), which now has bloody hands and brandishes its own weapons.

144–48   A standard list of horrible crimes, all of which violate apparently natural laws, such as those that are supposed to bond guests to hosts, and family members to one another.

144   *vivitur:* impersonal passive (see line 138, above): "it is lived," i.e., "people live." *raptum, raptī,* n.: plunder.

144–45   *non hospes ab hospite tutus [est], / non socer a generō [tutus est].*

146   *inminet:* "is intent on" (+ dat.). *inminet exitiō vir coniugis, [inminet exitiō] illa maritī. illa = coniunx.*

148   *ante diem:* before the appointed time (i.e., of his father's death); the son is unnaturally and sinfully eager to know when his father will die. *patriōs . . . in annōs = in annōs patris:* use of an adjective instead of a genitive noun; "the paternal years" = "the father's years."

149–50   *caede madentīs . . . terrās.*

150   *ultima caelestum . . . Astraea:* It appears that the rest of the gods have already moved to the heavens, after initially occupying the earth along with mortals. But human evil causes all the gods to separate themselves from humanity. The departure of Justice, here personified as the maiden Astraea, is a fitting consequence of the rampant crimes just described.

2. The Flood: 1.262–312

Jupiter has decided that all humanity has become too evil to save, as illustrated by the wickedness of Lycaon (1.163–252). Although the gods agree that humans should be destroyed, some gods worry that no one will be left to worship them. Jupiter promises that a new and different race will replace the old one.

Ovid's description of the flood has much in common with other descriptions of floods and storms in ancient literature. In particular, compare it with Vergil's description of the sea storm in *Aeneid* 1. Ovid's narrative focuses closely on the appearance and actions of the very anthropomorphic gods, such as Notus, Iris, Neptune, and Jupiter, and on the topsy-turvy nature of the flooded world. The passage also depicts several of the flood's human victims. Ovid does not emphasize their supposed guilt, but instead their bewilderment at the destruction of their homes and the metamorphosis of their landscape. Another description of a flooded landscape can be found at Horace, *Odes* 1.2.

262 *Aeoliīs . . . in antrīs: Aeoliīs* is an adjective (*Aeolius, a, um*) derived from the name of Aeolus, king of the winds, who lives with the various winds in a great cave. When ordered, he lets out one or more winds from the cave. (See Vergil's description of this arrangement in *Aeneid* 1, and compare Aeolus in Homer, *Odyssey* 10.) *claudit:* The subject of this sentence is Jupiter, who gets the flooding started with winds. Since Jupiter rules the sky, he can most naturally start a flood by calling up Notus, the wind that brings rain. Later (lines 274–84), his brother Neptune, who rules the waters on earth, will also contribute to the flood.

263 *fugant:* from *fugo, fugāre* ("to put to flight, cause to flee"); not to be confused with *fugio, fugere* ("to flee").

265 *terribilem piceā tectus cālīgine vultum:* note the word order, in which the first and last words agree, the ones next to them agree, and all depend on the central word. *terribilem . . . vultum:* accusative of respect with *tectus*. The participle *tectus* properly agrees with *Notus,* but Notus is not completely "covered with pitch-black fog"; rather, he is only covered "with respect to his terrible countenance." This Greek construction occurs frequently in Latin poetry.

266 *barba [est] gravis nimbīs. unda:* a standard poetic word for "water," or the "waves" of the sea, and a key word in this passage; note how often it appears (275, 290, 304, 305, 311). Note also the abundance of other words for water in this passage (e.g., *amnis, flumen, fons, aequor, gurges, pontus, mare*).

267 *sinūs:* nominative plural; here probably with the meaning "folds of the garments over the breast," or just "breast."

268 *ut(que)* here, with the indicative, means "when." *lātā:* from *latus, a, um. nubila:* neuter plural accusative. The neuter form of the adjective (*nubilus, a, um:* "cloudy") can often be used as a noun ("cloudy things" = "clouds"). Note also that the adjective *nubilus* is derived from the noun *nubes*. The poet uses a variety of words generally meaning "cloud" in these lines: *nubes, nimbus, cālīgo, nebula, nubila*.

270 *nuntia Iunonis:* Iris, the rainbow, serves as the messenger of Juno twice in the *Aeneid* (4.693–705 and 5.604–63). *variōs induta colorēs: induta* is an example

of a rare *active* use of the perfect participle of a nondeponent verb: "having put on" or "wearing." The participle thus takes an object (*colorēs*), as perfect participles of deponent verbs regularly do. (This usage can also be interpreted as a Latin usage of the Greek middle voice.)

271   The rainbow, which bridges earth and sky, is imagined to be drawing up water to feed the clouds.

272–73   *deplorata colonī / vota iacent: vota* is the subject, while *colonī* is genitive singular. The "farmer's prayers" are the things he has prayed for—i.e., his crops, etc. *Deplorata*, although it describes *vota*, is to be taken predicatively, as an adjective after the verb.

274   *contenta:* perfect participle from *contineo*, not *contendo. suō: suus* is supposed to refer to the subject of the sentence (here *ira*), but logic here demands that it refer to Jupiter (who possesses the *ira*). *illum = Iovem.*

275   *caeruleus frater [Iovis]* = Neptune; *caeruleus* is the regular color of water deities.

276   *qui postquam = postquam amnes:* use of the relative for connection; translate such a relative as a demonstrative or personal pronoun.

277   *intravēre = intravērunt.*

277–78   *non est hortamine longō / nunc . . . utendum:* Verbs that take a case other than the accusative must become impersonal when used in a passive construction; here, *utor* is used impersonally in the passive periphrastic (*non est . . . utendum*). The resulting nonsensical translation ("there must not be used") should be converted to the active voice ("I must not use" or "there is no need to use").

279   *opus est:* The *opus est* construction ("there is need") usually takes the dative of the one who needs and the ablative of the thing needed (e.g., *opus est mihi pecuniā*, "I need money"), but here it is used alone. *mole:* "the barrier."

280   *inmittite habenās:* "give full rein to . . ."

281   *hī = amnēs. fontibus:* dative of possession, equivalent to a genitive.

282   *defrenatō: frena* are the reins, which the river gods were urged to relax, so that the rivers would flood (*inmittite habenās*, 280). So now the rivers flow *defrenatō . . . cursū.*

283   *ipse:* Neptune; *illa* = the earth (*terram* in the previous clause).

284   *viās . . . aquārum:* Where Latin says "paths of waters," English says "paths for the waters."

286   *satīs: sata, satōrum*, neuter plural, "crops" (from *sero, serere, sevi, satus*, to sow).

286–87   What the rivers carry off (objects of *rapiunt*): *arbusta* (*cum satīs*), *pecudēs, virōs, tecta penetralia* (*cum suīs sacrīs*).

288   *si qua domus: qua = aliqua* "any." *Aliqui* and other such words beginning with *ali-* lose that prefix after the words *si, nisi, num*, and *nē*.

290   *pressae:* here meaning "submerged" (from *premo*).

292   *deerant quoque litora pontō: desum:* means "to be missing from something [dative]"; similar to the use of *sum* with a dative of possession, the sentence with *desum* can be turned around to mean "something [dative] lacks something [nominative]."

293   *hic . . . alter:* "one man . . . another man." Similarly, *ille* (295) and *hic* (296). These lines present several short images of humans caught in the flood. *cumbā . . . aduncā:* ablative of place where.

294   *ducit remōs:* i.e., rows his boat. *arābat:* note the imperfect, which here means "used to" and contrasts with the present *ducit.*

296   *summā . . . in ulmō:* *ulmus* is feminine, as are the names of all trees, even the second-declension ones ending in *-us.*

299   *quā:* "where." *carpsēre = carpsērunt.*

300   *ponunt:* "put (down)" or "lay (down)"; a common meaning of *pono, ponere.*

302   *Nereides:* The sea nymphs can now swim to visit places, such as cities and forests, which were previously on land and unavailable to them. *tenent:* "occupy" or "inhabit."

302–303   *altīs ... ramīs:* dative with the compound verb *incursant.*

304   These situations are famous *adynata,* or impossibilities, signs that the order of nature has turned upside down. (Compare Isaiah 11:6–9.)

305   *nec virēs fulminis aprō:* read *prosunt* (306) as the verb in this clause also. *prosunt* takes a dative. *fulminis:* the blow of the boar's tusk is called a "lightning bolt." For other descriptions of a boar's dangers, see the story of Adonis (*Met.* 10.529–559, 708–739), and of the Calydonian Boar Hunt (8.260–444); for "lightning bolts" in the boar's tusks, see 10.550 and 8.289.

306   *crura nec:* read *nec crura.*

307   *quaesitīsque diu terrīs:* ablative absolute. *ubi = in quibus [terrīs]. possit:* subject is the *volucris* in 308.

308   *decĭdit:* In compounds of *cado* ("fall"), such as *decĭdo,* the short "a" of the root verb weakens to a *short* "i." There is another verb *decīdo,* a compound of *caedo* ("cut"), in which the long diphthong becomes a *long* "i." (This distinction in vowel quantity is also essential in the perfect active forms: *cado / cecĭdi; caedo / cecīdi.*)

309   *licentia pontī:* the sea is depicted as having "freedom" from its usual restraints, as the rivers' "reins" were loosened at lines 280–82.

310   *novī:* here with its frequent meaning "strange"; these waves are "strange" to the mountains, which do not usually see the sea's waves.

311   *pepercit:* from *parco* (+ dat.).

311–12   Creatures who do not die by drowning eventually die of starvation, since their food supply has been taken away by the floodwaters.

312   *illōs:* "those [creatures]." *longa . . . ieiunia:* neuter plural. *victū:* from *victus, ūs:* (m.) "food."

3. Deucalion and Pyrrha: 1.313–415

Jupiter, having accomplished his mission of wiping out sinful humanity, now causes the floodwaters to recede. The sole survivors of this disaster are the pious couple Deucalion and Pyrrha. As the earth dries out, they are faced with the problem of surviving alone in the world. Eventually, they ask an oracle for advice and are given a mystifying response typical of oracles. But by following the oracle's instruction, they are able to repopulate the earth.

In the regeneration of humans from stones after this flood, Ovid depicts human origins as a type of metamorphosis, described in great detail, which contrasts with the two vague possibilities mentioned at 1.76–88 in the first (antediluvian) creation of humanity (there, humanity came either from the divine seed of the creator or from leftover heavenly seed within the earth). Thus, the Deucalion and Pyrrha story is a kind of fresh start for mortals. The last lines of the story, however, note the "hardness" of the rock-born humans; as often happens, a characteristic or personality is preserved after a metamorphosis. In several other stories, the metamorphosis goes the other direction: people who are "hard" as humans become rocks, and still display evidence after the metamorphosis of their premetamorphic nature.

The passage begins with a description of the land of Phocis and Mount Parnassus, where the boat of Deucalion and Pyrrha comes to rest.

313   *Aoniōs, Oetaeīs:* Phocis is between the land of the "Aonians," or Boeotians, and the "Oetean fields," or Thessaly.

314–15   *terra ferax . . . pars maris et latus subitārum campus aquārum:* renaming Phocis. Do not confuse *ferax* (from *fero*) with *ferox* (from *ferus*).

318   *cetera:* i.e., everything else but Mount Parnassus.

319   *consorte torī = uxore. parvā rate:* ablative with *vectus.*

320   *Corycidas nymphās:* the nymphs who live in the "Corycian" cave on nearby Mount Parnassus.

321   *Themin:* accusative singular, Greek form. Themis is an oracular goddess of the generation of the Titans. *quae tunc oracla tenēbat:* At the time of the Flood, the oracle at Delphi, below Mount Parnassus, belongs to Themis, and not yet to Apollo.

322   *illō:* ablative of comparison, referring to Deucalion.

323   *illā:* ablative of comparison, referring to Pyrrha. *metuentior:* comparative of the present participle from *metuo,* "more fearful."

324   *Iuppiter:* subject of both the verb in the *ut*-clause (*vidit,* 326) and the verb in the main clause (*disiecit,* 328). *ut:* followed by an indicative verb, *ut* can mean "when." *orbem:* = *orbem terrārum,* "the world."

324–26   *stagnāre, superesse, superesse:* infinitives in indirect statement after *vidit* in line 326.

325–26   *de tot modo milibus: modo* means "just now"; set in the middle of a preposi-
tional phrase, it modifies only the words in that phrase. "Out of [what had been]
just now so many thousands," i.e., out of the recent preflood population of the
earth. Note how little line 325 differs from 326.

326   *unam:* translate to reflect its gender. This passage has a number of such repe-
titions and parallel lines (e.g., 361–62), which emphasize the pair, Deucalion
and Pyrrha.

327   *ambo:* accusative.

328   *nimbīsque . . . remotīs:* ablative absolute. Note the additional ablative
(*aquilone*), connected to the passive participle, to express means/instrument.

328–29   Note the connectives carefully: the two verbs, *disiecit* and *ostendit,* are joined
by *-que* (in *nimbīsque*). *Ostendit* has two objects, joined by *et . . . et* (= "both . . .
and"). Each of the objects has a dative attached to it. Note the mirror-image
word order: *caelō terrās . . . aethera terrīs* (dative-accusative, accusative-
dative); this word order is called "chiasmus" and is a favorite device of Latin
poets.

329   *aethera:* accusative singular, Greek form.

330   *positō:* an instance where *pono* means "put aside" or "put down."

330–35   Again, note the use of connectives, especially *-que* as the link between whole
clauses or large parts of clauses, while *et* and *atque* link smaller elements. (Cf.
328–29.) The verbs linked by *-que* are: *manet, mulcet, vocat, inspirare iubet,*
and *revocare [iubet].* We can see the other pairs of words joined by *et* and
atque: exstantem atque . . . tectum (acc. participles modifying *Tritona,* a Greek
acc.); *fluctus . . . et flumina* (acc. objects of *revocare*).

331   *rector pelagī* = Neptune. *suprā profundum* = *suprā mare.*

332   *umerōs:* accusative of respect with the participle *tectum. innatō murice:* ablative
of means with the passive participle.

333   *Tritona* = accusative singular, Greek form. *conchaeque sonantī:* dative with the
compound verb *inspirāre* (334, "blow *on*").

334   *[Neptunus] iubet [Tritona] inspirāre.*

335   *illī:* dative of agent, a poetic usage.

335–38   Note, in these lines, how ablative nouns and their adjectives are separated:
turbine . . . ab imō; mediō . . . pontō; sub utrōque . . . Phoebō.

336   *in latum: latum* (from the adjective *latus, a, um*) is used here as an abstract
noun. This phrase goes inside the relative clause introduced by *quae,* which
describes the curve of Triton's horn.

337   *āera:* accusative singular, Greek form; from *āēr, āeris.*

338   *litora . . . sub utrōque iacentia Phoebō:* "the shores lying beneath either sun,"
i.e., shores where the sun rises and sets, in both the east and the west.

339   *ora . . . madidā rorantia barbā: ora* from *os, oris* (n.); *rorantia* is neuter plural
with *ora; madidā barbā* is ablative after *rorantia.*

340 *contigit, cecinit* (from *cano*): the subject of both verbs is still the *bucina*, which is also modified here by *inflata. receptūs:* accusative plural; "(signal for) retreat"; *cecinit receptūs* corresponds to the English idiom "sound the retreat."

341 *omnibus . . . undīs:* impersonal agent of the passive *audita;* "by all waters of land and sea," i.e., the rivers and the ocean, which will be spelled out together in the next line.

342 *quibus . . . undīs, coercuit omnēs:* supply *undās* with *omnēs;* Latin puts the noun inside the relative clause, although it is needed in the main clause, too. "It compels all the waters by which it is heard."

345 *decrescentibus undīs:* a good example of an ablative absolute with a present participle that should be translated as a "while" or "as" clause, with a present progressive verb: "while the waters are receding."

348–66 From a general description of the flood's departure, Ovid now turns to the reactions and laments of the two survivors, Deucalion and Pyrrha.

348 *redditus . . . erat:* a pluperfect passive verb form (from *reddo*), not a noun + *erat.* Note that there are two very similar Latin verbs that can be translated "return" in English: *reddo,* "give back" (a compound of *do*), and *redeo,* "come back" (a compound of *eo*). *quem* belongs inside the *postquam* clause and refers to the only noun that has appeared in the sentence so far. *vidit:* subject is Deucalion.

349 *agere:* indirect statement after *vīdit* (348). Translate *agere alta silentia* as "preserve deep silence."

352 *patruelis origo:* Pyrrha is the daughter of Deucalion's paternal uncle, *patruus;* hence the adjective *patruelis.* (See note for line 387.) Deucalion is the son of Prometheus, while Pyrrha is the daughter of Prometheus' brother Epimetheus. (See line 390, where they are both given patronymics.) The several references to their parentage in this story remind us that Prometheus was involved in the first creation of humanity (1.82–86).

353 *torus:* the "couch" or "bed" as symbolic of the marriage.

354 *occasus et ortus [solis].* The Latin words for the sun's rising (*oriri*) and setting (*occidere*) survive in the English words "Orient" and "Occident," which refer to the lands in the directions where these events occur.

356–57 Deucalion does not really believe that they are safe yet or that the weather has cleared up completely. Note the similarity in the meanings of *quoque adhuc* and *etiamnum* in the two clauses.

357 *mentem [meam].*

358–59 *tibi:* dative of possession. *foret = esset* "would be." All the verbs in lines 358–62 are imperfect or pluperfect subjunctive, because they are part of contrary-to-fact situations; e.g., "If you *had been* . . . (but you weren't), what *would* you do?" None of the actions expressed by these verbs have happened or are happening, in reality.

359–60   *quo . . . modo: quomodo* ("how?") is usually written as one word, but obviously has its origin as these two ("in what way?").

360   *quō consolante:* ablative absolute, with an interrogative pronoun (a form of *quis, quid*); this usage makes for very awkward English: "*While who is consoling* would you grieve?" For once, it works better *not* to translate the ablative absolute as a clause, but as a phrase: "*with whose consolation* would you grieve?"

361–62   Another pair of matched lines, ending with almost the same words; the contrast is in the *mē* and *tē*, to emphasize the parallelism of their situations.

362   *sequerer:* first-person singular, imperfect subjunctive (passive form, for deponent verb).

363   *possim:* present subjunctive, optative usage with *utinam.*

363–64   *paternīs / artibus:* another reference to his father Prometheus' creation of humans.

366   *sic visum [est bonum esse] superīs:* Forms of *videtur,* used impersonally, often mean "it seems *good*"; i.e., "it seems a good idea" = "they decide." Here you can guess the impersonal usage from the neuter form of the participle: *visum. superīs = dīs; superī* ("the ones above") is a common name for the Olympian gods in epic. *hominumque exempla [sola] manēmus:* note that this clause expresses approximately the same idea as that in line 365.

367   *placuit [eīs]:* used impersonally, *placuit* ("it was pleasing to them") is another way of saying "they decided."

369   *Cephisidas:* accusative plural adjective, Greek form. The adjective is formed from the noun *Cephisos* (-*i*), the name of a river in Phocis and Boeotia. At *Met.* 3.343, we are told that the river god Cephisos is the father of Narcissus.

370   *ut . . . sic:* "although . . . yet"; see also 1.15, 1.404.

371   *inroravēre: -ēre = -ērunt.*

372   *vestibus et capitī:* dative to complete the meaning of the compound verb *inroravēre* (371).

375   *ut:* followed by an indicative verb means "when." *tetigēre = tetigērunt,* from *tango. uterque:* "each one" (of them), i.e., Deucalion and Pyrrha; the verbs will be singular (*procumbit, dedit*), and the adjectives modifying the subject(s) singular (*pronus, pavens*) until line 377, when the subject is once again the more normal "they" (*dixērunt*). (Note that the singular adjectives, including *uterque,* are masculine, the default case when the people referred to are of mixed gender. Compare traditional English: "Let *each* person bring *his* own pencil.")

379   *Themi:* a Greek vocative. Themis, as we were told in 1.321, had an oracle near the place where Deucalion and Pyrrha landed.

379–80   *quā . . . arte: = quomodo,* indirect question.

380   *mersīs . . . rēbus:* dative.

384   *obstipuēre: -ēre = -ērunt;* from *obstipesco. silentia:* accusative plural.

385 *parēre:* takes a dative. Distinguish this verb, *pareo, parēre* (2nd conjugation), from the more common verb *paro, parāre* (1st conjugation).

386 *detque sibi veniam:* this clause is dependent on *rogat;* supply *ut* (indirect command).

387 *maternās . . . umbrās* = *matris umbrās;* Latin often uses an adjective where English prefers a genitive noun. Similar usages are *dē femineō . . . iactū* in line 413, *paternīs artibus* in 363–64 ("my father's arts"), and *patruelis origo* in 352.

389 *sēcum:* "to themselves" (Latin literally says "with themselves"); remember that the preposition *cum* attaches to the end of pronouns. *inter sēque* = *et inter sē* (not *inter et sē,* for *inter sē* seems to be considered a single unit). Note also that, again, *-que* joins two *clauses* (the ones with *repetunt* and *volutant*); cf. lines 328–29, 330–35.

390 *Promethides:* "son of Prometheus," a Greek patronymic ("father-name") form, nominative. *Epimethida:* "daughter of Epimetheus"; accusative, also a Greek patronymic; the nominative would be *Epimethis.*

391 *fallax . . . est sollertia nobīs: nobīs* here can be taken as a dative of possession; translate here as a genitive: "either *my* skill [at interpreting oracles] is deceptive, or . . . " (compare the English expression "Either my eyes deceive me, or . . . "). Since Pyrrha has offered no interpretation of the omen, Deucalion cannot be referring to "our" skill at interpretation; he must be referring to himself in the plural (a habit that is not restricted to kings and editors in Latin).

392 *pia sunt [oracula].*

394 *dici:* "are called"; rearranged: *reor lapidēs dici ossa in corpore terrae.*

395 *Titania:* since the father of Prometheus and Epimetheus was a Titan, their children and grandchildren are also called Titans. Note the feminine form here.

397 *diffidunt* + dative. *Fido, fidere* usually takes a dative, and so do its compounds.

398 *recingunt:* "ungird," "loosen." Note that the prefix *re-* can mean "un-" (as well as "back" or "again"). See also *cinctāsque resolvite vestēs* in line 382, where *resolvite* means "untie." The couple's actions exactly follow the instructions given by the oracle in lines 381–383.

399 *mittunt:* "throw" (a common meaning for *mitto;* here it corresponds to the instruction *iactate,* in line 383).

400 *credat, nisi sit: credat* is subjunctive in a rhetorical question; *sit* is often substituted for *esset,* the form normally expected in a contrary to fact condition ("*if there were not* Antiquity for a witness [*but there is*]").

401–402 *coepēre* = *coepērunt;* the infinitives *ponere, mollīrī,* and *ducere* depend on this verb. Beware of the connectives again: *ponere duritiem . . . suumque rigorem; mollīrīque morā; mollitiā ducere formam. mollīrī* is the passive of *mollio, īre* (and is not from *molior, īrī*). This verb and the abstract noun *mollitia* are both related to the adjective *mollis, e* ("soft"). *morā:* "with delay," i.e., "gradually."

403 *illīs:* dative with the compound *contigit* (404).

404   *ut . . . sic:* "although . . . yet"; see note for line 370. *ut quaedam [vidērī forma potest hominis], sic non manifesta.*

404–406   Ovid is comparing the new humans, gradually taking shape from the stones, to unfinished statues, in which the human forms appear to be "emerging" from the rock.

405   *uti = ut:* "as if."

405–406   "just as forms begun (*coepta [signa]*) from marble, but not fully drawn-out (*non exacta satis*) and very similar to crude statues."

407   *pars:* although the subject of *versa est* (408) and the antecedent of *quae,* the noun is placed "inside" the relative clause.

408   *corporis =* "flesh."

410   *vena:* a wordplay on the use of the same word for a "vein" of rock or metal and for a "vein" in the body.

412–13   Here, for a change, the two parallel processes (Deucalion's rocks become men, while Pyrrha's rocks become women) are *not* described in parallel sentences.

413   *dē femineō . . . iactū:* see note for line 387 (*maternās . . . umbrās*).

414–15   *inde:* a signal that we have reached the *aition,* the explanation that this story was meant to provide.

415   Reword: *documenta originis damus, quā simus natī. quā:* ablative of source, as usual with verbs of "being born"; compare Vergilian characters' habit of addressing Aeneas as *nate deā,* "one born *from* the goddess."

4. Daphne and Apollo: 1.452–567

This is the first erotic metamorphosis story in the poem and also the first of a series of stories about the gods' amatory adventures. While most of these other stories—Io, Europa, Callisto, and the rest—involve the rape (and usually impregnation) of a young woman by a god, the Daphne story tells of a god's unsuccessful pursuit of a woman. Daphne is transformed into a laurel tree (*daphnē* in Greek) before Apollo can catch her, and so escapes the literal rapes suffered by other objects of divine lust. However, Apollo does "possess" Daphne after her metamorphosis, for he claims the laurel tree as his own symbol. He proclaims at the end of the story that her service as his tree will substitute for service as his wife (1.557–58). Thus, the story of Daphne does fit metaphorically with the other rape stories.

The tale of Daphne is also important for its depiction of the gods. At the beginning, the archer god Apollo is shown deriding the power of Cupid's arrows, but by the end Cupid is proven to have power even over Apollo, as Apollo is forced to acknowledge (1.519–20). This lighthearted, humorous, and even irreverent depiction of the gods continues through most of the *Metamorphoses* and is especially prominent in the first five books.

452 *Phoebī = Apollinis. Peneia:* nominative singular adjective, modifying Daphne: "daughter of Peneus." Peneus is the river god who is Daphne's father.

454 *Delius =* Apollo, who is called "the Delian" after the island of Delos, his birthplace. *hunc = Cupidinem. victā serpente:* ablative of cause with *superbus.* In the preceding story (1.438–51), Apollo killed the giant snake Python.

455 *cornua:* the ends of the curve of the bow are referred to as "horns." The bow is bent *(flectentem)* as the string *(nervō)* is pulled back *(adductō)* toward the shooter.

456 *quid . . . tibi . . . cum fortibus armīs?* This fairly colloquial expression, from the proud and condescending Apollo to the playful and childish Cupid, could be rephrased as a construction with a dative of possession: *quid (negotiī) [est] tibi cum fortibus armīs?* "What business do you have with strong weapons?"

457 *ista . . . gestamina = sagittae.* Note the scornful *ista. nostrōs:* Apollo refers to himself in the plural. (See below: *possumus* [458], *stravimus* [460], *nostrās* [462].)

458 *quī dāre certa ferae, dāre vulnera possumus hostī = quī dāre certa vulnera ferae et hostī possumus.*

459–60 The object of *stravimus* is *Pythona* (a Greek acc.), modified by *prementem* (which has a direct object, *iugera*), and *tumidum* (with its attached abl., *innumerīs . . . sagittīs*).

459 *pestiferō tot iugera ventre prementem:* The immense Python, described here, was so big that it covered a large amount of ground when it lay stretched out. A *iugerum* is a Roman unit of land measure, similar to the English "acre," which may suffice as a translation here.

461 *face (. . . tuā):* from *fax, facis* (f.), "torch." Cupid has, in addition to his arrows, a torch with which to light the "fires" of love. *nescio quōs . . . amorēs:* literally, "I-don't-know-what love"; i.e., "some love or other (I really don't know or care which)." (The *nescio* does not serve as a main or subordinate verb, but is to be taken only with *quōs.*) This indefinite and informal expression reinforces the scornful tone of Apollo's address to Cupid. *esto:* Imperative form of *sum.*

462 *laudēs: laus* refers not only to praise itself, but to the source of the praise, the deed or virtue that inspires the praise. Here Apollo asks Cupid not to claim *(adsere)* expertise in the area that wins Apollo praise, i.e., archery.

463 *filius . . . Veneris = Cupido.*

463–64 *figat tuus [arcus] omnia . . . , tē meus arcus [figat].* Note the present subjunctive ("may").

464–65 *quantō . . . tantō . . . :* ablative degree of difference ("by as much as"); these two correlatives express a comparison. It is best, in English, to translate the main clause and its adjective *(tantō . . .)* first, then the subordinate clause, with "as" for the adjective there *(quantō . . .)*; i.e.: "Your glory is less than mine *by as much as* all the animals are inferior to a god."

464   *cedunt:* "are inferior to" ("yield to," "give way to").

465   *nostrā [gloriā]:* ablative of comparison after *minor.*

466   *elisō percussīs āere pennīs: elisō . . . āere* is an ablative absolute, while
      percussīs . . . pennīs is the ablative of means dependent on *elisō (āĕre* from *āēr,*
      āeris).

467   *impiger [Cupido]:* Cupid takes up a vantage point on Apollo's own Mount
      Parnassus to shoot his arrows of love. *umbrosā . . . arce:* ablative of place
      where.

468   *saggittiferā . . . pharetrā:* object of *ē* in *ēque.* The compound adjective
      sagittifera comes from *sagitta + fero:* "arrow-bearing." The suffix *-fer (-fera,*
      -ferum) is a common way of coining Latin adjectives; compare *opifer* in line
      521, below.

469   *hoc . . . illud:* "this one . . . the other one." *fugat hoc [telum] [amorem], facit*
      illud [telum] amorem. fugat comes from *fugo, fugare,* not *fugio, fugere.*

470–71 *[telum] quod facit, auratum est . . . [telum] quod fugat, obtusum est.*

472   *hoc:* "this one" or "the latter"; i.e., the arrow that drives love away. *illō:* "that
      one" or "the former"; i.e., the arrow that causes love. *nymphā Peneide:* Daphne,
      called by her patronymic "Peneis."

473   *Apollineās . . . medullās = medullās Apollinis.* Latin poets often make up
      adjectives from nouns, especially from proper names, rather than use the
      genitive of the name itself. Compare *Delphica tellus* (1.515, below): "Delphic
      land," as a roundabout way of saying "the land of Delphi."

474   *alter . . . altera:* "one . . . the other" (a frequent correlative use of forms of *alter*
      in pairs). We can tell which one is Daphne and which Apollo by the gender of
      the adjectives. Note the reverse word order of *alter amat, fugat altera,* reflecting
      the reverse meanings. *nomen amantis:* "the name of a lover" (*amans, amantis* is
      the normal Latin noun for "a lover," i.e., "one loving"). *Nomen amantis* here
      probably means "the very word 'lover'" or "the idea of a lover."

475–76 *latebrīs, exuviīs:* ablatives of cause with *gaudens:* "rejoicing *in* or *because of . . .*"

476   *Phoebēs:* Greek genitive form, from nominative *Phoebe.* "Phoebe," i.e., Diana
      (Greek Artemis), is the sister of Apollo, whom we have already seen called
      "Phoebus." Diana is the virgin (*innuptae*) goddess of the hunt and of wild
      animals.

477   *vitta:* a ribbon or headband worn by Greek women and girls; the carefree,
      solitary Daphne simply wears her hair in a headband, rather than in the
      elaborate coiffure that a city-dwelling, stay-at-home girl might affect. *sine lege:*
      "without (any) rule"; Daphne's hair is arranged (*positōs*) in a disorderly or
      "lawless" manner.

478   *multī [virī]. petiēre = petiērunt. aversata petentēs:* "having turned away the
      ones seeking (her)" or "her suitors"; since *aversata* comes from a deponent verb
      (*aversor*), it is a perfect *active* participle and can thus take a direct object
      (*petentēs*).

479 *virī:* genitive with the adjective *expers* ("free from"). *vir* can mean both "man" and "husband."

480 The *quid* clauses, all indirect questions, depend on *curat.* Rearrange as *nec curat quid [sit] Hymen, quid [sit] Amor, quid sint conubia* (Hymen is a god of marriage).

483 Rearrange as *exosa taedās iugalēs velut crimen. Exosa* is *ex-* plus the participle of the verb *odi, odisse, osus* ("to hate"); *exosa* acts like an active participle, in that it can take an object to complete its meaning: "hating *taedās iugalēs.*" *velut crimen:* a small-scale comparison: Daphne hates marriage torches "*as if they were a crime*" or "like a crime." The torch (*taeda*) was a standard feature of Roman wedding ceremonies. (Compare the ill-omened torch at the wedding of Orpheus and Eurydice, *Met.* 10.6–7.)

484 *pulchra . . . ora:* accusative of respect with the passive verb *suffunditur. ora =* "face"; a poetic singular for plural.

485 *cervice:* object of *in. blandīs . . . lacertīs:* ablative of means.

486 *dā:* "grant" + infinitive (*frui* in 487).

487 *frui:* One of the deponent verbs that take an ablative object (*perpetuā . . . virginitate*). (The other such verbs are *fungor, vescor, potior,* and *utor.*) *hoc:* "this [favor]" or "this [wish]." *pater . . . Dianae =* Jupiter. *ante:* adverbial: "previously."

488–89 *tē:* From here to the end of 489, the narrator addresses Daphne herself (the three second-person forms, *te . . . tuo tua,* emphasize this address) and points out ironically that, because she is a beautiful girl, she simply cannot have the perpetual virginity she wants. Beauty demands sexual attention and outweighs other considerations, such as lack of desire or consent. We will see this view of feminine beauty (which the poet himself may or may not endorse) again in this story in lines 527 and 530. Rearrange as *decor iste vetat tē esse quod optas.*

489 *repugnat* + dative (*votō . . . tuō*).

490 *conubia:* poetic plural for singular. *Daphnēs:* Greek genitive form; *conubia Daphnēs* should be translated "marriage *with* Daphne." *visae . . . Daphnēs:* A typically Latin way of expressing a prior action: "Apollo desires marriage with the *seen* Daphne"; i.e., "*once he has seen her,* Apollo desires marriage with Daphne."

491 *sua . . . oracula:* Apollo's own gifts of prophecy, as displayed at the oracle of Delphi. Just as Apollo's arrows are being proven less powerful than Cupid's in this situation, here one of his other great powers, prophecy, is of no avail. Later, at lines 521–24, he will observe that his powers of healing have also failed him, because they cannot cure the "wound" of love's arrow.

492 *ut* + indicative verb = "as"; introduces the simile in 492–94. (Compare line 531, below.) *demptīs . . . aristīs:* ablative absolute. Only the head of the grain was cut, and the stalks (*stipulae*) were left in the fields to be burned off later.

493–94   As line 492 offered one image of dry vegetation catching fire easily, these next lines offer another image, that of roadside hedges (*saepes*) that ignite from a torch carelessly brought too close by a passerby or left abandoned at daylight (*sub luce*). (The modern equivalent might be a grass fire started by a cigarette tossed from a passing car.)

493   *forte:* "by chance"; from the noun *fors, fortis*, not the adjective *fortis, forte*.

495   *in flammās abiit:* literally, "went away into flames"; i.e., "went up in flames" or "burst into flames." The metaphorical flames of Apollo's love mirror the actual flames in the comparisons in lines 492–494. *pectore totō:* ablative of place.

497   *spectat . . . pendere capillōs:* indirect statement; remember Daphne's unarranged hair (477).

498   *quid, si [capillī] comantur?* Exactly like the colloquial English question "What if . . . ?"

499   *oscula: osculum, -i* (n.) literally means "little mouth" (from *os, oris*, "mouth"), and usually means "kiss"; here, it seems to mean "lips."

501   *bracchia que et nudōs mediā plus parte lacertōs:* The arm is divided into two parts: the *bracchium*, or forearm, and the *lacertus*, or upper arm. Daphne wears very short sleeves, or no sleeves at all, so that her upper arms are "more than halfway" revealed. The words of lines 500–501 follow the line of Apollo's gaze, as it moves up Daphne's arm, from *digitos* to *manus* to *bracchia* to *nudos . . . lacertos*. Thus the narrative depicts the voyeuristic nature of Apollo's infatuation with Daphne (compare *visae,* 490; *spectat,* 497; *videt,* 498 and 499; *vidisse,* 500).

502   *qua = aliqua,* neuter plural (the indefinite prefix *ali-* drops off after *si*). *meliora [ea esse] putat. aurā:* ablative of comparison after *ocior.*

503   *illa* = Daphne. *revocantis [Apollinis].*

504   *Penei:* vocative of Daphne's patronymic *Peneis* (see line 472). *hostis:* nominative, appositive with the first-person subject.

505   *sic agna [fugit] lupum, sic cerva [fugit] leonem:* the verb for these subjects and objects is taken from the parallel construction in the next line (*aquilam . . . fugiunt . . . columbae,* 506).

507   *hostēs quaeque [fugit] suōs:* "each flees her own enemies." Note the gender of all the subjects in his examples: it is female animals (*agna, cerva, columbae, quaeque*) who flee predators.

508   *mē miserum:* accusative of exclamation. *ne . . . cadas:* present subjunctive used as an imperative ("don't fall") or as a wish ("may you not fall"). In this and the next lines, Apollo shows an ironic concern for Daphne's safety as she flees him; the potential rapist is concerned about his victim falling and skinning her knees, if she runs too fast.

508–509   *indignave laedī / crura: laedī* (passive infinitive from *laedo,* "injure") is to be taken closely with the adjective. *ne . . . notent:* present subjunctive expressing a wish; note the difference between the possibilities of the second-person construction (*nē . . . cadas*) and this third-person.

510–24   Apollo's speech on the run is ostentatiously rhetorical, with tightly linked verbal repetitions in almost every sentence: *moderatius* (510–11), *non* (512–13), *nescis* (514), *fugias/fugis* (515), *per me* (517–18), *certa/certior* (519–20), *nostra* (519), *prosunt* (524). In speech, as well as in grooming, Apollo prefers carefully crafted elegance, rather than the natural look.

510–11   Apollo now proposes to make a game of the pursuit: for safety's sake, Daphne may run more slowly, and he, the pursuer, promises also to slow down.

512   Here Apollo switches tactics; he speculates that Daphne must be running away because she thinks him one of the usual rustic humans (*incola montis, pastor*) who would chase a nymph in the woods. If she only knew his real identity, surely she would not flee. Hence, he reads her his divine résumé in lines 515–24. *incola, -ae:* the noun can denote a person of either gender, but here refers to a male inhabitant.

514   *horridus:* literally, "shaggy, rough," but also "uncultured, uncouth." Apollo is both well groomed and cultured.

515   *ideo:* "for that reason" (i.e., because you do not know).

515–16   *Delphica tellus et Claros et Tenedos et Patarea regia:* Delphi, Claros, Tenedos, and Patara were all famous centers of Apollo's worship. These nouns are individually the subjects of the singular verb *servit* (516); each of them "is subject to" Apollo (*mihi*, 515).

517   *genitor [meus].*

517–18   *quod eritque fuitque / estque:* literally, "what will be, what was, and what is"; i.e., the future, the past, and the present—revealed by Apollo's oracles. Note the three uses of *-que;* just as *-que* can be used in pairs (both . . . and), it can be used in threes for similar connections.

518   *per me concordant carmina nervīs:* Apollo refers to another of his domains, musical production on the lyre (whose strings are called *nervī*).

519–20   *certa quidem nostra [sagitta] est, nostrā [sagittā] tamen una sagitta / certior:* Apollo here alludes to his initial dispute with Cupid over the strength of their arrows, and he now admits that Cupid's arrow is *certior* than his own.

519   *nostrā [sagittā]:* ablative of comparison.

520   *in vacuō . . . pectore:* "in my [previously] free heart"; *vacuus* can mean "free of love" or "carefree" (a phrase repeated from *Amores* 1.1.26, where Cupid's arrow has conquered the poet's previously carefree heart).

521   *inventum . . . meum:* "my invention or discovery"; here, the neuter participle is used as a noun (literally, "the thing invented"). *opifer:* one of Apollo's epithets: "one who brings help (*opes*)." (See note on *sagittifera* in line 468.)

522   *herbārum . . . potentia:* Apollo is in charge of herbs because of their medicinal properties. *subiecta [est]. nobis = mihi.*

523   *ei mihi:* an exclamation of grief, such as "alas for me!" *quod:* "because" or "that." *nullīs . . . herbīs:* ablative of means with *sanabilis.*

524   *prosunt:* "are beneficial to" (+ dative). *artēs [medicinae].* Apollo laments that he, the master of the arts of healing, cannot heal himself.

525   *plura [verba] locuturum [Apollinem]: plura* is the object of *locuturum. Peneia:* Daphne (nom.).

526   *cumque ipsō verba inperfecta reliquit = ipsum et verba inperfecta reliquit.* Latin can say "A with B" as a substitute for "A and B."

527   *visa [est] decens.* The determining fact about Daphne continues to be her beauty, not her unwillingness; compare line 530, below. *corpora = corpus* (poetic plural for singular).

529   *retrō dābat:* "caused to go back."

530   *fugā:* ablative of means. *forma:* often means "beauty," rather than simply "shape" or "form." As in line 527 (*tum quoque visa decens*), Daphne's flight only increases her desirability in the eyes of her pursuer. *non . . . ultra:* "no longer." *sustinet:* "could not endure to"; followed by the infinitive *perdere* in the next line.

531   *iuvenis deus:* either *iuvenis* is here used as an adjective ("the young god") or it is a noun in apposition to *deus* ("the god, a youth"); in the latter case, the appositive might explain why he lacked the patience to continue. *ut* + indicative verb = "as." (Compare line 492, above, and line 533, below.) *movēbat [eum].*

532   *admissō . . . passū:* ablative of manner; *admissō* here means "having been let go, unrestrained."

533   *ut:* see note on line 531, above. Here, *ut* introduces a simile, or comparison, that continues until line 538. At line 539, with the word *sic,* the narrative returns from the world of the simile to the world of the story. Latin similes are usually marked by these introductory and concluding words. (Compare *ut . . . sic* in the simile at 492–95, above.) *cum:* "when." *canis . . . Gallicus:* a type of hunting dog.

534   *hic = canis Gallicus; ille = lepus. ille salutem [petit].*

535–37   *alter . . . alter:* "one . . . , the other"; here, the first alter refers to the hound, while the second refers to the hare.

535   *inhaesurō similis:* "like (similar to) someone about to hold on (i.e., dig his teeth in)." *iam iamque:* the adverb is repeated to add emphasis and a sense of urgency; it gives a kind of breathless tone.

536   *stringit vestigia:* "grazes (the hare's) heels." *rostrō:* the dog's snout.

537   *in ambiguō . . . an . . . :* "in doubt about whether . . ." *An* introduces "whether" clauses. The hare's margin of escape is so narrow that the hare cannot tell at the time whether it has been caught; it concentrates only on running.

539   This very intertwined word order can be rearranged: *sic deus et virgo: hic est celer spē, illa [est celeris] timore. spē, timore:* ablative of cause.

540 *[is] quī.*
541 *tergō fugācis [puellae]:* tergo is dative with *inminet* in the next line.
542 *cervīcibus:* ablative of place, depending on *sparsum.*
544 *Pēneidas undās:* the waters of the river Peneus (her father).
544–47 Lines 544–547 contain one of the most notorious textual problems in the *Metamorphoses;* hence the strange line numbering (the Loeb text reprinted here has no line 546). In some other editions (including Anderson's Teubner text, based on manuscript readings and emendations), the text of these four lines reads:

victa labore fugae, "Tellus," ait, "hisce vel istam	544
quae facit ut laedar, mutando perde figuram!	545
fer, pater," inquit, "opem, si flumina numen habetis!	546
qua nimium placui, mutando perde figuram!"	547

In the longer version, Daphne appeals for help both to the Earth (*Tellus*) and to her father, the river god Peneus. She asks them to take away the beauty that has been the cause of her misfortune. Since Peneus is the one who in fact helps her, and since manuscript readings conflict, some editors have been suspicious of the lines containing the appeal to Tellus.

545 *sī flūmina nūmen habētis: flumina* is nominative, in apposition with the second-person-plural subject of the verb. Daphne is speculating about the powers of rivers, such as her father, in general.
547 *nimium placuī:* Daphne thinks she has "pleased" Apollo "too much" by attracting his unwanted and aggressive attentions. *mutandō:* ablative of means.
548 *vix:* take closely with the ablative absolute *prece fīnitā.* English would say "scarcely had she . . . , when . . . "
549 *librō:* the word *liber, librī,* which we normally know as the word for "book," originally meant "the bark of a tree" (the inner part of which was used as a writing material).
550 *in frondem [crescunt] crīnēs.*
552 *ōra:* accusative plural = "face"; poetic singular for plural. (Compare line 484, above.) *ōra cacūmen habet:* "A treetop (*cacumen*) holds [the place of] her face." *nitor ūnus = nitor sōlus.*
553 *positāque in stipite dextrā [manū]:* ablative absolute.
554 *sentit adhūc trepidāre . . . pectus:* Either take as an indirect statement ("he feels *that* the heart still beats") or translate with an English participle ("he feels the heart still beating").
555 *conplexus . . . rāmōs:* the participle, from a deponent verb, has a direct object. *ut membra:* "as if they (the branches) were arms." (Or make your own word-play on "limbs.")
557 *cui:* the relative pronoun used as a connective; translate as *ei* or *huic.*

558–59   *habēbunt:* plural because of the list of subjects in line 559; each subject is accompanied by its own repetition of the object *tē,* for emphasis. (This rhetorical device—repetition for emphasis—is called "anaphora.")

560   *Triumphum:* we could put quotation marks around this word. The army of the victorious general shouted "Io Triumphe" during his triumphal parade. Apollo, as a god, is able to look into the future and see details of the Romans' civilization, which does not yet exist in the mythical era narrated here.

561   *Capitolia:* plural for singular; the triumphal procession ended at the temple of Jupiter on the Capitoline.

562   *postibus Augustīs = postibus Augustī.*

562–63   The emperor's house had two laurel trees (symbols of Apollo, a special god to Augustus) flanking its doorway and an oak wreath (the *corona civica,* granted for saving the lives of citizens) hung in the middle of the doorway.

564   *utque:* "and as . . ." *intonsīs . . . capillīs:* ablative of cause.

566   *Paean* = Apollo. *factīs modo . . . ramīs:* ablative of means; take *modo* closely with *factīs.*

567   *ut(que) caput:* "as if it were a head"; compare *ut membra* in line 555, above. *cacumen:* here "treetop," as in 552.

5. Io: 1.588–667

After the story of Daphne, Ovid describes how her father, the river god Peneus, mourned for her and was comforted by various other river gods and nymphs. But missing from the gathering was Inachus, a river from the region of Argos in the Peloponnese, for he was preoccupied with mourning for his own daughter, Io, who had been turned into a cow by Jupiter. Then follows the story of how Io became a cow and was eventually freed from this form.

In this story, which directly follows an erotic adventure of Apollo, Ovid tells his first story of an erotic adventure of Jupiter. Like Apollo, Jupiter is strangely unsuccessful in his attempts at seduction; his divine résumé (1.593–596) fails to impress the nymph, who flees him desperately. Unlike Apollo, Jupiter does not allow himself to be outrun; he brutally catches up with the nymph and rapes her.

Without focusing on the rape scene (this time—but compare the much more explicit rape in the Callisto story, 2.417–40), Ovid immediately begins to describe Juno's jealous anger. Attempting to hide his activities from his wife, Jupiter turns Io into a cow, but Juno tricks him into giving her the cow as a "gift." The Io story consists in large part of the tale of Io's life as a cow, a miserable, speechless possession of Juno, who puts her under the guardianship of the hundred-eyed monster Argus. Eventually Io is freed from her bovine life, after Jupiter's agent Mercury lulls Argus to sleep with the tale of another erotic adventure (Pan and Syrinx, 1.689–712) and kills him. Finally Jupiter manages to assuage Juno's anger, and Io, returned to human form, bears Jupiter's son Epaphus.

In addition to the divine rape story, this story introduces the theme of divine anger, which recurs throughout the poem. All of Jupiter's extramarital lovers incur the wrath of Juno, who punishes these women extensively and without regard for their level of consent; to Juno, rape victims are just as guilty of adultery as consensual lovers are.

The passage below does not cover the entire story of Io, or its inset stories, the death of Argus and the tale of Pan and Syrinx, but merely the first part of Io's adventures, the rape and her persecution by Argus. For the rest of her story, see 1.668–750.

588 *viderat:* this and other main verbs in the first part of this story are pluperfect, because the narrator is explaining the background cause of Inachus' mourning. *illam = Io.* The form of Io's name is the same, nominative and accusative; other cases do not occur in this story.

588–89 *a patriō . . . flumine:* her "paternal river" is, of course, her father the river god.

589–90 *virgo, digna, factura:* vocatives.

590 *nescio quem = aliquem.*

591 *et nemorum monstraverat umbrās:* a kind of stage direction, which tells what Jupiter did as he spoke. Compare *fugiebat enim* in line 597, below, which explains what Io was doing as Jupiter was talking.

593 *quodsi:* "but if." *sola:* take as part of the predicate: "If you are afraid to enter alone . . ."

594 *praeside . . . deō:* ablative absolute. *tuta:* Adjectives modifying the subject are often best translated as adverbs: literally, "you, safe, will enter . . . ," but, in better English, "you will safely enter . . ." *nemorum secreta [loca].*

595 *deō:* repeats the noun from the ablative absolute in the previous line.

595–96 *caelestia magnā / sceptra manū:* typical interlocked word order (acc., abl., acc., abl.), with both adjectives coming first, before either noun.

596 *teneo, mitto:* the first-person endings of these verbs give away "who" this god is. On first reading, we might begin the relative clause as "the god who . . . ," but when we reach the verb, we are forced to retranslate as "I, who . . ."

597 *nē fuge mē = nolī mē fugere.* Latin poetry frequently uses *ne* with the imperative to express negative commands, although prose uses *nolī(te)* + infinitive. *Lernae:* an area near Argos (see note on line 601).

598 *Lyrcea . . . arva:* another place-name meant to evoke Argos.

599 *inductā latās caligine terrās:* interlocked word order again; see above, lines 595–596.

601 *mediōs . . . in Argōs:* This story takes place in the Peloponnese, where the city of Argos is located; the river Inachus was named after the first king of Argos. Argos is also the special city of Juno. Here, the city's name is declined *Argī, Argōrum.*

602 *volucrēs:* adjective.

602–603 *mirata [est]:* governs the indirect statement *nebulās fecisse.*

603–604 *sensit* governs the two negative indirect statements: *non fluminis illās [nebulās] esse, nec umenti tellure [nebulās] remitti.* Juno suspects that these clouds are not caused by some kind of evaporation from a river or natural steaming of the earth.

605 *suus coniunx ubi sit* = *ubi suus coniunx sit:* indirect question, dependent on the question that is implicit in *circumspicit,* "she looks around (to see) . . ." *ut quae:* "as one who . . ."

606 *nosset* = *novisset. totiens:* take closely with *deprensi;* this is not the first time Jupiter has been caught in the act. *furta: furtum, -ī* (n.): "theft," and hence, "stolen or secret love"; the word Juno uses of Jupiter's affair with Semele at 3.266.

607 *quem* = *illum* (*maritum*); belongs inside the *postquam* clause. *fallor:* "I am deceived," i.e., "I am mistaken"; the less likely of the two alternatives. (Compare an English expression such as "Either my eyes deceive me *or* . . .")

608 *laedor:* Juno takes all of Jupiter's infidelities as a personal insult. The insult, as is implied in this whole scene, really comes from Jupiter, but since he cannot be punished, Juno blames the offense on the female involved in the infidelity, regardless of her actual guilt or consent. Vergil uses this same verb to describe Juno's "offended divinity," which caused her to persecute Aeneas (*Aeneid* 1.8: *quō numine laesō*).

609 *nebulāsque recedere iussit:* an interesting case of competing divine powers: Jupiter can summon the clouds, but Juno can order them away.

610 *praesenserat:* subject is Jupiter (the *ille* in line 611).

611 *Inachidos:* Greek genitive form; *Inachis* (nom.) = "daughter of Inachus" (a Greek patronymic).

612 *bos:* take as part of the predicate: "she was even beautiful *as a cow.*"

613 *nec non* = *et;* joins *probat* with *quaerit.*

613–14 *nec non . . . quaerit:* three indirect questions depend on *quaerit: cuius [vacca] sit, unde [vacca] sit, quō armentō [vacca] sit. verī quasi nescia:* modifies the subject of *quaerit,* Juno: "as if ignorant of the truth, she asks . . ." This phrase shows that Juno has seen through Jupiter's trick. *verī* is the neuter adjective used as an abstraction.

615 *Iuppiter [vaccam] ē terrā genitam [esse] mentitur.*

615–16 *ut auctor / desinat inquiri:* purpose clause.

616 *petit hanc Saturnia munus: munus* is appositive with *hanc:* "as a gift." *Saturnia* = Juno (daughter of Saturn).

617 *quid faciat [Iuppiter]?* Present subjunctive in a rhetorical or deliberative question: "what should he do?" *crudele [est] suōs addicere amorēs: addicere* = "surrender, abandon." *suōs . . . amorēs* = *suam . . . amantem. Amor* in the plural is often used in Latin love poetry to refer to the lover; English may refer to the lover as "my love," in the singular. (For a parallel, see Catullus 10.1–2:

Varus me meus ad suos amores / visum duxerat: "Varus took me to see *his girlfriend.*")

618–19   *illinc . . . hinc:* "from one side . . . from the other side." *Pudor:* "Shame" (embarrassment at being caught) urges Jupiter to hand over the cow, but Love urges him not to. Note the mirrored word order: *Pudor . . . suadeat illinc, hinc dissuadet Amor,* with contrasting pairs of nouns, verbs, and adverbs.

619   *victus Pudor esset Amore:* half of a contrary-to-fact condition (*victus . . . esset* = pluperfect subjunctive): "Shame *would have been* conquered by Love (but wasn't) . . ."

620   *sociae generisque torique: sociae* is dative. "The companion of both his birth and bed" is a way of expressing Juno's double relationship—sister and wife—to Jupiter. (Compare Juno's similar, but ironic, description of herself at 3.265–66: *Iovisque et soror et coniunx—certe soror*).

620–21   *leve . . . munus, vacca:* appositives again (as in line 616): "the cow, a small gift."

621   *poterat non vacca [esse] vidērī.*

622   *paelice donatā:* ablative absolute.

623   *diva = dea. anxia furtī:* the adjective *anxius, a, um* can take a genitive: "worried about *furtum*" (see note on line 606).

624   *donec Arestoridae [vaccam] servandam tradidit Argō. Arestoridae . . . Argō:* "to Argus, son of Arestor."

625   *luminibus = oculīs.*

626   *inde:* "from these (hundred eyes)." *bina [lumina]:* "two (eyes) at a time."

628   *constiterat quocumque modo:* "in whatever way he stood" (the verb precedes the words that introduce its clause). *Io:* accusative.

629   *Io:* accusative.

630   *luce = diē. sinit [eam] pascī.*

631   *claudit [eam]. indignō . . . collō:* dative with the compound verb *circumdat.*

632   *pascitur: pasco,* in the active, means "to feed or pasture (flocks), to allow (them) to graze." In the passive forms, the animals can be the subjects: "to be fed on . . . ," "to graze on . . ."; the food they eat is naturally in the ablative (here, *frondibus arboreīs* and *amarā . . . herbā*).

633–34   *terrae . . . habentī:* dative after the compound verb *incubat. gramen:* object of *habentī.*

635   *vellet:* "she would wish" or "she would like"; contrary to fact: she does not, in fact, hold out her arms.

636   *bracchia:* object of *habuit* and antecedent of *quae.*

637   *mūgitūs:* note the onomatopoeia (like the English word "moo").

638   *propriā . . . voce. propriā = suā.*

639–40   *ad ripās . . . Inachidas:* "to the shores of the river Inachus." (The short *a* in the adjective is a Greek form.)

640–41   *ut:* introduces the whole clause: *ut rictūs novaque conspexit in undā / cornua. rictūs: rictus* means "open mouth"; here perhaps it refers to the bovine look of

Io's mouth as she makes the terrifying mooing sounds mentioned in lines 637–638.

641   In the *Metamorphoses*, humans transformed into wild beasts often fear themselves or try to run away from themselves, as Io does. Compare the reaction of Callisto, who has been turned into a bear but still fears other wild bears (2.493–94). Metamorphosis as punishment involves the loss of one's human identity and the loss of recognition by other humans, as Io's family members do not recognize her (lines 642–43).

642–650   A sad and pathetic comparison can be made between this human-bovine encounter and the one in the Europa story; Ovid's depiction of the contrast between the mental states of the bovines is especially striking. Io's expressions of affection are attempts to communicate her identity and family sentiments; Jupiter's expressions of affection toward Europa and her maiden friends are attempts to hide his identity and his lustful intentions.

642   *naides:* the other water nymphs, sisters of Io and daughters of Inachus.

643   *quae sit:* indirect question after *ignorant* and *ignorat* in the previous line.

644   *sē:* take with both clauses: *patitur [sē] tangī sēque admirantibus offert.*

646   *patriīs . . . palmīs = patris palmīs:* an example of the Latin habit of using an adjective (*patrius*, "paternal") instead of a genitive noun (*patris*, "of her father").

647   *si modo:* "if only."

648   Note the subjunctives: Io does not actually ask for help or speak.

649   *duxit:* "drew."

649–50   Io is recognized by her father after she manages to draw the letters of her name in the dirt with her hoof. (Fortunately, Io has a short and simple name.) This scene is one of Ovid's brilliant and disturbing combinations of pathos and humor. With all of its implications about serious topics such as human identity and the cruelty of the gods, Io's situation is truly tragic, but at the same time the idea of written communication from a cow is ridiculous. Her father's lament, lines 651–63, is likewise an expression of real loss and grief, combined with silly comments about his bovine son-in-law and grandchildren. (Another instance of this combination is Narcissus' moment of self-recognition at 3.463–68.)

650   *indicium . . . perēgit:* "provided evidence."

651–52   Rearrange: *pendens in cornibus et cervice gementis et niveae iuvencae.*

654   *mihi:* dative of agent

654–55   Practically no distinction in meaning can be made between *invenio* and *reperio;* both mean "find." *Repertā* is ablative of comparison with *levior.* "Not found, you were a lighter grief than you [are now that you are] found." This state of bovine metamorphosis is worse than all the fates Io's father imagined for her when she disappeared.

655   *nostrīs [dictīs].*

656   *dicta = verba. tantum:* "only."

656–57   *altō . . . pectore:* "from deep in your heart" (not "from your deep heart").

657   *quodque unum potes [facere]:* refers rather loosely and parenthetically to the next whole clause: "the one thing that you can do: you moo . . ."

658   *thalamōs taedāsque:* symbols of a wedding.

659   *mihi:* dative of possession.

660   *habendus [est].*

661   *nec . . . licet . . . mihi:* "And it is not permitted for me (to . . .)"; i.e., "I am not permitted to . . ."

662   *esse deum:* subject of *nocet;* translate as an English gerund ("being a god").

663   *nostrōs luctūs = meum luctum;* Inachus refers to himself in the plural (*nostrōs*), and the noun *luctūs* is a poetic plural for singular.

664   *talia maerentēs:* "making such laments" (literally: "lamenting such things"). Refers to Io's family, her father and sisters. *submovet:* "drives away." *stellatus:* Argus is "starred" because his many eyes are scattered around his head like stars in the night sky.

665   *patrī:* dative of separation with *ereptam.*

666   *ipse* = Argus. Argus stations himself on the top of a mountain, where he can keep an eye on Io, no matter which direction she wanders.

6. Europa: 2.833–75

Jupiter's attention has fallen upon Europa, princess of the Phoenician city of Tyre, and he asks Mercury's help in approaching her. Mercury is to drive some cattle to the shore where Europa and her friends are picking flowers, while Jupiter disguises himself as an attractive bull in this herd. Deceived by the beauty of the bull, Europa comes too close and is carried off across the sea.

The abduction of Europa sets off a chain of stories that encompass multiple generations. Europa becomes the mother of King Minos, whose stories are told in Book 8 (1–182). She also becomes the excuse for stories of people persecuted by Juno, who out of jealousy punishes everyone related to her husband's lovers. Primarily, Juno's victims are the descendants of Europa's brother Cadmus, founder of the city of Thebes; these stories are told in Books 3 and 4. (Cadmus: 3.1–130, 4.563–603; Semele: 3.253–315; Ino: 4.416–562.)

The story of Europa ends abruptly in the last lines of Book 2, as the bull heads out to sea with Europa on his back, but Ovid recounts the tale twice more, in *Metamorphoses* 6.103–107 (on Arachne's tapestry), and in *Fasti* 5.603–618 (where the story picks up almost exactly at the point where *Met.* 2 leaves off). For a rationalized, demythologized version of this story, see the opening chapters of Herodotus' *Histories,* where the rape of Europa is one of a series of abductions that the historian uses to explain the long-standing hostilities between Europe and Asia.

833   *Hās . . . poenās:* In the preceding story (2.708–832), Mercury has punished the Athenian princess Aglauros for blocking his way to the bedroom of her sister, Herse, to whom Mercury wanted to make love. Aglauros said defiantly that she would never move from the doorway, so Mercury transformed her into a stone that *could* not move away. *verbōrum, mentis profanae:* objective genitives after *poenās.* Translate "punishment *for* the words and wicked mind." *Profanae* should probably also be applied to *verbōrum:* "wicked words and mind."

833–34   *poenās . . . cēpit:* In Latin, punishment is considered a fee to be paid to the person who has been wronged. So *capere poenās* means "to exact punishment," while *dāre poenās* means "to pay the penalty." (Note that these meanings are exactly the opposite of what we might expect from the literal translation of these phrases.)

834   *Atlantiades:* "Descendant (or grandson) of Atlas." A Greek patronymic form, which does not here really express paternity, but more generally descent. Mercury is Jupiter's son by Maia, daughter of Atlas. An epithet referring to a maternal ancestor is unusual. *dictās ā Pallade terrās* = Athens, named after Athena (Pallas), where the story of Aglauros took place.

835   *aethera:* accusative singular, Greek form.

836   *genitor:* Jupiter, Mercury's father. *causam . . . amoris:* Europa has apparently already attracted Jupiter's attention, although the poet does not narrate the time or place. Jupiter does not explain to Mercury the real reason he wants the cattle driven toward the shore: he wants to be able to join this herd near the spot where Europa is playing.

838   *pelle moram:* "drive away delay" = "hurry." *delabere:* imperative form of the deponent *delabor.*

839   *quaeque . . . tellus:* "the land which . . ."; the noun *tellus,* antecedant of *quae,* is included inside the relative clause and thus is attracted into the same case as the relative pronoun. *Tellus* is really the object of *pete* in line 841; the sentence could be reworded *pete hanc tellurem, quae. . . . tuam matrem:* Mercury's mother Maia, who is one of the Pleiades, a constellation that appears to Jupiter to be "on the left side" (*ā parte sinistrā*) as he looks at Europa's homeland from Olympus.

840   *[tellurem] Sidonida:* accusative singular, Greek form: "Sidonian." The two famous Phoenician towns of Tyre and Sidon are often used interchangeably.

841–42   *quodque . . . armentum regale:* As in line 839, the antecedent, *armentum regale,* is inside the relative clause; *armentum* serves as the object of the main verb *verte.* Rearrange: *verte armentum, quod . . . vides.*

846–47   *maiestas et amor* are two singular nouns that "add up" to a plural subject for the verbs *conveniunt* and *morantur.* This sentence could serve as a comment on all the erotic adventures of Ovid's gods, who seem unable to preserve their *maiestas* when in love.

848   *deum* = *deōrum. cui:* dative of possession, instead of the genitive; this use of the dative of possession is common with expressions for parts of the body (*dextra*).

848–49 *trisulcīs/ ignibus = fulmine.*

849 *qui nutū concutit orbem:* Traditionally, Jupiter's nod, by which he assents to and grants requests, is so powerful that it shakes the earth (or Olympus); see, for example, *Iliad* 1.528–30.

852 *nivis:* from *nix, nivis* (f.), "snow." *color nivis est:* either "he is the color of snow," or "his color is that of snow." *Nivis* is the antecedent of *quam.*

853 *calcavēre = calcavērunt. auster:* the south wind, which would naturally be warm and thus likely to melt snow.

854 *armīs:* from *armus, -ī* (m.), "shoulder, flank."

855 *cornua parva [sunt], sed [cornua] quae. . . . possis:* subjunctive because hypothetical: "you could . . ."

855–56 Reword: *possis contendere [ea cornua] facta [esse] manū:* an indirect statement follows *contendere; quae,* referring to the horns, is the subject of *facta [esse].*

856 *purāque magis perlucida gemmā.*

857 *nullae in fronte minae [sunt], nec formidabile lumen [est]. lumen = oculus.*

858 *Agenore nata:* "the daughter of Agenor," Europa. Literally, "the one born (nata) from Agenor" (hence the ablative). Agenor is the king of Phoenicia. See the note on 1.415.

859 *quod tam formosus [sit], quod proelia nulla minetur: quod* here means "because" or "that," after *miratur* (858). The *minetur* is subjunctive because the *quod* clause is part of Europa's thought ("she wonders that he is [as she thinks] so beautiful and that [as she thinks] he threatens no attacks"). This *quod* clause is "virtual" indirect discourse.

860 *quamvis mitem:* "however gentle he was . . ."

862 *amans:* the present participle *amans* is the standard Latin noun meaning "a lover." *dum veniat: dum* + subjunctive means "until," in clauses of anticipation or expectation.

863 *vix . . . vix:* the repetition illustrates Jupiter's impatience. *cetera = ceterās voluptatēs,* i.e., the rest of the lovemaking that he is anticipating, beyond just kissing the girl's hand. *differt:* "delays," "postpones."

865 *latus:* from *latus, lateris* (n.).

866 *metū demptō:* ablative absolute.

867 *plaudenda:* "to be patted" (gerundive expressing purpose), modifying *pectora* (866), and followed by the ablative *virgineā . . . manū.*

868 *inpedienda = impedienda:* "to be encircled" (gerundive, like *plaudenda* in line 867). *ausa est:* "she dared"; *audeo* is semi-deponent; i.e., in the perfect tenses, it has only passive forms, with active meanings.

869 *quem premeret:* indirect question dependent on *nescia.*

870–71 *cum . . . ponit:* a "*cum*-inversum" clause, with the indicative; the *cum* clause contains the main action of the sentence, rather than the background circumstances.

873 *praedam = Europam.*

874 *dextrā [manū]; altera [manus]. dorsō:* dative with compound verb (*inposita est,* 875).

875 Europa is frozen in this snapshot-like picture of the frightened girl looking back in trepidation at the shore, as her garments flutter about her.

7. Cadmus: 3.1–130

The story of Cadmus begins the chain of stories in Books 3–4 that treat members of the royal house of Thebes, most of them Cadmus' children and grandchildren. But the Cadmus story itself is an offshoot of the story of his sister Europa, abducted by Jupiter at the very end of Book 2. The opening lines of Book 3 show Jupiter arriving in his hideout on Crete with Europa, but Ovid then abruptly switches to the story of her brother Cadmus. Back home in Phoenicia, Cadmus has been sent out by his father, Agenor, to search the world for his vanished sister and is instructed not to return without her. Since Europa is thoroughly concealed on Crete, Cadmus' search fails, forcing him to seek a new homeland. The Delphic oracle advises him to follow a white heifer to the destined site of his future city. Sighting the omen, Cadmus arrives at the place that will become Thebes.

Near the site lives a monstrous snake, which attacks and kills Cadmus' companions. After Cadmus, at his most heroic, fights and kills the snake, a mysterious voice admonishes him that he, too, will someday be a snake. (For the story of Cadmus' metamorphosis into a snake, see *Met.* 4.563–603.) Upon the advice of Pallas (Minerva), Cadmus sows the land with the snake's teeth, which grow into a crop of armed men, born from the earth. These are the famous Spartoi ("Sown Men"), ancestors of all Thebans. By immediate, brutal infighting, the Spartoi narrow themselves to a crop of five, who make peace among themselves and help Cadmus establish the new city. Theban legend thus claims both a foreign, heroic founder and native origins.

The Cadmus story is notable for its use of heroic motifs, especially in Cadmus' duel with the snake, and for its imitation (or possibly parody) of Vergil's *Aeneid,* especially in certain details of the story of Cadmus' exile. The snake, too, owes much to Vergilian snakes, such as the snakes that kill Laocoön in *Aeneid* 2.199–227.

1 *deus* = Jupiter. *positā . . . imagine:* ablative absolute.

2 *Dictaeaque rura:* "the countryside of Dicte"; Dicte is a mountain in Crete, where Jupiter has taken Europa. *tenēbat:* "reached."

3 *pater ignarus:* Agenor, Europa's father, who does not know what has happened to her. *Cadmō:* dative after *imperat* (4); *imperat* is here followed by an infinitive (*perquirere*), not by the *ut*-clause we would normally expect. *raptam [puellam].*

4 *si non [eam] invenerit.*

4–5 *poenam . . . exilium:* appositives: "he adds a punishment, exile . . ." or "he adds exile as a punishment . . ."

5 *factō pius et sceleratus eōdem:* Agenor is *pius* toward his daughter, because he is determined to find her, but *sceleratus* toward his son, because he condemns him to exile.

6 *orbe pererratō:* this single ablative absolute covers all of Cadmus' heroic journey or wanderings. By fitting Cadmus into the model of Odysseus or Aeneas, we can see him not as a lonely wanderer, but as the leader of an expedition, in charge of a good-sized crew of men; otherwise, we are surprised to find (at line 22) that he is accompanied by an entourage. *pererratō:* the prefix *per-* means "thoroughly" or "completely."

6–7 *quis enim deprendere possit / furta Iovis?* A rhetorical question, with subjunctive verb: "who could catch . . . ?" After some of the previous episodes, such as the Io story, we know that the *furta Iovis* ("secret affairs of Jupiter") are frequently found out by Juno, but never by any mortal detective. On *furta,* see note on 1.606.

7 *profugus:* probably an echo of Vergil's description of Aeneas' epithet (*fato profugus*) in the opening sentence of the *Aeneid* (1.2). Like Aeneas, the exiled Cadmus is forced to search, with divine guidance, for a new homeland.

8 *Agenorides = Cadmus,* "son of Agenor" (a Greek patronymic form, nom. case); this heroic-sounding name also appears in lines 81 and 90. *Phoebī = Apollinis. oracula:* poetic plural for singular.

10 *tibi:* dative with *occurret. solīs . . . in arvīs.*

11 *passa, inmunis:* modify *bos* in the previous line; from the feminine form of *passa* we can see that the *bos* is a cow or heifer. The deponent participle *passa* is active and has *nullum . . . iugum* as its object. *inmunis* + gen.: "free of . . ."

12 *carpe viās:* "make your way." *quā . . . herbā:* ablative of place where.

13 *fac condas: facio* + (*ut*) + present subjunctive means "bring it about *that* [something happens]" or "see to it that . . ." *vocātō:* future imperative, which can be translated as a regular present imperative; the future imperative has a legalistic or archaic ring, appropriate to oracular pronouncements. *Boeotia:* the region around Thebes; the legend of the cow explains the origin of the region's name, from the Greek word for cow, *bous.*

14 *Castaliō . . . antrō:* ablative of place from which; the "Castalian cave" is the oracle of Delphi, called after the nearby Castalian spring.

16 *nullum servitiī signum:* object of *gerentem;* since this cow's neck is not marked by a yoke or plow, she appears to meet the specifications of the oracle.

17 *legit vestigia:* "he follows her tracks"

19 *Cephisī:* the Cephisus is a river in Boeotia. *Panopēs:* Greek genitive singular; Panopē is a town in Phocis, on the way from Delphi to Boeotia.

22 *comitēs . . . sequentīs* = Cadmus and his men.

23 *tenerā . . . in herbā.*

24 *agit gratēs = agit gratiās:* "gives thanks." Compare Aeneas' prayer of greeting and thanksgiving immediately upon realizing he has reached the land he was seeking *(Aen.* 7.120–147).

27 *libandās . . . undās:* "waters to be poured as offerings." *ē vivīs . . . fontibus:* only spring water, or some kind of flowing water, was pure enough to be used in a sacrifice.

28 *silva vetus stabat nullā violata securī:* the grove where the spring is found looks initially like a *locus amoenus,* the classic beautiful, inviting, and unspoiled natural setting. But in the *Metamorphoses,* danger often lurks in such places. Callisto is raped in just such a spot (2.405–40), and Narcissus finds his fateful pool in a similar grove (3.407–17). Often, there is a contrast between the virginal landscape (e.g., "violated by no ax") and the violation or destruction that takes place there. Here, the snake of Mars is quite a terrible intrusion into the picturesque grove.

29 *specus [erat] in mediā [silvā].*

29–31 The many ablatives in these lines must be attached to the correct words: *virgīs ac vimine densus, efficiens . . . conpagibus, fecundus aquīs.*

32 *praesignis:* "marked by, notable for" (+ ablative). *cristīs:* snakes in ancient literature often have "crests," perhaps to be imagined like the hood of a cobra or like the vertical crests depicted on the heads of dragons. (The Greek word for snake, sometimes used in Latin, is *dracon.*) Clearly, this snake is no real species; it is a fantasy mixture of everything terrifying about all types of snakes: flashy colors, strange-colored eyes, poison, quivering tongue, fangs, etc. This snake's closest literary ancestors are the snakes that attack Laocoön and his sons in *Aeneid* 2.199–27.

34 *trēs . . . linguae:* not three separate tongues, but a "three-forked" tongue.

35 *quem . . . lucum = illum lucum;* the relative used as a connective should usually be translated as an English demonstrative. *Tyriā . . . de gente profectī:* "the ones who had set out from the Tyrian race," i.e., Cadmus' Phoenician companions; Tyre, a city in Phoenicia, often stands for the whole region.

36 *tetigēre = tetigērunt* (from *tango, -ere*).

37 *urna:* a vessel that the men had brought to collect water for the sacrifice (lines 26–27).

38 *caeruleus serpens:* from Vergil on *(Aen.* 2.381), *caeruleus* is a standard color for Latin literary snakes. The color is usually a sort of dark bluish-green, but sometimes seems just to mean "dark." In line 63, this snake's skin is described as *atrae.*

39 *effluxēre = effluxērunt.*

40 *corpus:* "their bodies"; poetic singular for plural. *attonitōs . . . artūs.*

41 *ille = serpens.*

43 *mediā plus parte:* "more than halfway."

44 *tantōque . . . corpore:* ablative of description: the snake is "of such great body,"
i.e., "of such great size." *tantō . . . quantō:* "of such great size as . . ."

45 *si totum spectes:* "if you look at him as a whole (*totum*)." *[is serpens] qui
separat geminās arctōs:* the constellation Draco ("The Snake") lies between the
constellations of the Great Bear and the Little Bear. Silhouetted against the sky,
the *Martius anguis* looks as huge as that heavenly snake.

46 *nec mora = sine morā. Phoenicas:* Greek, masculine accusative plural; object of
the verb *occupat* (48).

46–47 *sive illi tela parabant / sive fugam [parabant]:* a figure of speech called *zeugma*
(or sometimes *syllepsis*), the use of unlike words in a similar construction: "they
prepared weapons or flight."

47 *utrumque:* "either one," i.e., the preparation of weapons or the preparation to
run away.

48–49 *necat* has three objects—*hōs, illōs,* and another *hōs*—which represent the three
groups into which the snake's victims fall; with each accusative is an ablative
word or phrase—*morsū, longīs conplexibus,* and *adflatū funestī tabe venenī*—to
express the means by which they are killed. (Note the increasing size and
complexity of the ablative phrases.) *adflatū, tabe:* take either as appositives
("his breath, the pestilence of deadly poison"), or add a conjunction such as *et*
("his breath *and* the pestilence . . .").

50 *fecerat exiguās iam sol altissimus umbrās:* it is high noon, so the shadows are
small.

51 *quae mora sit sociīs:* indirect question after *miratur. Agenore natus:* "the one
born from Agenor," i.e., "son of Agenor" (Cadmus); this is a Latin version of
the Greek patronymic used elsewhere (*Agenorides*). The construction *natus +*
ablative of source is most familiar from Aeneas' epithet in Vergil (usually found
in the vocative: *nate deā*).

52–53 The lion skin likens Cadmus to Hercules, the most famous monster-slaying
hero.

53–54 *telum [erat] . . . lancea . . . et iaculum (et) animus:* supply a dative of posses-
sion, *illi. Telum* is the general term, while the other nouns are specific: "his
weapon was . . ."

53 *splendenti . . . ferro:* ablative of description, with *lancea.*

55 *ut* + indicative = "when."

55–56 *letataque corpora vidit / victoremque suprā [corpora]:* "he saw the dead bodies
and, above the bodies, the victor . . ."

56 *victorem . . . hostem:* one of these should be taken as an adjective: "the victori-
ous enemy" or the "hostile victor." *spatiosī corporis:* genitive of description.

57 *tristia sanguineā lambentem vulnera linguā: vulnera* is the object of *lambentem;*
while *linguā* is ablative of means. Notice the arrangement of the words: the
adjectives come first, presenting the ideas of "grim" and "bloody" before we
know what exactly is grim (*vulnera*) and what is bloody (*linguā*).

58 *fidissima corpora:* vocative, addressed to the dead bodies of Cadmus' companions.

58–59 *aut . . . aut:* "either . . . or."

59 *aut comes [vestrae mortis]. dextrā [manū]. molarem:* Heroic warriors often throw huge stones at their enemies in battle; the ability to lift such a stone is used as a measure of the hero's prowess and of the general superiority of men in the heroic age to men in the current age: e.g., in *Iliad* 5, Diomedes lifts and throws a stone "which no two men could carry such as men are now" (Lattimore's translation); in the final battle of *Aeneid* 12, Turnus attempts to hurl a stone that "twice-six chosen men with bodies such as earth produces now could scarcely lift" (Mandelbaum's translation).

59–60 *molarem . . . magnum:* object of both verbs, *sustulit* and *misit.*

61 *illius [molaris].*

61–62 *cum turribus ardua celsīs / moenia = ardua moenia et turres celsae: cum* ("along with") can replace *et.* (See line 92, below, for another example.)

62 *mota foret = mota esset:* "would have been moved" (pluperfect subjunctive, as in a contrary-to-fact condition). *[sed] serpens sine vulnere mansit:* in contrast to the hypothetical destruction that would have been inflicted on the walls.

63 *loricae:* "breastplate"; the snake is imagined as armored, like a warrior.

63–64 *loricaeque modo squamīs defensus et atrae / duritiā pellis validōs cute reppulit ictūs:* the passive participle *defensus* has two ablatives of means associated with it (*squamīs* and *duritiā*); the main verb *reppulit* has an ablative of separation (*cute:* "from his skin").

65 Cadmus now throws his spear, which, unlike the rock, is capable of piercing the snake's skin. *at non duritiā iaculum quoque [serpens] vicit eādem: duritiā* is ablative of means.

66 *lentae spinae:* "supple back."

67 *ferrum:* the spear-head, made of iron. See line 71, below.

68 *ille = serpens. dolore:* ablative of cause with *ferox. terga:* poetic singular for plural.

70–71 The snake bites on the spear and manages to pull out the shaft, but the metal tip of the spear remains deep in the wound.

70 *id = iaculum* (object of *labefecit*). *vī multā:* ablative of manner. *partem . . . in omnem:* "on every side."

71 *vix = "barely."* Supply id (*iaculum*) as object of *eripuit. ferrum:* the iron tip of the spear, as opposed to the wooden shaft.

72 *accessit:* "was added to." *solitās . . . ad irās:* the snake is naturally an irritable creature (hence, *solitas*) and was already annoyed by the invasion of humans into his habitat, but the spear wound makes him especially angry.

73 *guttura:* poetic plural for singular; compare *terga* in line 68, above.

75–76 rearrange: *halitus niger, qui exit ore Stygiō, vitiatās inficit aurās.*

76 *ore Stygiō:* "his hellish mouth." *vitiatās inficit aurās:* the perfect participle represents the first of two verbal actions; the second is represented by the main

verb. The meaning of the Latin is quite close to a compound sentence: *vitiavit et inficit aurās.*

77–79   *modo . . . interdum . . . nunc:* these clauses describe various tactics the snake adopts at different times.

77   *spirīs facientibus:* ablative absolute; *inmensum . . . orbem* is the object of the present active participle.

78   *cingitur: cingo* can mean "to form a circle or ring"; here, the passive may be read as a reflexive: "he forms himself into a ring." Notice the repetition of words concerned with circles in this clause: *spirīs, orbem, cingitur. longā trabe:* ablative of comparison.

79   *ceu concitus imbribus amnis:* this phrase is the entire simile; the verbs in the sentence describe the actual movements of the snake.

80   *fertur:* a reflexive again, like *cingitur* in line 78: "he bears himself forward."

81   *Agenorides* = Cadmus.

81–82   *spoliōque leonis / sustinet incursūs:* Cadmus' lion skin, which he was wearing when he first entered the grove in lines 52–53, is more than just a Herculean affectation; it actually protects him like a kind of armor.

83   *cuspide praetentā:* ablative of means. *ille* = *serpens.*

85   *veniferō . . . palatō:* ablative of source with *manare.* (Do not confuse *mano, manāre* with *maneo, manēre.*)

88   *colla:* plural for singular. *dabat retrō:* "drew back."

88–89   *plagamque sedēre / . . . arcēbat:* "prevented the blow from lodging."

89   *cedendō:* ablative of means. *nec longius [plagam] īre sinēbat. longius:* "more deeply."

90–91   *coniectum in gutture ferrum . . . pressit:* again, the equivalent of a compound sentence; two consecutive actions, the first of which is expressed by the participle: *coniecit ferrum in gutture et pressit [ferrum]. sequens:* "following through."

91–92   *dum retrō quercus euntī [serpentī] / obstitit: obsisto* means "to get in the way of [dative]." Take *retrō* with *euntī.* The oak tree blocked the snake's fall, as he toppled backward from the blow.

92   *pariter cum robore:* "along with the oak tree"; Cadmus' spear pierces all the way through the back of the snake's throat, comes out the snake's "neck," and lodges in the wood of the tree against which the snake is leaning. This graphic description of the spear's path echoes (or parodies) some descriptions of human wounds in Homeric battle scenes.

94   *gemuit:* followed by indirect statement (*sua robora flagellārī*).

95   *spatium:* "dimensions." *victor victi . . . hostis:* The victor, Cadmus, is juxtaposed with the *victi . . . hostis,* the snake, in a foreshadowing of their parallel fates (see line 98).

96   *cognoscere:* infinitives are treated as neuter nouns; hence the gender of *promptum.*

97 *unde [vox venit]. quid:* "why?" *Agenore nate:* vocative of the patronymic phrase found above in line 51.

98 *spectabere = spectaberis* (the second-person singular, future passive indicative). *serpens:* take as part of the predicate: "as a snake." Note the mirror-image arrangement of words in this line: *serpentem . . . serpens, spectas . . . spectabere.*

99 *pariter cum:* "along with . . ." (as in line 92, above).

99–100 *pariter cum mente colorem / perdiderat:* another Ovidian zeugma; compare lines 46–47.

101 *virī = Cadmī.*

102 Pallas = Minerva.

102–103 *motaeque iubet [Cadmum] supponere terrae / vipereōs dentēs: motae . . . terrae* is dative after the compound verb *supponere.*

103 *dentēs, incrementa:* appositives; *incrementa:* "seeds."

104 *paret:* "he obeys." *ut* + indicative: "when."

105 *iussōs . . . dentēs:* "the teeth, as ordered"; note how this noun-modifier phrase is interrupted by an appositive phrase, *mortalia semina.*

106 *fidē:* ablative of comparison. *fide maius:* "a thing greater than belief," i.e., "something too great to believe," an editorial comment from the narrator, who sometimes expresses skepticism at his own story.

107 *acies . . . hastae:* the point of a spear, which is held upright and so stands far above the warrior's head.

108 *tegmina . . . capitum pictō nutantia conō:* plumed helmets.

111–14 The curtain (*aulaea,* n. pl.) in a Roman theater was raised from the floor to conceal the stage, and was lowered to the floor to reveal the stage. Thus, raising a curtain decorated with pictures of people caused the figures (*signa*) to appear gradually, heads first (*primumque ostendere vultūs*). Once the curtain had been raised to its full height, the complete figures were revealed (*tota patent*), appearing to "stand" at the edge of the stage (*imōque pedēs in margine ponunt*).

116 *nē cape [arma]:* poetic use of *nē* with the imperative, instead of the prose standard of *nolī(te)* with the infinitive (*nolī capere*). The same construction is used in the next line (*nē . . . insere*). *dē populō . . . unus:* Where English says "one *of*" a number or group, Latin says "one *from*"; the same construction is used in line 118 (*terrigenīs . . . de fratribus unum*).

119 *ferit:* the subject is the soldier (*unus*) who addressed Cadmus in 116–117; this soldier is also the *ipse* at the end of this line. (*ferit,* from *ferio, ferīre,* should not be confused with forms of *fero, ferre.*)

120 *hunc quoque [is] qui letō dederat, non longius illō / vivit:* the first soldier (from lines 116–17) is represented here by both *hunc* (object of *dederat*) and *illō* (abl. of comparison with *longius*); *qui* represents the soldier who killed him with a spear in line 119. The exchange could be represented as: Soldier A (*unus,* 116) kills Soldier B (*unum,* 118) with a sword; Soldier C then kills Soldier A with a spear (119); Soldier C is then also killed (120–21). These specific deaths

encapsulate the battle, which is then generalized into mass killings in the next lines (122–25), until only five men are left standing.

121 *exspirat modo quās acceperat aurās: exspirat* should be translated very literally: "breathes out." The soldier has hardly (*modo*) taken his first breath when he dies.

122 *exemplōque parī:* "in a similar manner"; compare the English expression "by the same token."

122–23 *suōque / Marte:* "by their own fighting" or "by fighting themselves." ("Mars" is often used to mean "war.")

124 *brevis vitae spatium sortita:* "having been allotted a short life-span." *sortita* modifies the collective noun *iuventus.*

125 *sanguineam . . . matrem = terram.*

126 *quinque superstitibus:* ablative absolute. *Echion:* Like the other four, one of the mythical ancestors of the Thebans. Echion marries Cadmus' daughter Agave and becomes the father of King Pentheus (for Pentheus' story, see *Met.* 3.511–733; see also Euripides' *Bacchae*).

127 *humō = humī* (locative). *Tritonidis = Minervae* (gen.).

129 *hōs . . . comitēs:* the five surviving earth-born soldiers. *Sidonius hospes:* "the Sidonian stranger," i.e., Cadmus. Sidon is one of the cities of Cadmus' native Phoenicia and is often used to refer to the entire region.

130 *iussus Phoebeīs sortibus:* "as ordered by the oracle of (Phoebus) Apollo," in line 13, above.

8. Semele: 3.253–315

In the story that just precedes this one, the hunter Actaeon inadvertently stumbles upon a woodland pool where the virgin goddess Diana is bathing (3.138–252). Angered that a man has seen her naked and that her purity has been even slightly violated, Diana changes Actaeon into a stag. Trapped helplessly in his animal form, Actaeon falls prey to his own hunting dogs.

The Semele story opens with the reactions of various people to Actaeon's death. Some think Diana was excessive in her vengeance, while others think she was merely expressing the stern nature of her virginity. Juno, however, takes another perspective, rejoicing at Actaeon's downfall because, as a member of the house of Cadmus, Actaeon was related to Jupiter's lover Europa. All members of Europa's family, however distant—even great-nephews, such as Actaeon—are hateful to Juno. In addition, Juno's hatred of the Theban royal family is now doubled, for Jupiter has had another love affair, this time with Cadmus' daughter Semele. Juno devises a plan by which to destroy Semele and her unborn child, who will be the god Bacchus.

Ovid here depicts Juno as an angry, embittered queen, ready to take bloody revenge on her rivals. Her references to her power and to her royal status recall

Vergil's depiction of her in the *Aeneid,* especially in her first angry speech at *Aen.* 1.37–49. Ovid, however, combines this epic tone with a less reverent one, poking fun at the myths about Juno, in the ironic references to her unsuccessful marriage (266) and to her unspectacular level of fertility (269). Other versions of the myth relate that when Semele's son Bacchus grew up, he rescued his mother from the Underworld. Ovid chooses not to include this belated happy ending, but instead follows the further adventures of the rest of her family.

253   *in ambiguō:* "in a state of ambiguity"; the adjective *ambiguō* is here used as an abstract noun (a rare usage in Latin). *aequō:* ablative of comparison; "what was fair."

253–54 *aliīs . . . aliī:* "some people" . . . "others" (the usual meaning of paired usages of forms of *alius*).

254   *dea:* Diana. *laudant: [deam].*

254–55 *[eam] dignam . . . vocant. dignus, a, um* takes an ablative.

255   *pars . . . utraque* = each side (each of the two factions of opinion about Diana).

256–57 *non tam . . . eloquitur, quam gaudet:* "she does *not so much* declare . . . *as* she rejoices"; *quam* here = "as," correlative with *tam. culpetne probetne:* indirect questions depending on *eloquitur; -ne . . . -ne* = "whether . . . or."

257   *clade:* ablative of cause. *domūs ab Agenore ductae:* "of the house descended from Agenore"; Agenor was the father of Europa (one of Jupiter's lovers) and of Cadmus (founder of Thebes and grandfather of Actaeon).

258   *Tyriā . . . paelice:* Europa, who originally came from Tyre, in Phoenicia.

259   *subit priorī [causae]:* "takes the place of the earlier one (i.e., reason)"; the dative is common after compound verbs.

261   *Semelēn:* accusative singular, Greek form. *linguam ad iurgia solvit: ad* = "for the purpose of"; *linguam . . . solvit* ("she loosened up her tongue") is a humorous metaphor for Juno's preparation for a vigorous verbal workout.

262   *profēcī quid . . . ?* = *quid profēcī . . . ?* In poetry, words introducing questions (and relative clauses) do not always come first in their clauses.

263–66 *ipsam . . . soror:* The sentence consists of the brief main clause (*ipsam . . . perdam*) and the three *si*-clauses.

263   *ipsa* = Semele. *mihi:* dative of agent with passive periphrastic.

264   *dextrā [manū].*

264–65 *decet:* Impersonal verb, followed by indirect statement: *me tenēre gemmantia sceptra.*

265–66 *regina Iovisque / et soror et coniunx:* a verbatim quotation of Juno's great *iurgium* in *Aeneid* 1. Ovid then completely deflates this gradiose Vergilian moment with Juno's sarcastic joke: *certē soror,* "well, sister, at least."

266   *et . . . et:* "both . . . and." *puto:* parenthetical. In this sentence, Juno seems briefly (and uncharacteristically) to consider overlooking this affair; perhaps,

she muses, it was just a brief fling, with no lasting consequences. But then she remembers Semele's pregnancy and returns to her usual state of rage.

266–67 *furtō . . . contenta: contenta* is followed by an ablative ("content *with . . .*").

268 *concipit:* "she conceives," i.e., she is pregnant. *id:* "that one thing" (i.e., the fact that she has conceived).

269–70 *mater:* predicate nominative after the linking verb *fieri. quod:* the somewhat vague antecedent is the *idea* of the whole main clause, i.e., the fact that Semele will become a mother by Jupiter. (Juno alludes to the fact that she herself, according to mythological tradition, had only one child with Jupiter; now Semele will have tied that record.) *mater . . . fieri:* "she wants to become a mother by Jupiter alone—a thing which has hardly happened to me." *unō = solō.*

271 *faxo = fēcero,* a rare and archaic future perfect form of *facio;* translate as a future tense. A form of *facio* introducing a subjunctive clause may mean "make it so that" or "bring it about that." *fallat: faxo [ut forma] fallat eam. Saturnia:* a frequent epithet for Juno in epic; Juno, like Jupiter, is the daughter of Saturn. By using it here, Juno suggests her traditional royal power; she is acting not just as a jealous wife, but as an angered queen.

273 *hīs [verbīs]. ab:* "after." Juno now undergoes a physical transformation, which Ovid describes in careful detail, much as he describes the metamorphoses of human characters. *soliō:* ablative of separation or place whence, after *surgit. fulvāque recondita nube:* the word meaning "hidden" (*recondita*) is surrounded, like Juno herself, by the "golden cloud" (*fulvā . . . nube*). Latin word order can mimic the ideas it is describing.

274 *Semelēs:* genitive singular, Greek form.

274–75 *ante . . . quam = antequam,* introducing *simulavit.*

275 *ad:* "at." *tempora:* "temples" (of her face). *canōs [capillōs].*

278 *Beroe:* name of Semele's nurse from Epidaurus. *Epidauria:* adj. *Semelēs:* see 274.

280 *venēre = venērunt. suspirat:* "she [Juno] sighs," as if concerned. Juno here plants the idea in Semele's mind that her lover may not really be Jupiter and should be tested.

281 *Iuppiter ut sit = ut Iuppiter sit.*

282 *nomine:* "under the name." *divōrum = deōrum. iniēre = iniērunt,* from *ineo, inīre.*

284 *verus [deus].*

284–86 *quantus . . . sumat:* "ask that, in the size and shape in which he is received by lofty Juno, he make love to you and that he first assume his own attributes." Literally, "ask that, in which size (*quantus*) and shape (*qualis*) he is received by lofty Juno, in such size (*tantus*) and shape (*talis*) he give you embraces (*det tibi conplexūs*)." *Quantus/tantus* and *qualis/talis* clauses often do not translate smoothly into English, because of their repetition; a natural English sentence omits the second of these paired words.

285   *rogātō:* future imperative; translate as a regular present imperative. Introduces indirect commands: *rogātō [ut] det, [ut] sumat.*

286   *ante:* adverbial, "beforehand"; before he comes to her again.

287   *Cadmeida:* accusative singular, Greek form, of *Cadmeis,* "daughter of Cadmus," Semele. Interpretations that put any blame on Semele for her own fate will have to take account of the adjective *ignaram.*

288   *formarat = formaverat. rogat . . . Iovem . . . munus: rogo* can take a "double accusative," of the person asked and of the thing asked for.

289   *patiere = patieris* (future indicative). The second-person-singular passive ending *-re* is an alternative to *-ris. repulsam:* from the noun *repulsa* ("refusal").

290   The first *quoque* is *quō + -que.* The second *(Stygiī quŏque conscia)* is the connective synonymous with *etiam. quō = ut,* when the purpose clause contains a comparative (such as *magis). suntō:* third-person-plural future imperative of *sum;* translate as if it were *sint,* a jussive subjunctive. The future imperative has the ring of solemn legal pronouncements and is often found in Latin legal language; it is appropriate language here for Jupiter's great binding oath by the river Styx.

291   *ille = Styx.* Rearrange the sentence: *ille est timor et deus deorum.* Since humans swear by the gods, and the gods swear by the Styx, it can be called the gods' "god."

292   *amantis = Jupiter. amans* (literally "the one [who is] loving") is used commonly as a noun for "lover."

292–93   Observe how *-que* is used to mark and divide the three consecutive adjectival phrases modifying Semele: *laeta malō, nimium potens, peritura amantis obsequiō;* also note that all three are ironic. *malō:* ablative of cause: "happy in (because of) her misfortune." *peritura:* future participle from *pereo. obsequiō:* ablative of cause; Jupiter's "obedience" to Semele's wish will be her destruction.

293–95   *qualem . . . talem:* compare the pairs *quantus . . . tantus* and *qualis . . . talis* in 284–85. Semele says, "Give yourself to me *in such as way (talem) as (qualem)* Juno is accustomed to embrace you."

294   *Veneris cum foedus initis:* Semele uses *Veneris foedus* to refer to the delicate subject of her lover's relations with his wife. *initis:* from *ineo;* see 282.

295   *tē:* "yourself" (reflexive). *ora* = "mouth"; poetic plural for singular. *loquentis [puellae].*

296   *vox = verba* (a common meaning).

297–98   *optasse, iurasse = optavisse, iuravisse.* Each infinitive is used absolutely (i.e., without an object) and depends on *potest,* so that there are two parallel clauses: *neque enim non haec optasse [potest], neque ille / non iurasse potest. Haec* and *ille,* of course, refer to Semele and Jupiter. Let *neque* negate each main verb and *non* negate each infinitive ("is *unable not* to have . . .").

299   *aethera:* accusative singular, Greek form. *vultūque:* Jupiter, who is essentially a sky god, can change the weather merely by changing his facial expression.

300   *quīs = quibus. fulgura = fulgora.*
302   *quā:* "as much as." *sibi:* dative of separation, after *demere.*
303–304 Take *igne* with *eō* in the main clause, as the antecedent of the relative *quō.*
     Read: *nec nunc armatur eo igne quo . . . deiecerat. Typhoea:* accusative
     singular, Greek form. Typhoeus was a huge and rebellious monster whom
     Jupiter destroyed with repeated blasts of lightning. The story of Typhoeus in
     Hesiod's *Theogony* 820–880 shows in great detail what Jupiter's thunderbolts
     can do when he is threatened. The tragedy of Semele's story lies in Jupiter's
     obliging himself to use his thunderbolts on someone quite unlike Typhoeus.
304   *feritatis:* partitive genitive; a normal Latin way of expressing quantity, where
     English does not always express the "of": e.g., "too much ferocity." *illō [igne].*
305   *dextra Cyclopum:* Jupiter's thunderbolts are manufactured by the Cyclopes.
306   *saevitiae flammaeque minus, minus . . . irae:* partitive genitive; see note on line
     304.
307   *superi:* a common epic term for the gods.
307–308 *domum . . . Agenoream:* Semele's house, so called after her grandfather Agenor.
     See line 257 above: *domus ab Agenore ductae.*
308   *donīsque jugalibus:* Ironically, this is the "gift" (*munus*) requested in line 288.
311–12 *patriō . . . femorī = patris femorī.* Latin prefers to use the adjective *patrius, a,*
     um as a modifier rather than the genitive of the noun *pater.*
312   *maternaque tempora:* i.e., the time his mother normally would have carried him.
313   *Ino matertera:* his aunt Ino, another of Cadmus' daughters. For her part in the
     nursing of Bacchus, Ino will be punished by Juno in Book 4.
314   *datum [Bacchum]. Nyseides:* the nymphs of Nysa, a place in Asia Minor where
     Bacchus is said to have spent his early years.
315   *occuluēre = occuluērunt. dedēre = dēdērunt.*

9. Echo and Narcissus: 3.339–510

The stories of these two characters interrupt the Theban stories of the house
of Cadmus; the only link to the preceding stories is the Theban prophet Tiresias,
who foretells the fate of Narcissus. Narcissus is to some extent a male version
of the "militant virgin," a character type already met in Daphne, Callisto, and
others; he refuses the romantic advances of all who approach him. (Another
famous celibate male is Hippolytus, son of Theseus; see Euripides' play
Hippolytus.) Unlike the others, however, Narcissus' celibacy is not given a
religious explanation, such as devotion to a virgin goddess, but seems to stem
entirely from his own pride and self-centeredness.
     Echo enters the story as an example of one of Narcissus' rejected lovers.
Her peculiar speech habits are explained in a flashback that alludes to untold
episodes of Jupiter's infidelity. As a penalty for her excessive talking, Echo can
only repeat the last few words she hears. It is in this restricted condition that

she courts Narcissus unsuccessfully and later wastes away until she is nothing but a voice. Finally, one of Narcissus' other rejected lovers prays that Narcissus may know the rejection he has inflicted on others. Nemesis, goddess of vengeance, answers the prayer by luring him into a beautiful place with a clear pool of water. It is in this pool that Narcissus sees his reflection and falls in love, with no hope of fulfillment.

The myth of Narcissus is one of the most famous in the *Metamorphoses*, because of its psychological insight and symbolism and its complex mixture of humor and pathos, beauty and silliness.

339–58 Narcissus is born, and a strange prophecy is received about his fate. He grows up to be extraordinarily beautiful but refuses the attention of all lovers.

339 *Ille* = Tiresias. *famā:* ablative of respect with *celeberrimus. Aoniās . . . urbēs:* "the cities of Boeotia"; Thebes is located in the region of Boeotia.

341 *fidē* = genitive (alternative form).

342 *caerula Liriope:* the epithet *caerula* suggests that Narcissus' mother Liriope was a water nymph. (The adjective is spelled either *caeruleus* or *caerulus.*)

343 *Cephisos:* nominative, subject of both *inplicuit* and *tulit.*

343–44 *[cui] clausae suīs Cēphīsos in undīs / vim tulit: clausae* is dative, modifying an implied relative (parallel to *quam* in line 342). Cephisos, the river god, "brought force to" (*vim tulit,* i.e., raped) the nymph, who had been "enclosed in his waters" (*clausae suīs in undīs*).

344 *enixa est:* "gave birth to."

345 *nymphē:* nominative singular, Greek form. *qui posset amārī:* relative clause of characteristic.

346 *Narcissumque [infantem] vocat. dē quō consultus* = *de hōc puerō consultus.*

346–47 *an esset . . . visurus:* "whether he would see" or "whether he was going to see"; this is the question that was put to Tiresias. *an* introduces questions that begin with "whether."

348 *fatidicus vates* = Tiresias.

349 *vox = verba. vana:* predicate adjective after *visa est. exitus* = "outcome." *illam* = *vocem.*

349–50 *exitus, res, letī genus, novitas furoris:* all subjects of *probat.*

351 *ter ad quinōs [annōs]:* "to three-times-five years." *Cephisius [puer]* = "the boy descended from Cephisos," i.e., Narcissus.

352 *poteratque puer iuvenisque vidērī:* take *puer* and *iuvenis* as predicate nominatives after *vidērī.*

353 *multī illum iuvenēs [cupiēre], multae [illum] cupiēre puellae:* The result of Narcissus' in-between age: he was sought as a lover by young men, who saw him as a boy, and by girls, who saw him as a young man. *cupiēre* = *cupiērunt.*

354 *sed fuit in tenerā tam dura superbia formā.* Take *tam* closely with *dura.*

355   *nullī illum [tetigēre] iuvenēs, nullae [illum] tetigēre puellae.*
Note the exact parallelism of this line with line 353, which brings out the contrast between the "many" who seek Narcissus and the "none" who obtain him. *tetigēre* = *tetigērunt* (from *tango*).

356   *hunc = Narcissum. trepidōs . . . cervōs:* object of the present participle *agitantem. trepidōs agitantem in retia cervōs:* Narcissus pursues the favorite sport of most young mythological heroes (e.g., Actaeon, Hippolytus; and some heroines, e.g. Daphne, Callisto): hunting. Here, he participates in a type of hunt in which deer are chased into net traps set up for them in the forest.

357   *reticēre:* "be silent in return to" or "make no answer to" (followed by the dative *loquentī [hominī]*).

358   *nec . . . didicit:* "did not know how to" (from *disco;* "has learned how" = "knows"). The sense of "learning" in the verb must be ignored, for Echo's deficiency is not actually due to a failure to learn but has been imposed on her by Juno. *resonabilis Echo:* renames the *vocalis nymphē* in the previous line.

359–401   The story of how Echo lost control of her voice and how she attempted to court Narcissus.

359   *Corpus adhuc Echo [habet].* At the time of her love for Narcissus, Echo had not yet become invisible, as she is now, but her voice had already become an "echo," as it is now.

360   *garrula [Echo]. oris = vocis.*

361   *ut* introduces the entire clause: *ut reddere dē multīs [verbīs] verba novissima posset,* a noun clause elaborating on *usum* (359): the use of her voice that Echo had was "that she could . . ." *novissima:* "last."

362   *cum . . . posset:* "when she (Juno) could have . . ."

362–63   *deprendere . . . nymphās:* Juno is out to catch the nymphs, not Jupiter. This sentence refers to more than one incident, because of the plural *nymphās,* the imperfect tense of *tenēbat* in line 364, and *saepe* in 363.

363   *sub Iove saepe suō nymphās in monte iacentīs:* a more explicit representation of Jupiter's sexual activity than Ovid's epic style usually allows. The phrase *sub Iove* holds a joke, for its most common usage is metaphorical ("under the sky," or "out in the open," with *Iove* standing abstractly for the sky, as Ceres stands for "food" in line 437). But the context of Juno's jealousy makes it clear that this time the phrase should be taken very literally.

364   *illa = Echo. tenēbat:* "used to hold back"; the imperfect tense implies repeated action. Every time Juno came to these regions in hopes of catching her husband's infidelity, she ran into Echo, who impeded her search with lengthy chatter.

365   *dum fugerent nymphae: dum* with the subjunctive means "until." *Saturnia =* Juno.

366   *quā:* ablative of means.

368   *rē:* "with action"; "in fact." *haec =* Echo.

369   *vocēs* = *verba*.

371   *incaluit [amore]*.

372   *quoque magis sequitur, flammā propiore calescit:* comparable to English expressions of the type "the more [one thing happens], the more [something else happens]." Here, the two comparatives are *quo magis* and *propiore flammā*. Literally, the translation does not fit well with the English idiom: "the more she follows, with a closer flame she burns"; the closest we can get is something like "the more she follows, the closer the flame with which she burns."

373   *non aliter quam* = *velut* (introducing a simile; compare the same phrase at line 483). *cum:* "when."

374   *admotās . . . flammās:* the fire does not actually have to be touched to the sulfur-smeared torch; fire that is merely moved near (*admotās*) causes the sulfur to ignite.

376   *mollīs . . . precēs:* the usual sort of entreaty made by a potential lover. *natura:* her nature (the one that Juno has imposed on her).

377   *nec sinit [ut] incipiat* = *nec sinit eam incipere. quod [natura] sinit:* "a thing which her nature does allow"; refers to the entire action described in the next clause.

379   Here begins Echo's encounter with Narcissus, after he has become separated from his hunting companions. As he calls, he thinks he is being answered by them. *forte:* from the noun *fors, fortis,* not the adjective *fortis, forte.*

381   *ut:* "as" (with indicative). *aciem:* "his gaze."

382   *[eum] vocantem*.

383   *nullō veniente:* ablative absolute. Narcissus is still expecting his companions to appear, but they are not there; he then speculates that they are avoiding him. *quid:* "why?"

386–87 *coeamus . . . coeamus:* Here, Echo's meaning begins to diverge from Narcissus', although she is still only repeating his own words. Addressing his hunting friends, Narcissus intends a very different sense of *coeo* than Echo does. This difference is heightened in their next exchange. *nullī . . . sonō:* dative after *responsura*.

388   *verbīs favet suīs:* "she supports (or backs up) her words"; *faveo* takes the dative. *egressa [ē] silvā*.

389   *speratō . . . collō:* dative with the compound verb *iniceret*.

391   *ante emoriar quam . . .* = *emoriar antequam . . . tibi:* dative of possession. *copia nostri:* "access to me"; *copia* can also mean "sexual availability." *nostrī* = *meī*.

392   *sit:* When Echo removes Narcissus' subjunctive verb from its subordinate clause and makes it a main verb, it becomes a positive *wish* ("may there be . . ."). Thus, the truncating process of her echoing plays with the possibilities of Latin syntax.

393   *[in] silvīs*.

394 *ex illō [tempore].*

395 *repulsae:* from the noun *repulsa, -ae.*

396 *vigilēs . . . curae:* "pain that makes one stay up all night"; sleepless nights are of course a standard sign of unrequited love, as is an emaciated look.

397 *adducit:* "contracts." *āera:* accusative singular, Greek form.

398 *tantum:* "only."

399 *ferunt:* "they say," followed by indirect statement: *ossa traxisse figuram lapidis. ferunt* is one of Ovid's ways of reminding us that this is only a story. *traxisse:* "took on," "acquired."

400 *videtur:* "is seen" (the passive meaning of *video,* not the more common idiomatic meaning "seems").

401 *[ab] omnibus.*

403 *hic* = Narcissus. *ante:* adverbial: "previously." *coetūs . . . virilēs* = *coetūs virōrum,* i.e., male lovers.

404 *aliquis despectus:* "some one scorned," i.e., one of the rejected lovers (apparently male). *manūs . . . ad aethera tollens:* a gesture of prayer and supplication. *aethera:* accusative singular, Greek form.

405 *licet* here introduces a concessive clause: "although." *amatō:* object of *potiatur,* which takes an ablative.

406 *Rhamnusia* = Nemesis, the goddess of vengeance, whose famous cult site was Rhamnus.

407–12 Description of the pool where Narcissus will meet his fate.

408 *pastae [in] monte.*

410 *turbarat = turbaverat.*

411 *gramen erat circā [fontem]. umor = aqua.*

412 *silvaque sole locum passura tepescere nullō:* i.e., the forest created shade, which kept out the heat of the sun. Note how Latin negates different words than does English: "allows the place to become warm with no sun" = "does not allow the place to become warm with sun." Compare *nullī . . . sonō* in lines 386–87, above.

413 *hīc:* the adverb ("here"), rather than the demonstrative pronoun. *et . . . et:* "both . . . and"; joining the two ablatives of cause *(studiō, aestū)* which depend on *lassus.*

414 *secutus:* "attracted by, pursuing." *faciemque . . . fontemque:* "both . . . and."

417 *spem sine corpore:* "a hope without substance," i.e., the dream boy in the reflection. *corpus putat [id] esse, quod umbra est:* as in the previous clause, the contrast is between substance *(corpus)* and something less solid, hope *(spem)* or shadow *(umbra).*

419 *ut:* "as." *Pariō . . . marmore:* marble from Paros was prized by sculptors for its pure whiteness.

420 *geminum . . . sidus = gemina sidera.* Poetic singular for plural (compare the opposite in line 422). The phrase is interrupted by the appositive, *sua lumina.*

421   *dignōs Bacchō [crinēs], dignōs et Apolline crinēs: dignus,* "worthy," takes an ablative (although English uses "of"); *et* here means "even." Bacchus and Apollo are two gods who have the long curls characteristic of young men.

422   *genās:* Although there are several *gen-* nouns (*gena, genus, gens, genū*), all are of different genders or declensions, so ambiguity is rare. *colla:* poetic plural for singular.

423   *in niveō mixtum candore ruborem:* The interlocked word order mimics the sense of the phrase; the words are mingled together, just as the colors are. This juxtaposition of pale skin and a red blush is often cited as a beautiful and erotic feature; Narcissus will notice it again in his "beloved" at lines 482–485, where two similes elaborate on the contrasting colors. Another famous instance, also containing a simile, is Lavinia's blush in *Aeneid* 12.64–69.

424   *quibus:* ablative of cause, referring to *cuncta* (neu. pl.).

424–26   Note the uses of paired words (*miratur-mirabilis, probat-probatur, petit-petitur*), illustrating Narcissus' confusing double situation: both subject and object, both active and passive.

426   *accendit [amorem] et ardet [amore].*

427–28   *quotiens:* exclamatory; take at beginning of the line.

428   *visum . . . collum:* object of *captantia.*

429   *in illīs [bracchiīs].*

430   Notice the difference between the indirect question clause, *quid videat* (subjunctive verb, introduced by interrogative pronoun), and the relative clause, *quod videt* (indicative verb, introduced by relative pronoun).

432   *credule:* vocative, addressed by the narrator to Narcissus. *quid:* "why?"

433   *avertere = averteris;* the passive form used as a reflexive (*avertes tē*). *quod amas, avertere, perdes: [si] avertere, perdes [id] quod amas.*

434   *repercussae:* "reflected."

435   *nil . . . suī:* "nothing of its own," i.e., no substance of its own. *-que . . . -que:* "both . . . and."

436   *possis = poteris.*

437–38   A compound subject, with the object (*illum*) repeated for emphasis: *non [cura] Cereris, non cura quietis abstrahere inde potest [illum];* i.e., Narcissus did not leave the image to eat or sleep.

437   *Cereris = cibī.*

438   *fusus:* "stretched out," "sprawled."

440   *levatus:* "raising himself"; the passive participle used as a reflexive.

441   *tendens sua bracchia:* the same gesture of supplication made by the rejected lover who called for the curse on Narcissus (see line 404, above).

442   *io:* an exclamation. *silvae:* Narcissus addresses the woods themselves, who have witnessed many love affairs. *Silvae* will be the implied subject of the second-person plurals *scitis* and *fuistis* in line 443.

443   *multīs [amantibus].*

444 *cum:* "since." *vestrae tot agantur saecula vitae: agere vitam* is a standard Latin idiom for "to lead life"; here, it is modified to *agere saecula vitae,* "to live ages of life."

446 *placet (mihi):* the verb is used impersonally, but is best translated as a passive with a personal subject: "I am pleased."

447 *tantus tenet error [me] amantem.*

448 *quoque magis doleam:* purpose clauses containing comparative words, such as *magis,* are introduced by *quo* rather than *ut.*

448–49 Lovers usually grieve because they are separated by geographical or physical barriers (seas, mountains, or locked doors). The lover standing alone outside the closed door of his mistress' house is a standard scene in Latin love poetry. In the *Metamorphoses,* this scene appears in the Iphis and Anaxarete story in Book 14, and a variation in the Pyramus and Thisbe story in Book 4. Narcissus sees that his situation ironically lacks these physical barriers, but his isolation is even greater, because he can see but not reach his beloved.

450 *exiguā prohibemur aquā:* the plural subject is amusingly ambiguous: it can be taken either as Narcissus' reference to himself in the plural (a common usage in poetry; "I am restrained [from him]"), or as a reference to the two "entities," Narcissus and his beloved ("we are restrained [from each other]")—but of course in either case, there is only one of them. See the similar mixture of plural and singular at lines 451 and 467–68. *ipse:* the boy in the water.

451 *porreximus:* the same ambiguous plural, because when "I" stretch out my lips, so do "we." But here, the two clauses of the sentence compare what "I" do (*porreximus*) with what "he" does (*nititur*). Narcissus still thinks of the boy in the water as a separate person.

451–52 *quotiens . . . totiens:* "as often as . . ."; with these correlatives, it is best to translate only the first one.

452 *hic [puer].*

453 *posse putes [eum] tangī. putes:* "you would think." *amantibus [nobis]:* dative after the compound *obstat.*

454–62 Narcissus addresses the boy in the water, leading up to the recognition of reality in line 463. Ovid continues one of his favorite devices, the use of two forms of the same word in the same sentence (lines 424–26, 458–60).

454 *quid:* "why." *puer unice:* (vocative) Narcissus uses *unice* to mean "peerless" or "matchless," but the word also reminds us that the boy is "singular."

455 *quōve petitus abis: petitus* might best be translated "when you are sought (by me)"; i.e., when I reach out my arms to the water and you vanish. *quō* means "where (to)" or "whither."

455–56 *certe nec forma nec aetas / est mea, quam fugias:* supply "it" as subject of *est;* take *forma* and *aetas* as predicate nouns.

456 *amarunt = amavērunt. quoque nymphae:* "the nymphs too." Now, Narcissus proudly boasts of his attractiveness to the nymphs whom he rejected.

457 *spem . . . nescio quam:* "I-don't-know-what-kind-of hope," i.e., "some sort of hope" or "some hope."

458 *porrigis [bracchia].*

460 *mē lacrimante:* ablative absolute.

461 *quantum . . . suspicor:* "as I suspect." *motū formosī . . . [tuī] oris:* When Narcissus talks, he sees the boy's lips move and assumes that the boy must be speaking to him.

462 *aurēs . . . nostrās:* object of *pervenientia; nostrās* here must be plural for singular ("my").

463 *iste [puer] ego sum:* the moment of truth. Henceforth, Narcissus himself will exploit the ambiguities of his situation, with a mixture of tragic and comic effects. Previously, only the narrator has been able to make fun of Narcissus' paradoxical love.

464 *meī:* objective genitive of the pronoun. *flammās moveoque feroque: moveo* is used to mean "I inspire the flames (of love)," while *fero* means "I endure the flames (of love)"; thus, I am both the cause of the love and the victim of it. Compare line 426: *accendit et ardet.*

465 *faciam, roger, rogem:* subjunctives in deliberative questions: "what *should* I do?" etc. With the two forms of *rogo,* the grammar plays a very literal part in the paradox: Narcissus is essentially asking, "Shall I be active or passive?"

466 *inopem me copia fēcit:* perhaps Narcissus' most famous paradoxical line. It depends on the etymological kinship between *copia* and *inopem* (both come from *ops, opis*).

467 *secedere:* "be separated from."

467–68 Narcissus switches between the singular and the plural first-person forms with a freedom that is not impermissible in Latin poetry, but that, in his case, may reflect his confusion about his double identity.

468 *vellem [ut id] quod amamus abesset:* this sentence, along with the wish in the previous line, is the *votum in amante novum.* Narcissus observes that lovers do not usually wish to be further divided from their beloved; compare his comments in lines 458–60 on the closeness of his lover, in contrast to the distance that usually separates unhappy lovers. *abesset:* translate the imperfect subjunctive as if it were in a contrary-to-fact condition: "I wish it *were absent* [but it's not]."

469–73 Narcissus predicts his own death (and, naturally, that of his lover).

469 *dolor virēs [meās] adimit.*

470 *primō . . . in aevō:* "in my earliest years."

471 *mihi . . . positūrō morte dolorēs: positūrō* modifies *mihi* and has its frequent meaning of "put down" or "lay aside"; as a future *active* participle, it has *dolorēs* as its object. *morte:* "in death."

472 *vellem [ut] hic [puer], qui diligitur, diuturnior esset.* Although he himself welcomes death, Narcissus wishes only that his beloved might live longer.

473   *[nōs] duō concordēs:* subject.

474   *male sanus = insanus.*

476   *quam cum vidisset abīre = cum eam [formam] vidisset abīre:* Latin uses the relative pronoun as a connective more than is possible in English; English cannot put a relative pronoun in a subordinate clause (this clause would literally read: "when he saw which . . ."); English must say "when he saw it . . ."

477   *quō refugis:* The falling of Narcissus' tears into the pool has disturbed the image, which is now breaking up. Notice that in this address Narcissus has returned to speaking of the image as if it were another "person"; if he fully acknowledged it as a reflection of himself, he would not speak of it as "fleeing" or "deserting" him. *crudelis:* vocative.

478–79   *liceat . . . adspicere:* The impersonal verb *licet* takes an infinitive to complete its meaning. The present subjunctive indicates a wish or a prayer.

478   *quod tangere non est = [id] quod tangere non licet:* this clause is the object of *adspicere* in 479.

479   *miserō praebere alimenta furorī:* Narcissus knows that looking at the reflection only makes him more infatuated ("feeds my madness," as he puts it), but he still wants to continue.

480   *summā . . . ab orā:* "from the top edge."

483   *non aliter quam:* understatement (technical term: *litotes*); in introducing a simile, "not otherwise than . . ." means "just as . . ." This is in fact a double simile ("like apples *or* grapes"), and the second alternative, the grapes, is introduced by *ut,* "as" (484).

483–85   *non aliter quam poma solent . . . aut ut . . . solet uva . . . ducere purpureum . . . colorem:* The two fruits (*poma, uva*) are introduced by *non aliter quam* and *ut;* each is subject of the same verb (*solent, solet*), which takes the complementary infinitive *ducere* ("take on"). *Poma* is modified by two relative clauses: *quae candida [sunt aliā] parte, [et quae aliā] parte rubent; uva* (which here means "a *bunch of* grapes") is modified by the ablative phrase *variīs . . . racemīs* and by *nondum matura.* The image is of ripening fruit that is delicately shaded from light to dark on different sides, as the flush of redness is spreading over Narcissus' white skin. The idea of "ripening" is also suggestive of Narcissus' age and incipient sexuality. (See note above on line 423.)

486   *quae:* neuter plural. The relative as a connective again, as in 476; object of *adspexit. simul = simul ac:* "as soon as," introduces the whole clause, as if it were placed at the beginning of the line, before *quae. liquefactā rursus in undā:* the water had been disturbed by his tears but is now cleared up (*liquefactā rursus*), so that the image can once again be seen plainly.

487   *non tulit ulterius:* just like the English expression: "he could bear it no longer." *ut:* "as."

487–89   Another double comparison: *ut flavae . . . cerae matutinaeque pruinae.* As in lines 483–85, the verb is *solent* plus an infinitive (*intabescere . . . solent*). Each subject is accompanied by an ablative phrase that tells what melts it: *cerae* are melted by *igne levī*, and *pruinae* by *sole tepente.*

490   *ignī:* Note the two different ablative singular forms of the i-stem *ignis: ignī* here and *igne* in line 488.

491   *mixtō candore:* ablative of description; *ruborī* is dative after *miscere.*

492   *quae modo visa placēbant: visa* can be taken as the antecedent of *quae:* "those sights (literally 'things seen') which just now (*modo*) used to be pleasing." Notice the imperfect tense of *placēbant: "used to be* pleasing (but aren't any more)."

493   *quondam quod = quod quondam.*

494   *quae:* "these things," i.e., all these happenings; object of *vidit. ut [Echo] vidit: ut* here, with the indicative, means "when." *quamvis irata memorque:* modifiers of Echo.

496   *haec* = Echo, who is able to show her continuing care for him by echoing his laments.

499   *spectantis [Narcissī].*

501   *dictōque "valē":* ablative absolute. *Valē* may be left untranslated: "when *valē* was said [by him]." *inquit et Echo:* "Echo, too, said . . ."

503   *lumina = oculōs. dominī:* the possessor of the eyes is said to be their "master." *formam:* object of *mirantia.*

504   *tum quoque:* "even then." *[in] infernā sede:* in the underworld.

505   *in Stygiā . . . aquā:* As in other stories, the transformed person retains some of the character he displayed before his metamorphosis: Narcissus continues to gaze at his reflection even after his death. (Compare how the weeping Byblis becomes a spring, the talkative Pierides become magpies, and Clytie, who loved the sun god, becomes a heliotropic flower.) Narcissus' situation is slightly different, because his spirit actually dies and descends to the Underworld, while only his body seems to have been transformed into a flower (see lines 509–10). *planxēre = planxērunt.*

505–506   *sororēs naides:* since Narcissus' mother was a water nymph, so were his sisters. *posuēre = posuērunt;* his sisters dedicated locks of their hair to him, in a gesture of mourning.

507   *plangentibus:* dative with the compound verb *adsonat.*

510   *medium:* object of *cingentibus.*

10. Pyramus and Thisbe: 4.55–166

Just as Book 3 ends with the punishment of King Pentheus, who refuses to worship Bacchus, Book 4 opens with another group of nonbelievers, the daughters of Minyas. While all other Thebans take a holiday from work to celebrate the rites of Bacchus, these three women remain at home, continue with their weaving, and tell stories to pass the time. Their stories all have romantic themes: the lovers Pyramus and Thisbe; several of the sun god's lovers; and Salmacis and Hermaphroditus. At the end of these stories, the daughters of Minyas are transformed into bats, in punishment for their continued denial of Bacchus.

Ovid's version of the story of Pyramus and Thisbe is the earliest one found in classical literature; if Ovid got it from an earlier source, that source is unknown to us. The story seems to be of Near Eastern origin, since it is set in Babylon. Ovid's version is presented as an aetiology, a tale that explains the origins of something, in this case the red berries of the mulberry tree. This story is also one of the first in the *Metamorphoses* in which both lovers are mortal; earlier amatory stories have mainly treated nymphs or mortal women involved with gods.

This story is familiar to English-speaking readers from Shakespeare's humorous retelling of it in *A Midsummer Night's Dream*. That version demonstrates Shakespeare's detailed knowledge of Ovid's text.

55–56 *alter, altera:* "one . . . , the other . . ."

56 *puellīs [omnibus].*

57 *tenuēre = tenuērunt;* here, with the meaning "occupied." *contiguās . . . domōs:* the feminine gender of *domus* reflects its fourth-declension origins, although in some cases (such as this acc. pl.), the second-declension endings are more common. Pyramus and Thisbe live in houses that share a party wall, rather like a modern duplex.

57–58 *altam . . . urbem:* Babylon.

58 Semiramis was legendary queen of Babylon, who built its famous brick walls. She was the wife of King Ninus, whose tomb serves as a landmark for the lovers in this story (see line 88, below).

59–60 At first, Pyramus and Thisbe became acquainted merely as neighbors, but eventually fell in love.

60 *coissent:* like the apodosis of a contrary to fact condition: "[if their fathers had permitted,] they *would have* come together . . ." *taedae . . . iure:* "by the law of the torch," i.e., "in marriage." Torches, carried at Roman wedding ceremonies, symbolize marriage.

61 *vetuēre = vetuērunt. potuēre = potuērunt. quod non potuēre vetāre:* "a thing which they could not forbid"; refers to the action in the next line.

62 *ex aequō:* "equally" or "mutually." *captīs [amore] . . . mentibus.*

63 *conscius omnis:* "every accomplice." Negative expressions in Latin often differ from those in English: Latin says "every accomplice was absent," while English says "there were no accomplices."

64 *quō(que) magis . . . magis:* parallel to the English construction "the more [one thing happens], the more [something else happens]." Supply *ignis* as subject of *tegitur.* This line expresses metaphorically the cliché that hiding one's love makes it grow more intense.

65 *tenuī rimā:* ablative of means.

66 *quam [paries] duxerat: duxerat* here means "developed" or "acquired." *fieret:* take here as the passive of "make," not with its specialized (but common) meaning "become."

67 *nullī:* dative with *notatum.*

68 *primī vidistis amantēs:* the narrator addresses the lovers directly: "you lovers first saw . . ."

73 *invide . . . paries:* vocative; the lovers are now addressing the wall. A certain penchant for this sort of rhetorical address will be noticed throughout the story. *quid:* "why?" *amantibus:* dative after the compound verb *obstas.*

74 *quantum erat:* "how much (i.e., how little) would it be . . ." or "how small a thing would it be"; followed by the *ut*-clauses (*ut sineres . . . aut . . . pateres*) as objects. *totō . . . corpore:* ablative of manner.

75 *hoc si nimium est = si hoc nimium est ad oscula danda:* gerundive phrase expressing purpose.

76 *nos debēre:* indirect statement after *fatemur.*

77 *quod . . . aurīs:* this entire clause is the object of *debere:* "we confess that we owe to you *the fact that (quod)* . . ." Notice the two uses of the English "to": the dative indirect object (*verbīs*) and the prepositional phrase for motion in space (*ad amicās . . . aurīs,* "to loving ears").

78 *talia:* neuter plural object of *locutī. diversā . . . sede:* ablative of source (translate "from . . ."). In this phrase, Ovid seems to play with the ridiculous nature of the rhetorical situation—the lovers in unison address the wall from their respective sides of the crack.

79 *sub noctem:* "as night fell" (contrast the uses of *sub* with the acc. and with the abl.). *dixēre = dixērunt. dedēre = dedērunt.*

79–80 *dedēre . . . quisque:* "they each gave"; the subject, while singular, obviously refers to *both* of the lovers, so the verb is plural.

80 *contrā:* "to the opposite side"; adverbial, not a preposition.

81–82 Pyramus and Thisbe apparently communicate through the fissure only during the day, not under cover of darkness, as one might think. Ovid is unclear about the location of this fissure within the houses; perhaps it is in a garden wall, as suggested by the reference in line 82 to the sun's drying of the grass.

83 *coiēre = coiērunt.*

84 *multa . . . questī: multa* may be translated either adverbially ("having complained much"), or as a noun reflecting its neuter plural form ("having made many complaints"). *nocte silentī:* ablative of time when.

84–88 *statuunt ut . . . :* the series of present subjunctive verbs (*temptent, relinquant, conveniant, lateant*) constitute the lovers' plans and should be translated as such: "they decide that they *should* . . ."

87 *nēve sit errandum . . . spatiantibus:* "so that they may not make a mistake (i.e., miss each other) as they wander about." The verb is used impersonally, with a dative agent. *[in] latō . . . arvō.*

88 *ad* = "at." *ad busta Ninī:* Ninus was a legendary king of Babylon (and husband of the Semiramis mentioned in line 58); the rendezvous at his tomb adds some local color to the story. (Recall Shakespeare's wonderful phrase "Ninny's tomb": *A Midsummer Night's Dream,* Act V, Scene 1.)

89 *arbor [erat]. niveīs . . . pomīs:* Before the deaths of Pyramus and Thisbe, the mulberry had white fruit. The staining of the fruit to red constitutes the metamorphosis in this story.

90 *ardua mōrus:* all names of trees are feminine in Latin. Some easily confused words: *mōrus, -ī* ("mulberry tree"), and the much more common *mōs, mōris* ("custom") and *mora, -ae* ("delay"). (The word for the mulberry fruit, *mōrum, -i,* appears in line 127.)

91 *pacta:* "the plans"; neuter plural, from *paciscor.* The participle, though deponent, is used in a passive sense. *placent [eīs]. lux, tardē discedere visa:* The night the lovers are eagerly anticipating seems to come very slowly.

91–92 *lux . . . praecipitatur aquīs:* the sun appears to set in the ocean, which is in the west, while darkness also appears to arise from the ocean.

93 *Callida:* applied to Thisbe, this adjective seems to imply something about the way she opened the door (abl. abs.: *versatō cardine*). As often, a nominative adjective modifying the subject can be translated as an adverb.

94 *suōs:* literally, "her own people," i.e., the people in her household. *adoperta vultum:* "having covered her face," i.e., wearing a veil (*vultum* is acc. of respect).

95 *dictā sub arbore:* "beneath the appointed tree."

96 *audacem [eam] faciebat amor.*

97 *boum:* genitive of *bos, bovis. spumantīs . . . rictūs:* accusative of respect with the participle *oblīta* (from *oblino;* the participle of *obliviscor* has a long *i: oblītus, a, um*).

98 *depositura sitim:* the future participle can be used to express purpose after a verb of motion: the lioness "came to slake her thirst."

99 *quam* = *leaenam. ad lunae radiōs:* "by the light of the moon."

101 *velamina:* the veil that Thisbe was said to be wearing in line 94. Poetic plural for singular.

102 *ut* + indicative: "when." *multā . . . undā:* ablative of means.

103–104 *inventōs forte sine ipsā . . . tenuēs . . . amictūs:* the *tenuēs amictūs* (poetic plural; see line 101) are Thisbe's veil, again. The lioness just happens upon the veil (*inventōs forte*), without its owner (*sine ipsā [puellā]*).

104 *ore cruentatō:* ablative of means; as noted in lines 94–95, the lioness had just made a kill, so had the blood of fresh meat on her mouth.

105 *serius egressus:* "coming out later" (from home); the same verb was used of Thisbe's departure from her home (94: *egreditur*).

107 *ut:* "when."

108 *una duōs . . . nox perdet amantēs:* an excellent illustration of the flexibility of Latin word order, which allows the two contrasting adjectives (*una duōs*) to be

juxtaposed; also an example of interlocked word order, in which two pairs of nouns and adjectives are arranged *abab*.

109   *ē quibus:* "of whom" (i.e., of the two lovers). *illa:* Thisbe. *longā dignissima vitā: dignus, a, um* takes an ablative to complete its meaning, although English says "worthy *of*."

110   *nostra = mea;* poetic plural for singular. Pyramus is taking all the blame for the tragedy. *miseranda:* vocative, addressed to the absent Thisbe.

110–11   *quī iussī [ut] venires in loca plena metūs nec [quī] prior hūc vēnī:* the antecedent of *qui* is *ego,* hence, the first-person verbs. The use of an *ut*-clause after *iussi* is unusual; an infinitive would be used in prose. Translate a single *nec* as "and . . . not."

112   *nostrum = meum* (see line 110). *divellite:* Pyramus now addresses all the local wild beasts whom he thinks have killed Thisbe.

113   *scelerata . . . [mea] viscera.*

114   *o quicumque . . . habitatis . . . leonēs:* "O you lions who dwell . . ." (literally: "whichever lions . . .").

115   *timidī:* genitive of quality: "it is *characteristic* of a fearful man . . ." *optāre necem = exspectāre necem;* Pyramus means that waiting for the lions to eat him is more cowardly than committing suicide. *Thisbēs:* genitive singular, Greek form.

116   *[illa velamina] fert.*

117   *utque dedit notae lacrimās, dedit oscula vestī = ut dedit lacrimās et oscula notae vestī.*

118   *accipe . . . haustūs:* "take a drink." *nostrī = meī.*

119   *quō(que):* the relative *quō* refers to *ferrum* (the relative often precedes the antecedent).

120   *nec mora = sine morā. traxit [ferrum].*

121   *ut:* "as." *humō = humī* (locative).

122   *non aliter quam cum = velut cum;* the expression "not otherwise than when . . ." (i.e., "just as when . . .") introduces a simile. This is one of Ovid's most famous and maligned similes; critics have charged that the image of a leaking water pipe makes an inappropriate, unromantic point of comparison with the dead lover's lifeblood. *vitiatō . . . plumbō:* "when its lead has been damaged"; Roman water pipes were made of lead. This very Roman image of water spurting from a burst pipe contrasts with the exotic Babylonian setting of the story.

123–24   *longās . . . aquās:* "long streams of water."

124   *āera:* Greek accusative form, from *āēr.*

125   *arboreī fetūs:* the fruit of the mulberry tree.

125–26   *in atram . . . faciem:* It seems strange to us that blood should turn the berries to a color we usually call "black," but *ater* may be translated as "dark." *Ater* is in fact a regular color of blood in Latin epic (although in line 127, the berries are described as *purpureō*).

126–27 *madefactaque sanguine radix / purpureō tinguit pendentia mora colore:* *sanguine* is an ablative of means after *madefacta*, and *colore* after *tinguit.* The adjective *purpureō* might modify either *sanguine* or *colore*—or perhaps both. *mōra* is from *mōrum, -i* ("fruit of the mulberry tree"; see note on line 90).

128 *metū nondum positō nē fallat amantem:* the fear clause (*nē fallat amantem*) depends on *metū. positō* here has it common meaning "put down or aside." For the meaning of *fallat* ("escape the notice of"), compare line 94.

129 *illa:* Thisbe.

130 Rearrange: *gestit narrāre quanta pericula vitarit. gestio, īre:* "desire eagerly, long." *vitarit = vitaverit.*

131–32 *ut . . . sic:* "although . . . yet . . ."

131 *visā . . . in arbore:* She has seen the tree before, on her first visit to the rendezvous (line 95).

132 *facit [eam] incertam pomī color. haeret an haec sit: an* introduces "whether" questions. The basic meaning of *haereo* is "stick, cling"; here, its meaning is metaphorical: "get stuck, be at a loss." "She is at a loss [about] whether this is it."

134 *solum:* from *sŏlum, -i,* "ground." (The quantity of the vowel distinguishes this noun from the adjective *sōlus, a, um* and the noun *sōl, sōlis.*) *retrōque pedem tulit:* "she recoils." *ora:* poetic plural for singular.

134–35 Two comparisons are used in close proximity to describe Thisbe: her face is paler than boxwood, and her shudder is like the quivering of the ocean's surface. Notice the two ways of introducing these comparisons: the first with a comparative adjective (*pallidiora*), and the second with the word *instar* ("equal to" + genitive).

136 *exiguā cum summum stringitur aurā = cum summum [aequor] stringitur exiguā aurā:* The image is of a calm surface of the sea ruffled by a light breeze. Thisbe shudders gently here just because she has seen a dead body; when she realizes it is Pyramus, she will have a much more violent reaction.

137 *suōs . . . amorēs = suum amantem* (a common poetic usage).

139 *comās:* accusative of respect with the participle *laniata* ("torn with respect to her hair"; or more naturally, "tearing her hair"). *amplexa:* active participle from a deponent verb.

140 *fletum = lacrimās.*

142 *mihi:* dative of separation.

145 *Thisbēs:* genitive singular, Greek form.

146 *recondidit [oculōs]:* "closed his eyes." *visā . . . illā [puellā]:* ablative absolute.

147 *quae:* the relative used as a connective; translate as *illa,* and as subject of the *postquam* clause.

147–48 *ense . . . vacuum:* "empty of its sword."

148–49 *tua . . . manus . . . amorque perdidit:* two singular subjects with a singular verb.

149–50 *est et mihi fortis . . . manus: mihi* is a dative of possession; *et* is used as an intensifier. "*I, too* have a brave hand . . ." *in unum . . . hoc:* "in this one thing alone" (i.e., suicide). *est et [mihi] amor:* same construction as the previous

clause. *dabit hic [mihi] in vulnera virēs: hic* refers to *amor; in vulnera virēs:*
"strength for [inflicting] wounds."

151   *persequar [te] extinctum.*

152–53   *[tu] quī . . . poteras. morte . . . sola:* ablative of means with the passive infini-
tive *revellī. ā mē:* "from me."

153   *poteras, poteris:* the juxtaposition of two forms of the same verb is one of
Ovid's favorite types of wordplay. *nec morte:* "not even by death." When they
were both alive, Pyramus and Thisbe probably swore that only death could part
them; now they have an opportunity to be together in death.

154   *estōte rogatī:* a future imperative (second-person plural, passive): "be asked,"
addressed to *parentēs* (vocative in line 155). *hoc:* "this thing" (to be elaborated
on by the *ut* clause that begins in line 156). *ambōrum:* "both of us."

155   *multum:* adverbial with *miseri:* "very miserable." *meus illiusque parentēs =
meus parens et illius [Pyramī] parens: parentēs* here seems to refer only to one
parent of each lover (hence the singular *meus*), no doubt the father (see line 61:
vetuēre patrēs).

156   *ut:* the request introduced in line 154: "be asked this, (namely) that . . ." *[nōs],
quōs certus amor [iunxit], quōs hora novissima iunxit. novissima:* "last."

157   *[nōs] componī [in] tumulō non invideatis eōdem: invideo* here can be translated
"begrudge that . . . ," followed by the indirect statement (*[nōs] componī*).

158–59   *tu . . . :* a vocative address to the mulberry-tree. "You, tree, who . . ."

159   *[et quae] mox es tectura [miserabilia corpora] duōrum.*

160   *pullōs:* "dark, gloomy" (from the adjective *pullus, a, um*, not the noun *pullus,
-ī*, "chicken"). Thisbe asks the tree to retain the color that its berries have been
stained by Pyramus' blood.

161   *fetūs:* "fruit." *monimenta:* appositive to *fetūs.*

162   *aptatō . . . mucrone:* ablative absolute; *mucro* is the point of the sword.

163   *incubuit:* "she fell on." *ferrō:* dative with the compound verb. *ā caede [Pyramī].*

164   *tetigēre = tetigērunt. deōs, parentēs:* Thisbe made two requests; one, about their
burial, had to be fulfilled by the lovers' parents, while the other, about the mul-
berry fruit, had to be fulfilled by the gods (although we must presume it also
took the gods' intervention for the parents to be informed of the burial request).

165   *ater:* see note on line 125, above.

166   *[id] quod rogīs superest:* "that which remained from the funeral pyre," i.e., their
bones. By Roman custom (which seems to override the Babylonian setting
throughout this story), Pyramus and Thisbe would have been cremated and their
bones then collected and placed in an urn. *unā . . . in urnā.*

11. Perseus and Andromeda: 4.663–752

This episode is one of a series featuring the hero Perseus. Ovid's treatment
of the complex of Perseus stories is in many ways typical of his treatment of

epic heroes. Perseus is first introduced in the middle of his adventures, after his most famous adventure, the slaying of Medusa; at 4.615, he appears on his return journey, bearing the monster's head, which drips blood onto the sands of Libya and generates the snakes thought to be typical of that country (4.617–20). Thus the heroic slaying of Medusa is featured only as the source of an aetiological (explanatory) metamorphosis. Next, Perseus encounters Atlas, described as a gigantic king of a western land, whom Perseus turns to stone with Medusa's head (4.621–62). In the next episode, the longest of Perseus' adventures in Book 4 (and our Latin passage here), the hero performs what appears to be a heroic exploit, but in the service of a romantic cause, the rescue of the beautiful princess Andromeda from a sea monster (4.663–752). In the Andromeda episode, Ovid undercuts Perseus' heroism with overblown rhetoric (e.g., his initial address to her, 4.678–79) and with realistic details (e.g., the technical problem Perseus experiences with his winged sandals, 4.729–31). A prime focus of the episode is the sea monster, an amalgam of various other literary snakes and monsters (especially the snake fought by Cadmus in *Met.* 3.28–98 and the snakes that populate Vergil's *Aeneid*). Ovid also plays with the melodramatic scene of the maiden's rescue, in the depiction of Andromeda's parents and in their "negotiation" with Perseus for his services (4.695–705).

663 *Hippotades* = son of Hippotas, Aeolus, king of the winds. The patronymic at the opening of the episode sets a grand epic tone, for the name also appears at the beginning of Odysseus' Aeolus adventure (*Od.* 10.2). Aeolus also appears prominently in the first major episode of Vergil's *Aeneid* (1.50–63). In Ovid's Perseus episode, however, Aeolus takes no part in the action, but is merely alluded to in a description of the weather. As in Vergil, Aeolus is said to keep all the winds imprisoned under a mountain, from which only a few are released at a time. *[in] aeternō carcere.*

664–65 *admonitorque operum . . . Lucifer:* Lucifer, the "light-bringer," is the morning star, whose rise signals the time to get up and start work.

664 *[in] caelō . . . altō.*

665 *ille* = Perseus. *pennīs . . . resumptīs:* ablative absolute. Perseus is wearing the winged sandals given him by Mercury for his adventures.

666 *parte ab utrāque:* "on both sides," i.e., on both his feet. *telō . . . uncō:* the curved sword with which he had decapitated Medusa; it is called a "hook" at line 720 and a "scythe" at 727. *accingitur:* the passive form used as a reflexive: "girds himself with . . ."

667 *āera:* accusative singular, Greek form, from *āēr. talaribus:* here, "winged sandals."

668 *gentibus . . . relictīs:* ablative absolute. Perseus' flying journey takes him around the far reaches of the known classical world, from Atlas in the far west to Andromeda's Ethiopia in the far south. *circumque infrāque:* adverbial; *-que . . . -que:* "both . . . and."

669 *Cephea . . . arva:* the lands of Cepheus (Andromeda's father).

670 *maternae . . . linguae = matris linguae.*

670–71 *pendere . . . poenās:* a common idiom meaning "pay the penalty."

671 *Andromedan:* accusative singular, Greek form. *Ammon:* the North African version of Jupiter.

672 *quam simul . . . vidit = simul illam . . . vidit:* the main clause on which the *simul* clause depends is *trahit . . . ignēs* (675). *religatam bracchia:* "tied with respect to her arms," i.e., "with her arms tied."

673 *Abantiades:* Perseus, descendent of Abas (his great-grandfather). *nisi quod:* "except for the fact that . . ."; the conclusion of this condition is *ratus esset* in line 675.

674 *lumina = oculōs.*

675 *marmoreum ratus esset [illam esse] opus:* conclusion of a contrary-to-fact condition; "he *would have thought* she was a marble statue (but he didn't)." *trahit . . . ignēs:* "he caught fire (with love)."

677 *oblītus est:* from *obliviscor.* The picture of the hero struck dumb with love is here taken to a new level, as Perseus, forgetting to flap his winged sandals, almost crashes to the ground while staring at the beautiful girl. (Compare *Amores* 2.5.51–52, where an especially good kiss is said to be able to cause Jupiter to drop his thunderbolts.)

678 *ut:* "when" (with indicative).

678–79 *o . . . digna . . . :* These two lines make up Perseus' vocative address to Andromeda; *digna* ("[you who are] worthy *of*") is followed by two contrasting ablative phrases, *non istīs . . . catenīs* and *[catenīs] quibus inter sē cupidī iunguntur amantēs.* The comparison of Andromeda's current actual chains to the metaphorical "bonds" between lovers adds a touch of ridiculous rhetoric, in view of the maiden's crisis situation; this is no time to try to impress a girl with elegant words. *istīs:* a good example of the scornful force of *iste:* "not *those* chains."

680 *requirentī [mihi]. nomen terraeque tuumque = nomen terrae et nomen tuum.*

681–86 Andromeda's maidenly modesty at first outweighs the emergency of her situation. She is too well brought up to speak to a strange man, even one who could save her life, and she would normally have covered her face with her hands or a veil, but, prevented by her chains, she weeps instead. Perseus has to ask several times (*saepius instantī*) before she will answer, and she finally does so merely to preserve his good opinion of her, to keep him from thinking it is some crime of her own that has brought about her situation.

681 *vincla = vincula. illa =* Andromeda.

682–83 *manibusque modestōs / celasset vultūs, si non religata fuisset:* contrary-to-fact condition. *modestōs . . . vultūs:* poetic plural for singular.

683 *si non = nisi.*

684 *quod potuit:* "what she could do"; refers to the entire action of the line.

685 *saepius instantī [virō]:* completes the meaning of the main verb *indicat* in 688.
nē: negative purpose clause. *sua* modifies *delicta;* its placement at the beginning of the clause gives it emphasis.

686–88 *indicat* (688) has two types of objects: the noun phrase *nomen terraeque suumque* and the indirect question *quantaque maternae fuerit fiducia formae.*

687 *maternae . . . fiducia formae:* "confidence in maternal beauty," i.e., "her mother's confidence in her beauty." Andromeda had been ordered sacrificed to the sea monster because her mother boasted too much of her own beauty (see lines 670–671).

688 *nondum memoratīs omnibus:* Take *nondum* as part of the ablative absolute; *omnibus* is neuter plural ("everything," i.e., Andromeda's entire story).

689 *inmensō . . . pontō:* dative after the compound *inminet.*

690 *possidet:* "fills up."

691 *unā:* adverb.

691–92 *genitor . . . et . . . mater adest:* two singular subjects, to be taken individually with the singular verb (rather like English "her father was there, and her mother was, too"). *genitor* is a poetic equivalent of *pater.*

692 *iustius illa [misera]: illa* refers to Andromeda's mother, who was "more rightly" unhappy, because she was the cause of her daughter's impending doom.

693 *nec sēcum auxilium [ferunt]. dignōs tempore fletūs:* "tears suitable for the occasion." This line seems to mock the situation as a standard scene; the parents wept in the way parents normally do when their daughter is about to be eaten by a monster.

695 *hospes:* Perseus.

695–96 *manēre:* "await."

696 *ad opem . . . ferendam:* gerundive expression of purpose.

697–701 A contrary-to-fact condition (imperfect subjunctive in both clauses: *si peterem . . . , praeferrer*). Note all of the nominative phrases in apposition to *ego: Perseus Iove natus et illā; Gorgonis anguicomae Perseus superator; alīs aeriās ausus iactatīs ire per aurās.* Perseus uses this elaborate boast to introduce himself to Andromeda's parents and says that if they merely knew his identity they would immediately give him their daughter. In lines 701–703, he will, almost as an afterthought, offer to win her hand by rescuing her from the sea monster.

697 *hanc ego si peterem = si hanc [puellam] ego peterem:* placing the two pronouns together at the front of the clause emphasizes them and their (potential) relationship. *Iove natus et illā: natus* with ablative of source is a common epic way to express parentage: "the one born *from* . . . ," i.e., "son of . . ."

697–98 *illā, / quam clausam inplevit fecundō Iuppiter aurō:* refers to Perseus' mother Danaë, who was imprisoned (*clausam*) in a tower to preserve her chastity; Jupiter entered through the tower's window as a shower of gold and impregnated her (*inplevit fecundō . . . aurō*).

699 *anguicomae:* "snaky-haired."

699–700   *alīs . . . iactatīs:* ablative of means.

701–702   *tantīs / dotibus:* Perseus speaks of his prior heroic reputation as his "dowry" or "wedding gifts."

702   *et meritum:* "a service, too." *[si mihi] faveant modo numina.*

703–705   *paciscor:* Perseus seems to be offering to make a deal with Andromeda's parents; they look upon his offer as a *legem* ("contract," 704), and make their own, even better, offer (*promittuntque super regnum dotale*).

703   *ut mea sit servata meā virtute:* noun clause that is the object of *paciscor; mea sit* is the main part of the clause ("that she be mine"), while *servata* modifies the implied subject.

704   *quis enim dubitaret?* Subjunctive in a rhetorical question.

705   *super:* adverbial: "in addition, on top of that"; i.e., in addition to the reward suggested by Perseus himself, the princess' hand.

706   *Ecce:* returns attention to the threat approaching from the sea.

707   *iuvenum:* the ship's rowers.

708   *sic fera [sulcat aquās]:* like a ship, the beast "plows" or cuts through the sea water. *dimotīs . . . undīs:* ablative absolute; *inpulsū:* ablative of means dependent on *dimotīs.*

709   *tantum aberat scopulīs, quantum . . . :* "it was as far away from the rocks as . . ."

709–10   *mediī . . . caelī:* a partitive genitive with *quantum;* this phrase must be expanded to fit into the rest of the clause: "as the distance in the middle of the sky which a *Balearica funda . . ." Balearica tortō funda potest plumbō . . . transmittere:* warriors of the Balearic Islands (Majorca and Minorca) were famous for their use of the slingshot in battle. Translate: "which a Balearic sling can cross (*transmittere*) by means of its hurled leaden bullet (*tortō . . . plumbō*)."

711   *iuvenis* = Perseus. *pedibus tellure repulsā:* ablative absolute, with ablative of means attached. Perseus pushes off of the ground with his feet, so that he can fly up high into the air. This much detail about the exact technicalities of using winged sandals may undercut their magic aura a bit. Compare also lines 729–730, where the wings malfunction.

712   *arduus:* translate adverbially. *ut* + indicative: "when."

713   *visā . . . in umbrā: in* here must mean "against"; *in* with this meaning is more commonly followed by the accusative, but Ovid uses both accusative and ablative.

714   *utque Iovis praepes: ut* ("as") introduces a simile, which will be concluded by the corresponding *sic* in line 718. The "bird of Jupiter" is the eagle.

715   *Phoebō:* "Phoebus" is here used as a synonym for the sun.

716   *occupat aversum:* "attacks from behind." *neu saeva [draco] retorqueat ora:* negative purpose clause; *ora* is poetic plural for singular.

717   *[in] squamigerīs . . . cervicibus:* again, a poetic plural for singular. The suffix *-ger* (from *gero*) is often used by authors to form new adjectives meaning "_____-bearing." Compare the similar suffix *-fer,* as in *anguiferum* (741).

718-20 *sic . . . Inachides . . . :* the narrative now returns from the simile to the story, and the parallels become clear: Perseus, in his winged sandals, corresponds to the eagle (his father's symbol), while the sea monster corresponds to the snake. Like the eagle, Perseus will swoop down on the monster and strike its neck from behind to avoid being bitten.

718 *per inane:* "through the void (i.e., air)."

719 *terga:* poetic plural for singular. *ferae . . . frementis:* take this genitive phrase with both clauses: *terga ferae [frementis] pressit* and *dextrōque frementis [ferae] in armō . . . ferrum . . . abdidit. armō:* from *armus, -ī* (m.)

720 *Inachides* = Perseus. The Inachus is a river in Argos, where Perseus was born. (Inachus is also the father of Io.) *curvō tenus . . . hamō:* "as far as the curved hook"; Perseus is using his scimitar-like sword (see line 666: *telō . . . uncō,* and 727: *falcatō . . . ense*), and buries the entire blade in the monster.

721-22 *modo . . . modo . . . modo:* more than one *modo* is used to introduce a series of actions done and repeated in turn: "now [it does one thing], now [it does another thing], and now [it does another thing]." Compare *nunc, nunc, nunc* in the description of Perseus' corresponding actions at lines 725-727.

721 *laesa [fera].*

722 *subdit [sē] aquīs:* the dative *aquīs* completes the meaning of the prefix in the compound verb (literally, "places itself under the water").

722-23 *more ferocis . . . aprī: more* ("in the manner of") plus the genitive is another way of introducing a simile. Just as in lines 714-720 Ovid compared the fight between Perseus and the monster to an encounter between an eagle and a snake, here he compares them to other animals, a wild boar confronted by a pack of hunting dogs.

723 *circumsona:* an adjective made up by Ovid; the *sonus, a, um* portion is equivalent to *sonans.*

724 *ille* = Perseus.

725 *quāque patet:* "wherever it [the monster] is exposed"; while the monster is diving, rearing, and turning, it exposes various portions of its body to Perseus' blows. *terga cavīs super obsita conchīs: terga* is poetic plural for singular; *super* should be taken adverbially; *cavīs . . . conchīs* is associated with *obsita* (from *obsero, ere,* "cover"). Like a ship (to which it was compared in line 706), the monster has small shells growing on its skin.

725-27 *nunc terga . . . , nunc laterum costās, nunc quā . . . :* all three are objects of *verberat* in line 727.

726-27 *nunc quā . . . :* "now [the place] where . . ."

727 *desinit in piscem:* "comes to an end in [the form of] a fish"; whatever the rest of the monster is, its tail is that of a fish. *falcatō . . . ense:* another expression for Perseus' curved sword; *falcatus* is related to the noun *falx, falcis,* "scythe, sickle."

728 *fluctūs* = aquam.

729 *maduēre* = *maduērunt. gravēs . . . pennae:* An example of Ovid's method of undercutting heroic scenes with realistic details: Perseus' winged sandals do not operate well when wet, and he is forced to stop relying on them.

730 *nec:* take with *ausus credere.*

732 *stantibus exstat aquīs, [sed] operitur ab aequore motō:* the contrast is between *stantibus . . . aquīs,* calm waters, and *aequore motō,* rough waters; the rock's peak is visible when the water stands calm, but is hidden when rough waves crash around it.

733 *nixus:* from *nitor, niti,* + ablative. *eō [scopulō]. sinistrā [manū].*

734 *repetita:* "repeatedly attacked."

735 *cum plausū clamor:* the subject is treated as if it were *plausus et clamor,* and hence has a plural verb, *inplevēre.*

736 *inplevēre* = *inplevērunt. generumque [eum] salutant:* "they greet him as their son-in-law"; since Perseus has defeated the monster, he may now marry Andromeda, according to his agreement with her parents.

737 *[eum esse] auxilium domūs servatoremque fatentur.*

738 *Cassiopē* (nom.): Andromeda's mother.

740 *ipse* = Perseus. *manūs haustā victricēs . . . undā:* note the interlocked word order. The noun *victrix* is used as an adjective. *haustā . . . undā* ("drawn water") is ablative of means. The picture of the hero making use of a washbasin immediately after his heroic victory is another overrealistic and antiheroic Ovidian touch.

741 Take *nē* at the beginning of the entire line. Perseus must improvise a resting place for Medusa's head while he washes up. This scene reminds us that Perseus has been carrying the Gorgon's head all along, although he did not use it to his advantage during the battle with the sea monster.

742 *natās sub aequore virgās:* "plants born beneath the sea"; i.e, seaweed or perhaps live (soft) coral, which will be made stony by contact with Medusa's head. (Do not confuse *virga, -ae* with *virgo, virginis.*)

743 *Phorcynidos:* genitive singular, Greek form; Medusa was the daughter of Phorcos, son of Neptune. *ora* = *caput.*

744 *virga recens bibulāque etiamnum viva medullā: medullā* ("marrow, pith") is ablative of specification with *viva.*

746 *percepit:* "acquired."

747–52 The origin of the coral in the sea is now explained: the nymphs saw the effects of Medusa's head on a few twigs of seaweed and produced more hardened plants by this same method; they then "sowed" these twigs throughout the sea to generate coral, which is soft in the water (when alive, like its plant origin) but becomes hard outside the water (when dead, like objects petrified by Medusa).

749 *iterant:* "multiply"; the original twigs thrown into the sea are the source ("seeds") of all future coral plants.

750   *nunc quoque:* a phrase that often brings an aetiological story up to the present
      day: "even now . . ." *[in] curaliis.*
751   *ut:* noun clause explaining *eadem natura:* "the same nature, [namely] that
      they . . ." *tactō . . . ab āere:* it was thought that coral became hard only through
      contact with the air.
751–52   *[id] quod vimen . . . erat, fiat . . . saxum.*

12. The Lycian Farmers: 6.313–81

This story, like many of Ovid's, skirts the edges of another famous work of
literature, in this case, the *Homeric Hymn to Apollo.* The *Hymn* recounts the
wanderings of Latona, the mother of Apollo and Diana, as she looks for a safe
haven in which to give birth to the twin gods. She is eventually taken in by the
island of Delos, which becomes sacred to Apollo. In Ovid's sequel, Latona
travels with her newborn children from Delos to Lycia in Asia Minor, where
she stops in search of a drink of water. The local farmers, unaware of her
identity, mock her and prevent her from obtaining any refreshment. In
vengeance, she turns them to frogs.

Although this brief story is not one of Ovid's best known, it makes an
interesting contrast when read alongside other stories of divine punishment and
vengeance in the *Metamorphoses.* The preceding books have been full of
stories of mortals punished or metamorphosed by divinities (usually goddesses),
sometimes for no offense, sometimes for foolishness or pride. In many of these
stories, the reader is left wondering if justice has been done, or if the avenging
divinity has gone too far. Book 6 begins with two stories of mortals who
challenge goddesses and pay dearly, perhaps excessively, for their pride:
Arachne (6.1–145) and Niobe (6.146–312). Niobe, mother of fourteen children,
boasts that she is more worthy of worship than Latona, mother of only two; at
Latona's request, Apollo and Diana mercilessly strike down each one of
Niobe's children before her eyes. In the Lycian farmers episode, however, the
same goddess Latona appears as an almost pitiful figure, a new mother of twins,
exhausted from a long journey and desperate for a drink of water. The
punishment of her human opponents, who have no redeeming virtues, seems
quite just.

The narrative setting of this story is also notable: after Niobe's fate has
demonstrated Latona's power, the people of Niobe's city tell other stories about
the goddess, and one citizen in particular recounts the story of Latona and the
Lycian farmers, which he heard in his youth from an old Lycian. Neither the
narrator nor his informant is identified by name, so it is difficult to judge their
credibility or motivation. Another such story, told by a seemingly minor
character to illustrate a point about divinities, is the story of Baucis and
Philemon (8.611–724).

313   *tum:* after the fate of Niobe. *numinis = Latonae.*

314   *femina virque:* At the beginning of the Niobe episode, the women of her city had been ordered to worship Latona; only Niobe had resisted. Now, after Niobe's punishment, all citizens, male and female, zealously worship Latona's power.

315   *gemelliparae:* "twin-bearing," an adjective apparently made up by Ovid for the occasion. It is a compound of *gemellus* ("twin") and *pario* ("give birth"; as in the English derivative "oviparous").

316   *utque fit:* "as happens." *ā factō propiore priora [facta] renarrant:* "after a more recent deed, they recount earlier ones"; recent events inspire people to recall similar events from the past.

317–30   The citizen sets up the story by describing how in his youth in Lycia he met an old man with whom he visited a site sacred to Latona.

317   *ē quibus unus:* "one of whom"; this is the only identification of the narrator: he is one of the citizens who now worship Latona. *agrīs:* ablative of description with *fertilis.*

318   *non inpune:* "not with impunity," i.e., not without punishment. This rhetorical device, a kind of understatement, is called litotes and is often stronger than a simple positive statement ("very definitely *with* punishment"). *sprevēre = sprevērunt.* From the verb *sperno.*

319   *ignobilitate:* ablative of cause. The narrator claims this story lacks fame because of the lowly status (moral and social) of the people involved.

320   *mira tamen [res est]. -que . . . -que:* "both . . . and."

320–21   *vidi praesens . . . notum:* The narrator cites his credentials: you can believe his version of this story because he saw the site himself. For other such narrative claims, see, for example, Nestor at 12.182–88.

321   *grandior aevō:* "rather advanced in age."

322   *inpatiens viae:* "intolerant of the journey"; the narrator's father (*genitor*), now too old to make the cattle drive himself, sends his son, along with an experienced local guide.

323   *inde:* from the region of Lycia in question.

324   *gentis illius:* of the Lycian people. *euntī [mihi].*

325   *[in] lacū mediō. sacrōrum nigra favillā:* "blackened with the ashes of sacrifices."

327   *faveas mihi:* the optative subjunctive, in a prayer; can be translated as an imperative: "be favorable to me."

329–30   *Naiadum Faunīne foret tamen ara rogabam / indigenaene deī:* indirect questions dependent on *rogabam* and introduced by the *-ne* particles ("whether . . . or") on *Faunīne* and *indigenaene.* "I asked whether it was an altar of the Naiads or of Faunus or of a native god."

329   *foret = esset.*

330   *talia rettulit:* "gave the following answer."

331–81 The old Lycian tells our nameless narrator the origin of the altar in the pool. Latona's transformation of the farmers is an illustration of her power, which the altar now commemorates.

332 *suam vocat hanc [aram]. cui:* refers to *illa* (Latona). *regia coniunx* = Juno, wife of Jupiter. Angry at Latona for becoming pregnant with Jupiter's children, Juno prevented her from finding any land that would accept her; no land wanted to be the birthplace of Latona's children. Latona is a sympathetic figure in this story partly because she is first depicted as the victim of an angry goddess and only later as a vengeful goddess herself.

333–34 *erratica Delos . . . cum levis insula nabat:* according to the story of Apollo's birth, Delos was a "floating" island, not anchored to any place in the sea, until Apollo honored it for its hospitality to his mother and gave it a secure resting place.

335 *cum Palladis arbore palmae* = *palmae et arborī Palladis;* the "tree of Pallas" is the olive. A standard detail of the story of Apollo's birth is the tree (or trees) upon which Latona supported herself during the delivery. *palmae:* dative after the compound *incumbens.*

336 *invitā . . . novercā:* ablative absolute, to be taken with adversative force: "although their stepmother was unwilling." Juno is said to be the "stepmother" of Jupiter's children by other mothers.

337 *hinc quoque:* from Delos, too. *puerpera:* "new mother." *fertur:* "is said"; a common way to report a story.

338 *portasse* = *portavisse. numina* = *deōs.*

339–40 *Chimaeriferae . . . finibus in Lyciae* = *in finibus Chimaeriferae Lyciae.* Lycia was the home of the monster Chimaera; the adjective "Chimaera-bearing" was made up by Ovid for this situation.

340 *longō . . . labore:* ablative of cause with *fessa; labor* can refer to Latona's actual "labor" (childbirth) and the "work" of making the journey to Lycia.

341 *sidereō . . . ab aestū:* "from the sun's heat"; *sidereus* comes from *sidus* ("star"), and the sun is a star. *sitim collegit:* "built up thirst."

342 *ebiberant:* note the prefix: the twin babies "had drunk out" or "had drunk dry" their mother's breasts. The picture of Apollo and Diana as greedy nursing infants (*avidī . . . natī*) is a typically light Ovidian view of the gods, with its roots in Hellenistic literature. (Compare Theocritus' *Idyll* 24 about baby Hercules, or Callimachus' portrait of the young Artemis in the *Hymn to Artemis.*)

343 *forte:* ablative from *fors. mediocris aquae:* genitive of description with *lacum.*

344 *agrestēs:* the *colonī* of line 318. *legebant:* the primary meaning of *lego* is "choose"; hence, it can mean "pick," as it does here. Its extended meanings such as "read" and "elect" are variations on the primary meaning.

345 *vimina cum iuncīs* = *vimina et iuncōs.*

346 *Titania:* Latona is the daughter of the Titan Coeus; at line 366 she is called *filia Coei. positō genū:* ablative absolute.

348 *rustica turba* = *agrestēs* (see line 344). *adfata [est] vetantīs [agrestēs].*
349 *quid:* "why?" *quid prohibetis [me] aquīs. usus communis aquārum est:* In lines
     349–51, Latona, although desperate for water, first makes a philosophical
     argument: water is public property, a commodity that all are entitled to use.
350–51 *proprium* applies to all the accusative nouns: none of these elements can be
     proprium, "one's own" or "private."
350 *āera:* accusative singular, Greek form, from *āēr.*
351 *publica munera:* a pool of drinking water is a gift bestowed on the public at
     large by nature. In Rome, the water supply was a part of the "public works"
     provided by the state.
352 *quae* = *haec publica munera;* the relative used as a connective. *quae tamen ut
     detis, supplex peto* = *supplex peto ut detis [mihi haec publica munera]* The *ut*-
     clause is an indirect command after *peto. tamen:* Even though Latona has
     explained why taking a drink of water is her right, "nevertheless" *(tamen)* she
     will ask politely and humbly *(supplex peto)* for the farmers' permission.
352–54 Latona assures the locals that she is not going to contaminate the water by
     washing in it, but that she only wants a drink. The locals would be justified in
     preventing someone from bathing in their supply of drinking water.
354 *os [meī] loquentis:* "my mouth as I speak." *umore:* ablative after *caret.*
356–57 *vitamque fatebor accepisse simul* = *fatebor me accepisse vitam cum aquīs.*
358 *hī:* the babies, Apollo and Diana, whom she is carrying with her. *nostrō* = *meō.*
359 *casū . . . tendēbant bracchia natī:* It was a common, indeed trite, habit for
     defendants in court to display their children in order to gain sympathy from the
     jury. Ovid plays with this convention by having Latona point out her babies,
     who make what could be construed as a gesture of supplication (stretching out
     the arms) at just the right moment.
360 *potuissent:* a rhetorical question: "whom *would* the goddess' charming words
     not *have been able* to move?"
361 *hī:* the farmers. *[deam] orantem.*
361–62 *mināsque, nī procul abscedat:* "threats (of what they will do) unless she with-
     draws far away."
362 *insuper:* adverbial; in addition to the threats. Both *minae* and *convicia,* of
     course, are very dangerous ways to speak to a goddess.
363–64 *ipsōs . . . lacūs:* poetic plural for singular.
364 *turbavēre* = *turbavērunt.*
365 *movēre* = *movērunt. huc illuc:* "this way and that."
366 *filia Coeī* = Latona; the epithet emphasizes her divine status.
367 *indignīs:* dative after *supplicat;* the farmers are "unworthy" of Latona's suppli-
     cation, although she has humbled herself before them. *ultrā:* adverbial.
368 *verba minora deā:* "words lesser than (i.e., unworthy of) a goddess"; Latona's
     humble words of her previous speech are now replaced by the commanding
     words of an angry divinity.

369 *aeternum:* adverbial. *stagnō . . . in istō:* an example of the scornful force of *iste;* Latona no longer wants anything to do with their pond.

370–81 The farmers are transformed into frogs, although Ovid does not name the animal until the last word of 381. He seems to enjoy dropping hints about the animals' habits and appearance, before finally revealing their name.

370 *optata:* nominative neuter plural; *deae:* genitive. *iuvat [colonīs]:* impersonal use of the verb, followed by the infinitives in 370–374.

371 *[in] cavā . . . palude.*

371–72 *modo . . . nunc . . . modo:* introducing various activities done at various times by the frogs.

372 *[in] summō . . . gurgite. nāre:* from the verb *no.*

374 *nunc quoque:* a phrase often introducing a feature that has remained the same from the premetamorphosis character; frogs, like the farmers, still make ugly sounds.

375–76 *litibus, pulsō pudore, maledicere:* comparison is made between the sound of frogs' antiphonal croaking and the type of speech used by the farmers to Latona (*minās, convicia,* 361–362).

377 *quoque iam:* like *nunc quoque* in 374.

378 *ipsaque dilatant patulōs convicia rictūs:* the act of croaking (the continuation of the farmers' *convicia*) causes the frogs' already wide mouths to spread out.

379 *colla intercepta [esse] videntur.*

13. Boreas and Orithyia: 6.675–721

Boreas, the god of the north wind, loved the Athenian princess Orithyia, but when he could not win her father's consent to their marriage, he carried her off unexpectedly to his home in the northern land of Thrace. Much of this story's significance comes from its position in the narrative and from its contrast with other stories. The immediately preceding story tells of another Thracian rapist, King Tereus, who also married an Athenian princess, Procne, but brutally raped and mutilated her sister Philomela (6.412–674). Tereus marks a new development in Ovid's rape theme—the mortal rapist, unlike the divine ones of earlier stories. In the present story, Boreas' speech justifying and defending his use of force (*vis*) to obtain the woman he wants might be considered a manifesto for all the rapists of the *Metamorphoses,* or perhaps only for the immortal ones.

The story of Boreas also provides a transition from the long episode of Tereus in Book 6 to the next major series, the stories of Jason and Medea in Book 7 (1–403). The Tereus-Procne-Philomela story is linked to Boreas-Orithyia by a genealogical link (Procne's father, Pandion, is the grandfather of Orithyia) and a geographical link (both Tereus and Boreas come from Thrace).

Boreas and Orithyia provide the link to the stories of Book 7 by becoming the parents of the winged boys Zetes and Calais, who sail away with Jason and the Argonauts in the final lines of Book 6.

675   *hic dolor:* the fate of Pandion's daughters Procne and Philomela. To avenge her husband Tereus' rape of her sister Philomela, Procne killed her own young son Itys and fed him to Tereus for dinner; afterwards, Tereus and the two women were all metamorphosed into birds. *ante diem:* "before his time"; *ante* also governs *extrema . . . tempora.*

676   *Pandiona:* accusative singular, Greek form; in the last story, King Pandion was the father of Procne and Philomela.

677   *rērum . . . moderamen:* "government of the state."

678   *iustitiā dubium validīsne potentior armīs: dubium* is adverbial with *potentior,* followed by two alternative ablatives of respect: *iustitiā* and *validīs . . . armīs.* The alternatives are joined by the *-ne* on *validīs;* prose might join these with *utrum . . . an.* It was "doubtful" or unclear whether Erechtheus was stronger in respect to his justice or his military prowess.

679   *crearat = creaverat.*

679–80 *totidem . . . femineae sortis:* "an equal number of the feminine lot," i.e., a number of daughters equal to the number of his male offspring (4).

681   *ē quibus:* "of these" (the two outstanding daughters mentioned in 680). *Aeolides Cephalus:* Cephalus, grandson of Aeolus (god of the winds), marries Erechtheus' daughter Procris; the story of their tragic marriage is told by Ovid in *Met.* 7.690–862 and in *Ars Amatoria* 3.657–746. *tē coniuge:* ablative with *felix:* "happy with you as his wife"; addressed to Procris (682).

682   *Procri:* vocative. *Boreae:* dative after *nocēbant. Boreae Tereus Thracesque nocēbant:* King Erechtheus is reluctant to give his daughter Orithyia to the Thracian Boreas, because of the tragic outcome of the last Athenian-Thracian marriage, that of Procne and Tereus.

683   *dilectā . . . Orithyiā:* ablative after *caruit.*

684   *precibus, viribus:* ablative after *ūti.*

685   *agitur nil:* "nothing is accomplished." *horridus irā:* "bristling with anger"; *irā* will be the antecedent of the relative *quae* in 686.

686   *nimium domestica:* "very familiar." *illī . . . ventō:* take these two words together, after both *solita* and *domestica.* It is normal for Boreas, as the North Wind, to display *ira,* since the North Wind generally brings harsh weather. Here and in the following speech, Ovid plays with the concept of a quasi-anthropomorphic god of a natural feature such as a wind. This "wind" speaks, has feelings, and falls in love, but also blows and gusts. (Compare Ovid's treatment of several river gods, such as Book 8's Achelous, who, in his anthropomorphic aspect, entertains dinner guests, while his river aspect is in flood and prevents them from traveling.)

687   *meritō:* "deservedly"; Boreas will argue that he has a right to use force to obtain Orithyia, because force is his usual instrument (*mea tela,* as he calls it in this line). *quid:* "why?"

689   *dedecet:* although *dedecet* is often used impersonally (with "it" as a subject), here it is used personally with *usus* as subject.

690–701   Note the repetitive structure of the rest of Boreas' speech: 690–92: two clauses beginning with the ablative of means, *vī,* illustrating what he does "with force"; 693–99: two sentences beginning with *idem ego, cum . . . ,* illustrating what is characteristic of him as a god; and 700–701: a final sentence beginning with *hāc ope* (i.e., *vī*), again describing his use of force.

691   *freta = mare. robora:* "oak trees."

692   While lines 690–91 allude to the effects of Boreas' blowing (chasing off clouds, churning up the sea, and overturning trees), 692 seems to allude to the effects of his coldness (snow, hail).

693   *fratrēs:* the other winds. *[in] caelō . . . apertō.*

694   *is = caelum apertum. campus:* The open sky is compared to the Campus Martius, a park in Rome used as an exercise field. Boreas suggests that the clashing of the winds is just their way of "working out" strenuously.

695–99   Ancient science sometimes attributed thunder, lightning, and earthquakes to the effects of clashing winds (as in the sixth book of Lucretius), but here one of the winds himself explains the process.

697   *subii:* "enter."

698   *ferox:* Nominative adjectives modifying the subject may often be translated as adverbs. *mea terga:* poetic plural for singular. *imīs . . . cavernīs:* dative to complete the meaning of *sub* in *supposui.*

700   *debueram . . . petiisse:* "I ought to have sought." *thalamōs:* "marriage."

700–701   *socer / non orandus erat, sed . . . faciendus [erat]:* "should not have been *asked* to be my father-in-law, but should have been *made* my father-in-law."

701   *mihi:* dative of agent with the passive periphrastic construction (*orandus erat*). *Erechtheus:* father of Orithyia.

702   *haec [verba] . . . aut hīs non inferiora:* After Boreas' vivid speech, we are reminded that the poet does not necessarily have access to Boreas' exact words. But Ovid claims that his own words, even if they are not entirely accurate, are at least as good as any words that Boreas might actually have spoken. *hīs [verbīs]:* ablative of comparison with *inferiora.*

703–707   In this description of Boreas' abduction of Orithyia, he is both man and wind. As a winged man (as his sons will be), he wears a cloak, embraces his beloved, and burns with the "fires" of love. But the beating of his wings and the flapping of his cloak cause winds to blow.

703   *iactatus, -ūs* (m.): "movement, beating."

705   *pulveream . . . pallam:* the cloud of dust (*pulvis*) raised by the wind as he goes is described as his cloak.

706 *metū:* ablative of cause with *pavidam.* This phrase is the only hint we get of the
victim's perspective, but it recalls the considerable attention paid to Philomela,
the victim in the previous rape story. *caligine:* ablative of instrument with *tectus.*

707 *Orithyian:* accusative singular, Greek form. *amans:* "the lover," Boreas.

708 *ignēs:* the metaphorical flames of love, which act like literal flames, for they
are fanned and further inflamed by the movement of Boreas' flight.

709–10 *prius . . . quam:* tmesis (division) of *priusquam,* which introduces the second
clause: *nec suppressit priusquam tenuit.*

709 *āeriī cursūs:* genitive. *suppressit habenās:* another metaphor: "rein in."

710 *Ciconum:* the Cicones are a people of Thrace. *tenuit:* "reached." *raptor:* here Boreas
is finally called, literally, a rapist. The word is withheld until the end of the line.

711 *Actaea:* Athenian (woman).

711–12 *et coniunx . . . et genetrix:* Orithyia immediately became both wife and mother
(*et . . . et* = "both . . . and").

712 *partūs enixa gemellōs:* "having given birth to twin sons."

713 Read: *quī cetera matris [habērent], pennās genitoris habērent.* The relative
pronoun is frequently postponed one position (*cetera qui = qui cetera*). *cetera*
(neu. pl. acc.): "the rest of the features." The sons resembled normal humans,
except for their wings, which they inherited from their father. The next five
lines (714–18) describe how the boys were not born with wings, but grew them
only at puberty, along with their beards. *habērent:* subjunctive in a relative
clause of characteristic.

714 *memorant:* "they say that . . ."; an indirect statement follows: *hās [pennās] non
natās esse unā cum corpore. unā:* (adverb) "together."

715 *rutilīs subnixa capillīs:* "beneath their golden hair" (a strange use of *subnixa,*
which normally means "supported by").

716 *inplumēs:* "wingless." *Calais, Zetes:* the names of the sons of Boreas and Orithyia.

717–18 *pariter . . . pariter:* "at the same time as" (translate only once).

717 *coepēre = coepērunt.*

718 *flavescere [coepēre] malae. malae:* "cheeks"; their cheeks become "tawny"
because their beards are the color of their hair, said above to be reddish (*rutilīs,*
715).

720 *cum Minyīs:* the Argonauts are called "Minyans" because many of them were
related to King Minyas. *vellera . . . nitidō radiantia villō:* the Golden Fleece;
vellera is poetic plural for singular.

721 *non notum = ignotum. [in] primā . . . carinā: carina = navis.* The *Argo* was said
to be the first ship ever built (e.g., Catullus 64.11). *petiēre = petiērunt.*

14. Medea's Magic: 7.251–349

Ovid seems to have had a special interest in the story of Medea. He wrote a
tragedy about her—the only one of his major works that has not survived. He

wrote a letter from her perspective in the *Heroides*. In the *Metamorphoses*, Ovid depicts, in addition to the story of Medea's initial passion for Jason, some less familiar episodes from Medea's story: her rejuvenation of Jason's father Aeson, her murder of Jason's evil uncle Pelias, and her escape from Greece. The most famous episodes in the story of Jason and Medea—the voyage of the Argonauts, the retrieval of the Golden Fleece, and Medea's infanticide—are either ignored or treated only cursorily. These episodes were well known to Ovid's readers through Euripides' tragedy *Medea* and Apollonius' *Argonautica*.

After Jason and Medea return to Greece with the Golden Fleece, they find Jason's father, Aeson, weakened by advanced age. Jason asks Medea to take some of his remaining years of life and give them to his father, but Medea offers something better: she will magically make Aeson young again (7.159–78). Ovid describes at great length Medea's incantations and her journey around the world in search of magic herbs (7.179–250). The first part of the passage below describes the process Medea uses to rejuvenate Aeson (7.251–93). Next (7.297–349), Medea takes vengeance on one of Jason's enemies, the evil king Pelias, who had sent him on the quest for the Golden Fleece. Pelias' daughters are induced to kill their aged father so that he can be rejuvenated like Aeson, but Medea omits the crucial herbs from the potion this time.

251 *quōs ubi placavit = ubi illōs deōs placavit:* in the previous lines (234–50), Ovid has described Medea's sacrifices and prayers to Hecate and to Iuventa (Youth), in preparation for her treatment of Aeson.

252 *ad aurās:* "into the open air."

253–54 A good example of Latin's use of participles to describe a series of actions. Although this sentence contains only one main verb, *porrexit* (254), it describes three distinct actions, the first two of which are expressed by perfect participles (*resolutum*, 253, and *stratīs*, 254). *in plenōs resolutum [eum] carmine somnōs* describes how Medea puts Aeson to sleep with a chant; *stratīs . . . in herbīs* describes how she spreads out magic herbs; finally, *porrexit* describes how she lays Aeson's sleeping body out on the herbs. Latin verb tenses express very precisely the order in which events happen.

254 *exanimī:* from *exanimis, e,* dative after *similem.* The description of Aeson as "similar to a dead man" becomes especially ironic when we read the next episode, in which Pelias is actually killed by this treatment.

255 *Aesoniden:* "son of Aeson," Jason. Greek accusative form. Note the chiastic word order in the line: *hinc procul . . . procul hinc.* Jason and his attendants are ordered to withdraw far from sight of the secret ritual.

256 *monet arcanīs [eōs] oculōs removēre profanōs.*

257 *passīs . . . capillīs:* "with her hair let down."

258 *flagrantīs . . . arās:* the two altars of Hecate and Iuventa that Medea had built before bringing out Aeson.

259 *in fossā sanguinis atrā:* Near the two altars, Medea had dug ditches (*fossās,* 245), into which she had poured the blood of a black sheep which she sacrificed. Now she dips her torches into this blood before she lights them at the fire on the altars. *sanguinis = sanguine.* Ovid here uses the genitive where we would normally expect an ablative of specification ("dark *with* blood").

260 *infectās [facēs sanguine].*

261 *lustrat:* "purifies"; note the triple use of the magic number three.

262 Medea will now prepare a potion by boiling herbs in a cauldron (*[in] positō . . . aēnō*). In lines 219–233, Medea flew to lands around the world to gather herbs for this potion.

264 *Haemoniā . . . valle:* "from a valley in Thessaly"; the Greek region of Thessaly was famous for its witches, later described most famously in Lucan's *Civil War* VI.

267 *Oceanī:* to the ancients, the "Ocean" meant the Atlantic, an exotic location at the edge of the world. The *lapidēs* in line 266 come from the far East (*extremō . . . Oriente*), while the sand comes from the far West.

268–71 The verb *addit* has three objects, *pruinās, alās,* and *prosecta,* linked by *et, et,* and *-que.*

268 *exceptās lunā . . . pruinās:* frost was believed to drop down from the moon during the night. *lunā pernocte:* ablative of source, dependent on the participle *exceptās. pernocte* comes from the adjective *pernox,* "all-night."

270–71 rearrange: *prosecta ambiguī lupī solitī mutāre vultūs ferinōs in virum.* The wolf is called *ambiguī* because of its ability to change shape. *in virum:* i.e., *in vultum virī.*

271 *nec defuit:* "nor was there lacking . . ."; i.e., "and there was also . . ." Double negative to express a positive. *illīs:* dative with *defuit.*

272 *Cinyphiī . . . chelydrī:* "Cinyphian" = Libyan; the chelydrus is an amphibious snake found in northern Africa.

273 *quibus insuper:* "on top of which . . ."

274 *novem cornicis saecula passae:* since *passae* ("having endured") comes from a deponent verb (*patior*), it is active and has *novem saecula* as its object. Note the interlocked word order.

275 *postquam:* take at the beginning of the line; introduces all of lines 275–276. *hīs et mille aliīs . . . rēbus:* ablatives of means.

276 *propositum . . . mortalī [propositō] . . . maius:* a *propositum* is a "plan"; *mortalī [propositō]* is ablative of comparison with *maius. barbara* = Medea.

277 *iampridem:* take with *arentī;* the branch has been drying out for some time, just as Aeson has long since grown old.

278 *omnia confudit:* "she stirred it all up." *summīs inmiscuit ima:* "she mixed the lowest (portions) with the highest"; Medea uses the branch to fold together all the ingredients in her cauldron.

279 *ecce:* draws attention to the miracle.

280   *nec = et non;* take the *non* closely with *longō. longō tempore:* ablative of time within which.

280–81   Note the three markers of the time sequence of the transformation: *primō, nec longō tempore,* and *subitō.*

282   *quācumque:* "wherever."

285   *quae:* (neu. pl.) "these things," i.e., the events described in the last few lines; the relative pronoun is here used as a connective, equivalent to a demonstrative such as *haec. recludit:* "opens up"; an example of the *re-* prefix meaning "un-"; *recludo (re + claudo)* literally means "un-close."

286   *senis:* Aeson.

286–87   *exire:* dependent on *passa* (nom., modifying Medea).

287   *replet [iugulum] sucīs;* Medea's potion from the cauldron replaces Aeson's aged blood in his veins. *quōs = sucōs.*

289   *canitiē positā:* ablative absolute; *positā,* as is often the case, means "put aside (or down)."

291   *adiectō . . . corpore:* ablative absolute; *corpore* = "flesh" (to fill in the wrinkles).

293   *quater denōs:* "four times ten" (a common poetic method of expressing numbers). *hunc se [fuisse] reminiscitur:* "he remembers that this is the man he was . . ."

294–96   Here Ovid inserts a three-line account of another story of rejuvenation: Bacchus (here called Liber), inspired by Medea's treatment of Aeson, uses the same technique on his old nurses. It is unusual for a god to learn from, or be inspired by, a mortal; through this practice of magic and through her flight around the world, Medea seems to have become a nearly divine figure.

295   *iuvenēs annōs:* "youthful years"; subject of *posse reddi* in the indirect statement.

296   *capit hoc . . . munus:* Ovid gives no details of how Bacchus might have received the secret of the potion from Medea. *Colchide:* "the woman from Colchis," Medea.

297   *Nēve = et nē* (negative purpose clause).

297–98   *odium cum coniuge falsum / Phasias adsimulat:* As a pretense for her appearance at Pelias' home, Medea claims to have had a dispute with Jason. This false breakup substitutes, in Ovid's narrative, for the real one still in the future. Ovid only obliquely alludes to the very famous ending of the relationship, when Jason's divorce of Medea prompted her to murder their children (7.394–397). In the present story, a pretended divorce is the excuse for another vengeful murder.

298   *Phasias:* another name for Medea; the Phasis is a river in Medea's homeland, Colchis. *Peliae:* genitive; Pelias had usurped the throne from Jason's father Aeson and had sent Jason on the quest for the Golden Fleece.

299   *ipse:* Pelias himself.

300–301   *callida . . . Colchis:* "the clever woman from Colchis," i.e., Medea.

302   *inter meritōrum maxima:* "among the greatest of her services."

302–303   *refert . . . demptōs / Aesonis esse situs: refert* ("she reports") is followed by an indirect statement. *situs, -ūs* (m.): "physical deterioration, decay"; poetic plural for singular.

303   *hāc in parte:* "on this part [of the story]."
304   *virginibus Peliā . . . creatīs:* dative with the compound verb *est . . . subiecta;* "the daughters of Pelias" (literally, "the maidens begotten by Pelias").
305   The indirect statement (*suum . . . revirescere posse parentem*) depends on the noun *spes* in the previous line ("the hope *that . . .*").
306   Understand *illam* (i.e., Medea) as the object of *iubent. sine fīnē:* "without limit"; if Medea agrees to rejuvenate their father, the daughters of Pelias will promise Medea any reward she asks.
307   *brevī spatiō:* ablative used to express duration of time.
308   *fictā gravitate:* ablative of means.
309   *quō:* in a purpose clause containing a comparative (*maior*), *quō* replaces *ut.*
310   *maximus aevō:* "greatest in age," i.e., "eldest."
311   *dux gregis:* i.e., "the ram," subject of *fiet. agnus:* predicate with *fiet.* Medea proposes to demonstrate her magic first, by using an old ram, which she will turn into a young lamb.
312   *laniger:* "woolly [ram]." *effetus:* like Aeson in line 252 (*effetum . . . corpus*), the ram is weakened and worn out by old age.
314   *cuius = huius;* the relative used as a connective. Latin can use a relative to connect two separate sentences, but such relatives should be translated as demonstratives, especially when they occur in subordinate clauses (as here, in an *ut*-clause).
314–15   *ut . . . fodit et . . . maculavit: ut* + indicative here means "when."
315   *exiguō . . . sanguine:* the aged, being "dried up," are said to have less blood than the young. When Ovid narrates the fall of Troy, King Priam is said to have *exiguum . . . cruorem* (13.409).
316   *pecudis:* the ram. *venefica:* "the sorceress," Medea.
317   *ea:* nominative; "these things" (the magic potions).
318   *nec non:* "and also."
319   *[ē] mediō . . . aenō.*
320   *[illīs] balatum mirantibus:* "while they were wondering at the bleating" (abl. abs.).
321   *fugā:* "in its flight."
322   *obstipuēre = obstipuērunt;* from *obstipesco. satae Peliā:* "the daughters of Pelias" (compare the similar expression with *creatīs* in line 304). *promissa:* neuter plural, subject of *exhibuēre* in the following line.
323   *exhibuēre = exhibuērunt.* Medea's trick with the ram has demonstrated the *fides* of her claims (*promissa*) about her ability to restore youth. *inpensius:* comparative adverb from *inpensē. [filiae] instant:* "insist."
324–25   *ter iuga Phoebus equīs in Hiberō flumine mersīs / dempserat:* a picturesque poetic expression; a more prosaic sentence might read, "Three days passed." Phoebus, the god of the sun, drives a chariot across the sky every day, dives into the ocean in the west, and takes his horses to be unhitched. *equīs . . . mersīs* is dative with the compound verb *dempserat* (from *demo,* "take [something]

away from"). The "Spanish River" (*Hiberō flumine*) is the Atlantic Ocean, thought by the ancients to be a large river that surrounds the known land; from the perspective of Greeks and Romans, the sun sets out in the ocean beyond Spain, the westernmost land in the Mediterranean area.

325 *quartā . . . nocte:* ablative of time when.

326 *fallax Aeetias:* "the deceptive daughter of Aeëtes," Medea (nom.).

327 *laticem = aquam.* *sine viribus herbās:* This time, Medea does not use her magic plants, so the spell does not work on Pelias as it did on Aeson and on the ram.

328 *similis:* modifies *somnus* in the following line. *resolutō corpore:* ablative absolute. Note the similarity of the language here to that describing Aeson at lines 252–54.

330 *[somnus] quem dederant cantūs magicaeque potentia linguae:* Medea had performed incantations to put Pelias into a deep sleep.

331 *Colchide:* Medea (abl.).

333 *haurite:* "drain out." In this case, Medea wants the daughters to cut their own father's throat (a deed that she did not require of Jason for the rejuvenation of his father; see lines 285–87).

335 *vita est aetasque parentis:* the singular verb is used individually with each of the two subjects: "your father's life is in your hands, and his age is, too."

336 *pietas:* Medea's use of this serious Roman word is ironic here; she convinces the daughters that it is "loyalty" (*pietas*) and "duty" (*officium*) for them to kill their father. *nec = et nisi.* *agitatis:* "ponder." *spēs . . . inanīs:* accusative; ironic, because the women's hopes really are empty.

337 *praestate:* imperative; "perform, fulfil." *telīs:* ablative of means (from *telum, -ī,* neu., "weapon").

339 *ut:* "as." *ut quaeque pia est, . . . inpia prima est:* "as each [woman] is *pia,* she is first to be *inpia.*" In other words, the most *pia* of the daughters strikes first, and the others in order according to their relative degrees of *pietas.*

340 *nē sit scelerata, facit scelus:* another paradox, like the *pia/inpia* contrast in the previous line.

340–41 *haud . . . ulla = nulla [filia]* (subject). *ictūs . . . suōs:* object of *spectare.*

342 *caeca . . . vulnera:* "unseen wounds."

344 *[ā] torō.*

344–45 *inter / tot medius gladiōs:* note the word order: the word *medius* is, like Pelias, "in the middle of so many swords."

346 *gnatae = natae, filiae. quid:* "why?" *in fata parentis:* "for your father's death."

347 *cecĭdēre = cecĭdērunt;* from *cado. illīs:* dative of possession with *manūs* and *animī;* equivalent to a genitive (*illārum*). The hands and the spirits "fall" in rather different ways; this use of two incongruous nouns (*manūs, animī*) with the same verb is called zeugma (or syllepsis).

348 *plura:* neuter plural; object of *locuturō. locuturō:* ablative of separation with *abstulit* in the following line. *cum verbīs guttura = verba et guttura;* another zeugma. *guttura:* poetic plural for singular. *Colchis:* Medea. When Pelias'

complaints affect his daughters' resolve, Medea seizes the knife, cuts his throat, and throws him into the boiling water. Since the water has no magic powers, this is the end of Pelias. Medea escapes punishment by flying away in her magic chariot (lines 350ff.).

15. Daedalus: 8.183–259

Daedalus, the royal builder and engineer for King Minos of Crete, appears in several stories connected with the Cretan royal family. When Minos' wife, Pasiphae, fell in love with a bull, Daedalus constructed an artificial cow in which she could conceal herself in order to approach the bull. After this deception, which resulted in the birth of the Minotaur, Minos prevented Daedalus from leaving Crete, so that Daedalus had to use his ingenuity to devise a means of escape from the island for himself and his son Icarus. The story of their attempt to fly is the best known of the stories of Daedalus. (This story is also told by Ovid in the *Ars Amatoria* 2.19–98.)

As a pendant to the tragic story of Icarus, Ovid tells the story of Perdix, Daedalus' nephew, who was apprenticed to Daedalus but aroused his jealousy by inventing the saw and the compass; after Daedalus threw the young man off a cliff, Minerva rescued him and changed him into a partridge (*perdix*). This story, like that of Icarus, also depicts the discovery of new technology and the death of a young man, but presents a much less sympathetic picture of the master craftsman himself. Perhaps the tender and loving father of the first episode is not completely innocent and his invention not completely benign. We can also see parallels between Daedalus' nephew, who is thrown down and becomes a bird, and his son, who falls to his death trying to fly like a bird. These two stories illustrate the way Ovid can comment on one story by juxtaposing it with another.

Both of these stories conclude with *aitia,* which explain the origins of natural phaenomema (the "Icarian" sea and the *perdix,* or partridge).

183 *Crētēn:* accusative singular, Greek form. *perosus:* participle from *perodi, -odisse;* the prefix *per-* has its common meaning "thoroughly."
184 *exilium, locī natalis:* Daedalus spent many years in Crete but was originally an Athenian.
185–86 *licet [ut] obstruat terrās et undās:* subject of *obstruat* is Minos.
187 *āera:* accusative singular, Greek form, from *āēr, āeris* (m.), "air." The vowels *ae-* in this word are pronounced separately, not as a diphthong as they are in *aes, aeris* (n.) "bronze." *omnia possideat, āera non possidet:* note the parallel constructions in the two clauses that nearly rhyme; each verb has a metrically equivalent three-syllable object (*om-ni-a, a-e-ra*), to emphasize the contrast between what Minos controls and what he does not.

189   *novat: novo, novāre* means "to make *novus*" (i.e., to make "new" or "strange").
      Daedalus both recreates nature anew and makes an unusual facsimile of it, since
      a flying man is not a faithful representation of nature.

190   *ā minimā [pennā].*

191   *ut [in] clivō [pennās] crevisse putes. crevisse:* from *cresco.*

191–92   *sic . . . avenīs:* Ovid compares the graduated arrangement of the feathers on
      Daedalus' wings to the slope of the reeds on a panpipe.

195   *puer Icarus: puer* has special force here, because Icarus is depicted as an
      extremely young, playful, and foolish child. Note that he is called *puer* again
      in line 223, just as he begins to disobey his father's instructions.

196   *sua sē tractāre pericla:* indirect statement dependent on *ignarus* ("not knowing
      that . . .").

197–98   *modo . . . modo:* a pair like *et . . . et* ("both . . . and") or *alius . . . alius* ("one . . .
      another"); "now [he does one thing] . . . and now [he does another]."

198   *captābat:* from *capto, captāre,* a frequentative verb (meaning "to do something
      repeatedly"), based on *capio: "capere* over and over," "keep chasing after or
      catching." The imperfect tense here adds to the suggestion of repeated and
      incomplete action.

199–200   *mollibat, impediebat:* Again, imperfect tense to signify repeated action. The
      curious and pesky little Icarus *kept on* playing with the materials and getting in
      his father's way.

200   *manus ultima:* "finishing touch." *coeptō:* dative after *inposita est;* participle
      from *coepi:* "a thing begun," i.e., "an undertaking." (See the inscription on the
      back of the U.S. one-dollar bill: *annuit coeptīs.*)

201–202   Alone, Daedalus takes the wings on a test flight before advising Icarus of the
      techniques he has learned (203–208).

202   *motāque . . . in aurā:* "in the moved air"; the air is moved by the flapping of
      his wings.

203   *instruit et natum = et instruit natum. curras:* cannot mean "run" here literally,
      but "run [on your wings]" and hence, "fly."

203–205   Reword: *moneo ut [in] mediō limite curras, nē unda gravet pennās, si demissior
      ibis, [et nē] ignis adurat [pennās], si celsior [ibis].* The *ut*-clause is an indirect
      command after *moneo;* the two *nē*-clauses are negative purpose clauses, each of
      which has a *si*-clause attached to it. The purpose clauses explain why Icarus
      should fly *mediō limite.*

206   *inter utrumque [limitem] = inter duōs limitēs.*

206–207   *nec . . . iubeo:* A poetic liberty. Negatives with *iubeo* are not usually allowed in
      prose; *veto* must be used instead. *Boōtēn, Helicēn:* accusatives, Greek form. Bootes,
      Helice, and Orion are all constellations. Ancient sailors used stars for navigation,
      but Daedalus wants his son to look not to the stars but to his father for guidance.

208   *mē duce:* ablative absolute. *pariter = simul.*

209   *umerīs [Icarī].*

210 *genae . . . senilēs = genae senis.* Perhaps referring to Daedalus as an "old man" emphasizes the difference in both age and wisdom between him and his son. *Genae* is from *gena, ae* (f.), "cheek," and should not be confused with several other similar words (*genus, gens, genu*). *maduēre = maduērunt.*

211 *patriae . . . manūs = manūs patris; patriae* from the adjective *patrius, a, um.* *patriae manūs* and *genae senilēs* are both examples of the Latin tendency to use adjectives instead of genitive nouns to show possession; e.g., "paternal hands" instead of "the father's hands."

212 *repetenda:* in its original function as a future passive participle ("not to be sought again" or "which will not be sought again"), without the sense of obligation common in this form.

213 *ante:* adverbial, "in front [i.e., of Icarus]." *comitī = Icarō.*

213–14 *ales . . . quae:* Although *ales* can mean a bird of either sex, the gender of the relative pronoun that refers to *ales* here reveals that this is a mother bird.

215 *hortaturque [Icarum] sequī:* Subject of *hortatur* is Daedalus.

216 *et movet ipse suās [alās] et natī respicit alās:* The combination *et . . . et* indicates that Daedalus was doing these things simultaneously.

217–19 Three people see Daedalus and his son in flight (*hōs . . . vidit et obstipuit*): *aliquis* (who is identified with the *dum-*clause), *pastor,* and *arator.*

218 *pastor [innixus] baculō. aut . . . -ve = aut . . . aut.*

219–20 Rearrange: *crēdidit eōs, quī aethera carpere possent, esse deōs.* Note the use of *credo* with indirect statement: the subject of the infinitive is accusative, as in any indirect statement (despite the fact that *credo* takes a dative of the person believed).

219 *possent:* Relative clauses within indirect statement have subjunctive verbs. *aethera:* accusative singular, Greek form.

220–21 *laevā parte:* ablative of place where.

221–22 All these islands (Samos, Delos, Paros, Lebinthus, and Calymne) are located in or near the "Icarian Sea," where Icarus will fall.

221 *Samos, Delos, Paros:* All these names of Greek islands are feminine, as we can see from their adjectives (*Iunonia, relictae*). Samos is "Junonian" because it is the center of Juno's worship.

224 *ducem = patrem.*

226 Note how the adjective-noun phrase *odorātās cērās* is interrupted by its appositive, *pennārum vincula.*

227 *ille = Icarus.*

228 *remigiōque carens: careo* takes an ablative.

229–30 The subject of *excipiuntur* is *ora* (a poetic plural), modified by *clamantia.* The object of the participle *clamantia* is *patrium nomen* (= *nomen patris;* see note on *patriae manus,* in line 211). *caeruleā . . . aquā:* ablative with the passive verb.

230 *aqua, quae . . . ab illō:* the "Icarian" Sea.

231 *nec iam:* "no longer." Daedalus is no longer a *pater* because he has just lost his son (although he does not yet know).

232   *quā . . . regione:* ablative of place where.

235   *tellus ā nomine dicta [est] sepultī [puerī]:* This is the island of Icaros (or Icaria), just to the west of Samos.

236   *hunc* = Daedalus. *corpora:* poetic plural. *[in] tumulō.*

237   *elice:* from the rare word *elix, elicis* (m.): a drainage ditch.

239–40   *nec visa prioribus annīs, / factaque nuper avis:* This particular bird is the only (*unica*) partridge in existence at the time, because the metamorphosis of Perdix inaugurated the species. Note that the metamorphosis seems to have involved a change of gender, too: the bird *perdix* is consistently given feminine adjectives (*garrula, testata, facta, ignara,* etc.), although it is created from a male human. *longum . . . crimen:* The partridge stands as a reminder of Daedalus' guilt, a constant indictment of his action.

241   *huic* = *Daedalō. docendam:* gerundive to express purpose: "to be taught."

242   *germana [Daedalī]. suam . . . progeniem* = Perdix, the *puerum* of the next line.

242–43   *natalibus actīs / bis . . . sēnīs: natalis* = *natalis dies,* "birthday." *Sēnī, ae, a* = "six at a time"; here *sēnīs* goes with *bis* ("twice") to express the number twelve ("two times six"), in a common poetic circumlocution for numbers.

243   *animī . . . capacis:* genitive of characteristic, describing the boy Perdix. *ad praecepta:* dependent on *capacis.*

245   *traxit in exemplum:* "took as an example."

247   *primus et* = *et primus. duo ferrea bracchia:* the compass.

248   *illīs distantibus:* ablative absolute.

249   *staret* = "stand still." *duceret orbem* = "trace or draw a circle."

250   *sacrā ex arce Minervae:* This episode evidently takes place back in Daedalus' native Athens ("the citadel of Minverva [Athena]"), before he went to Crete.

251   *praecipitem [eum] mīsit: mitto* here has the meaning "throw." *[eum] lapsum [esse] mentitus:* By claiming the boy's death was accidental, Daedalus tried unsuccessfully to avoid prosecution but was convicted and exiled from Athens. Hence his sojourn in Crete (*longum exilium,* line 184).

254   *quondam:* understand closely with *velocis.*

255   *nomen, quod [erat illī] et ante. et:* "also." *ante:* adverbial.

256   *corpora:* poetic plural.

257–59   The death of the boy Perdix by falling from a great height explains the tendency of the partridge to stay on the ground. The metamorphosed creature often retains some memory of the experiences it had in human form.

16. Orpheus: 10.1–85

Book 10 is entirely concerned with Orpheus. The book opens with the story of Orpheus' loss of Eurydice and his subsequent mourning, and then goes on to set the stage for the song sung by Orpheus, which continues for the rest of the book (10.148–739) and includes the stories of Hyacinthus, Pygmalion,

Myrrha, and Adonis. Book 10 thus appears to be one of the most unified books in the *Metamorphoses*, because all of its stories either concern Orpheus or are narrated by him. The prominence of this figure of the poet-singer also makes Book 10 an important piece of evidence for Ovid's view of poetic activity. The first story, the famous tale of Orpheus' unsuccessful journey to the Underworld to rescue his wife, serves to characterize the singer and his concerns. His song in the Underworld shows his concern with love, a topic prominent in the stories he sings after his return to earth (see his preface to the longer song at 10.148–54). He does have an uncanny effect on all who hear his music, from Cerberus to Pluto himself, but despite this poetic accomplishment, Orpheus is unable to accomplish the rescue of his wife. In fact, his supposedly moving song seems rather unimpressive, even comic. It displays a number of literary associations. Orpheus alludes to the Rape of Persephone (the Latin Proserpina), by which the King of the Underworld obtained his own wife, as recounted originally in the *Homeric Hymn to Demeter* and twice in Ovid's works (*Met.* 5.341–661and *Fasti* 4.417–620). Ovid's story of Orpheus also alludes extensively to another account of Orpheus' journey, in Vergil, *Georgics* 4.453–527; Ovid reverses several Vergilian details (compare Eurydice's words as she departs in each version) and augments Vergil's account in several places (where Vergil mentions one famous sinner, Ovid mentions five).

1 *inde:* Book 9 ends with the joyous wedding of Iphis and Ianthe, attended by Hymenaeus, the god of weddings. From that wedding, Hymenaeus journeys to attend the ill-fated marriage of Orpheus and Eurydice. *croceō . . . amictū:* "saffron" was the traditional color of a Roman bride's veil.

2 *aethera:* masculine accusative singular, Greek form; object of *per* in line 1. *Ciconum:* (gen. pl.) the Cicones are a people of Thrace; Orpheus is a Thracian.

3 *Ortheā:* adjective with *voce.* Equivalent to a genitive noun. *nequiquam . . . vocatur:* Hymenaeus is traditionally invoked for luck at weddings, but this time, in spite of his invocation, the marriage ends in tragedy.

6 *fax:* Torches, a traditional part of a wedding ceremony, often symbolize marriage in general. Here, the god of marriage himself holds the torch, but it does not burn auspiciously.

7 *nullōsque invēnit motibus ignēs:* Shaking the torch did not cause the smokiness to give way to a clean flame.

8 *exitus [erat] auspiciō gravior:* The outcome (the bride's tragic death) was even worse than the omens suggested. *nupta:* subject of the *dum* clause.

9 *turbā:* ablative dependent on the participle *comitata* (nom.)

10 *occidit:* Eurydice's death is reduced to this one word, which is then explained only by the rather cool ablative absolute in the rest of the line. Throughout the story, Ovid reduces the chances for real pathos or sincere tragic feeling.

11 *quam* = *illam. postquam:* take at the beginning of the line.

11–12 *Rhodopeius . . . vates:* "the Thracian poet," Orpheus.

12   *nē non temptaret et umbrās: nē* introduces the negative purpose clause, while
      non negates the verb itself. *"Lest* he leave even the Shades *un*tried." *et* =
      "even."

13   *Taenariā . . . portā:* Taenaros is a promontory in the southern Peloponnese,
      where a certain cave is said to be the entrance to the Underworld.

14   *lĕvēs populōs:* the ghosts of the Underworld. *sepulcrō:* ablative with the
      participle *functa* (from *fungor,* one of the handful of deponent verbs that take
      an ablative).

15   *Persephonēn:* accusative, Greek form.

16   *pulsīs ad carmina:* "plucked to accompany his song." *nervīs:* the strings of the
      lyre.

18   *quicquid mortale creamur:* a tricky combination of third person and first
      person: "whoever of us is created a mortal [thing] . . ." The pronoun, which we
      would expect to be masculine (*quisquis*), is attracted into the neuter to agree
      with the neuter adjective *mortale.* The verb is subjunctive in a relative clause
      of characteristic.

19   *falsī positīs ambagibus oris:* ablative absolute; *positīs* here means "put aside,
      discarded." Orpheus claims to be speaking the "straight" truth, not the "winding
      ambiguity" (*ambagibus*) characteristic of a persuasive orator or a poet.

20   *vera loqui [me] sinitis. vera:* neuter plural. *hūc:* to the Underworld. *vidērem:*
      Orpheus has not come to the Underworld as a mere sightseer, as did, for
      example, Aeneas.

21   *uti = ut.*

21–22 *uti villosa colubrīs / terna Medusaeī vincirem guttura monstrī:* the *Medusaeī . . .
      monstrī* is Cerberus, who has three heads (Ovid says "necks") which, like
      Medusa's, are adorned with snakes. *vincirem* is from *vincio, vincīre,* not *vinco,
      vincere.*

25   *temptasse = temptavisse.*

26   *[me] vīcit Amor. deus hic = Amor.*

27   *an sit [Amor notus] et hīc, dubito: an* means "whether": *dubito an:* "I am
      uncertain whether . . ." *et hīc:* "here, too" (in the Underworld); *hīc* is the adverb,
      not the demonstrative from *hic, haec, hoc. sed et hīc tamen auguror [Amorem
      notum] esse; auguror:* "I guess" (deponent; literally, "foretell").

28   *fama . . . veteris . . . rapinae:* "the story of the ancient Rape [of Persephone]." It
      is amusing for Orpheus to doubt the veracity of this story, which was narrated
      by the Muse herself in *Metamorphoses* 5. Ovid sometimes has his characters
      question stories that have already been told elsewhere in his poem or in the
      poems of others. Compare Scylla's charge, at *Met.* 8.119–25, that Europa was
      not the mother of Minos and was not seduced by a bull, although Ovid recounts
      this very story at *Met.* 2.833–75. At 13.733–34, Ovid raises the possibility that
      all poets are liars, including, we may presume, himself and Orpheus.

29 *vos:* Pluto and Persephone. *per:* "by, in the name of." *ego:* subject of *oro* in line
    31.
31 *Eurydicēs:* genitive singular, Greek form. *retexite:* "reweave"; since one's fate
    is depicted as a thread spun out by the Parcae, returning someone to life can be
    depicted as repairing this thread.
32 *omnia debemur:* With the neuter adjective *omnia,* Orpheus could again be
    referring to "us" as things, as he does in line 18 (*quicquid mortale creamur*);
    many texts remove this problem by reading *omnia debentur.*
33 *serius aut citius:* "sooner or later." *sedem . . . ad unam:* i.e., to the Underworld.
36 *haec* = Eurydice.
37 *iuris . . . vestrī:* "in your power"; possessive genitive in the predicate. *pro
    munere . . . usum:* Orpheus contrasts *usus* (temporary use or enjoyment, similar
    to a loan) with *munus* (an outright gift); both are Roman legal terms. He argues
    that he only wants to "borrow" Eurydice for a little longer, since Pluto will get
    her back soon enough.
38 *quodsi:* "but if."
38–39 *certum est . . . mihi:* impersonal passive (from *cerno,* "determine, decide");
    equivalent to "I have decided."
39 *[me] nolle redīre [ad terram]. duōrum:* i.e., both Orpheus and Eurydice.
    Orpheus vows either to return to earth with Eurydice or to remain in the
    Underworld with her.
40 *dicentem, moventem:* modifing an understood *eum* (Orpheus), object of *flebant*
    ("wept for") in the next line; as present participles, *dicentem* and *moventem* take
    their own objects (*talia, nervōs*). *talia [verba]. ad verba:* "to accompany his
    words"; compare *ad carmina* in line 16 above.
41–44 Ovid now describes the effects of Orpheus' song on five famous sinners
    found in the Underworld. Tantalus, punished for serving human meat to the
    gods, is condemned to strive for food and drink that remain just out of reach.
    Ixion, punished for murder and attempted rape, is tied to an eternally
    revolving wheel. Tityos, a giant punished for offenses against Apollo and
    Diana, is afflicted by vultures who continually eat away his liver. The
    Belides, more commonly called Danaids, are punished for murdering their
    husbands; they must carry water in leaky jars. Finally, Sisyphus, for a variety
    of crimes, must attempt to roll a rock up a hill. All of the effects described in
    lines 41–47 qualify as *adynata* ("impossibilities"), events that no one would
    have thought possible: the eternal punishments cease, the Furies weep, and
    Pluto feels pity.
42 *captavit:* from *capto, captāre,* a frequentative form of *capio;* frequentative
    verbs mean "to do [an action] over and over." Tantalus, of course, repeatedly
    reaches for his elusive drink. *refugam:* adjective; "fleeting."
43 *carpsēre* = *carpsērunt.* The story of Tityos is so famous that Ovid need not
    specify whose liver is being eaten by birds. *vacarunt* = *vacavērunt.*

44   *Belides:* "descendants of Belus." Belus was the father of Danaus, who was the
     father of the forty-nine daughters who murdered their husbands. They are usually
     referred to as Danaids, after their father. Part of their story is told in Aeschylus'
     Suppliant Women. Sisyphe: the poet here varies his construction with an address
     to one of the sinners. He also contrives a noticeably alliterative phrase.

45   *primum:* adverbial. *lacrimīs:* ablative with *maduisse* in the next line. *carmine:*
     ablative with the participle *victārum.*

46   *Eumenidum:* (gen. pl.) the Furies, spirits of punishment who reside in the
     Underworld, most famous from their appearance in Aeschylus' tragedy
     Eumenides. To make these cruel and pitiless goddesses weep is indeed an
     amazing feat. *regia coniunx:* Persephone (Latin Proserpina), wife of Pluto.

46–47 Rearrange: *nec regia coniunx nec [is], qui regit ima [loca], sustinet negāre
     orantī.*

47   *sustinet . . . negāre:* "bear to deny [his wish to him]." *orantī:* modifies Orpheus.

48   *Eurydicēn:* accusative, Greek form.

48–49 *umbrās . . . recentēs / inter = inter umbrās recentēs.*

49   *dē vulnere:* "because of her wound" (the snakebite that caused her death). There
     may be an echo of Vergil's description of Dido's shade, still showing the mark
     of her suicide: *recens a vulnere (Aen.* 6.450).

50   *hanc* = Eurydice. *hanc simul et legem . . . accipit:* the use of the same verb with
     two very different types of noun is called zeugma or syllepsis. Orpheus "receives"
     his wife and the rule in rather different senses. *Rhodopeius:* Thracian.

50–52 *legem* is restated by two indirect constructions: *nē flectat sua lumina,* and *inrita
     dona futura [esse].* The rule *(lex)* imposed on Orpheus had two parts: (1) do
     not look back until you have exited the Underworld (a command, represented in
     indirect speech by a subjunctive clause) and (2) if you do, the gift will be void
     (a statement, represented in indirect speech by the accusative-plus-infinitive
     construction).

51   *lumina = oculōs. donec = dum;* with the subjunctive, means "until."

51–52 *Avernās . . . vallēs:* Avernus, a lake in the region of Naples, was said to be an
     entrance to the Underworld; it is the point through which Aeneas descends in
     Aeneid 6. Here, *valles* is modified by the adjective *Avernus, -a, -um,* which
     probably simply means "infernal."

53   *adclivis* (or *acclivis*): "upward sloping." *carpitur:* note that this word, basically
     meaning "pick out," is used to describe the action of the vulture, as it eats
     Tityos' liver *(carpsere,* line 43), and of Orpheus and Eurydice, as they carefully
     pick their way along the dark path out of the Underworld; it will also appear to
     describe a metaphorical "plucking" of flowers (below, line 85).

56   *nē deficeret:* fear clause, dependent on *metuens.* Either Orpheus or Eurydice
     could be the subject ("fearing that she was faltering" or "fearing that he was
     failing her"). *avidus videndī:* "desirous of seeing" or "eager to see"; *avidus*
     implies greedy longing.

57   *amans:* the application of the epithet "lover" to Orpheus explains, to some
     degree, his desire to look at Eurydice too soon.

58–59   The act of attempting to embrace the dead and finding only empty air fits a
        common pattern in epic, displayed by Odysseus (*Odyssey* 11.204ff.), Aeneas
        (*Aeneid* 2.790ff., 6.700ff.), and Vergil's Orpheus (*Georgics* 4.500f.).

60–61   *non est . . . quicquam / questa:* "she does not make any complaint" (*est questa*
        from *queror, queri, questus*).

61   *quid enim nisi se quereretur amatam?* Rearrange: *quid enim quereretur nisi se
     amatam [esse]?* The verb is subjunctive in a deliberative (i.e., rhetorical)
     question: "what would she complain about?" *nisi se . . . amatam [esse]* serves
     as an object of the verb: "except *the fact that* she was loved."

62   *vale:* Eurydice's quoted "good-bye" functions as the object of *dixit* in line 63
     and as the antecedent of *quod* in line 62. (This usage is exactly paralleled in
     English: "a last good-bye.")

63   *eōdem:* "to the same place," i.e., back into the Underworld.

64–71   Ovid now compares Orpheus to two other mythological figures: *Orpheus
        stupuit non aliter quam [is stupuit] qui vidit . . . [et is stupuit] qui in se crimen
        traxit.* The first is an unnamed man who was turned to stone by the shock of
        seeing Hercules bringing Cerberus out of the Underworld. The second is Olenos,
        who was granted his wish to be turned to stone to share his wife's punishment.
        Together, these stories convey the ideas that Orpheus was temporarily frozen
        in shock and that he wished to join Eurydice in death.

64   *geminā nece:* ablative of cause after *stupuit.*

64–67   The man who saw Hercules with Cerberus is otherwise unknown, although
        within the world of mythology, it can easily be imagined that one witnessing
        such an event might turn to stone.

65   *mediō [collō] portante catenās:* Apparently, when capturing the three-headed
     dog, Hercules put a leash on only one of the heads.

66   *canis = Cerberī.*

66–67   *quem non pavor ante reliquit, / quam natura prior = quem non pavor reliquit
        antequam natura prior [eum reliquit]. natura prior* refers to his human state.

67   *saxō per corpus obortō:* ablative absolute.

68   *quique in se crimen traxit:* The second mythological comparison, parallel with
     the *qui vidit* clause in 65–66. Olenos' wife Lethaea seems to have boasted
     excessively of her beauty (*confisa figurae,* 69) and been punished with petrifica-
     tion; after attempting to draw the blame onto himself, Olenos was allowed to
     share her punishment and thus remain with his wife.

69   *tu . . . confisa:* vocative. *figurae:* dative with *confisa; confido* (like *fido*) takes a
     dative.

70–71   *iunctissima . . . pectora:* "most devoted hearts," i.e., Olenos and Lethaea
        (*iunctissima* = literally, "most joined").

71   *umida . . . Idē:* Mount Ida.

72 *orantem, volentem:* modify Orpheus. *transire [flumen].*

73 *portitor:* the "doorman" of Hell is Charon, who rows souls across the Styx in his boat; he will not permit Orpheus to follow Eurydice back into the Underworld. *septem . . . diēbus:* ablative to express duration of time.

74 *in ripā:* on the bank of the Styx. *Cereris sine munere:* the "gift of Ceres" is grain; Orpheus remains on the banks of the Styx for seven days without eating.

75 *alimenta:* predicate nominative. *fuēre = fuērunt.*

76 *Erebī:* another name for the Underworld.

77 *Rhodopēn:* feminine accusative singular (Greek form). Rhodope is a mountain in Thrace and the source of Orpheus' epithet *Rhodopeius* (lines 11, 50). *Haemum:* Mount Haemus, another mountain in Thrace.

78 *tertius:* translate adverbially: "for the third time." *inclusum Piscibus annum:* the old Roman calendar began with March, when the sun passes through the sign of Pisces.

79 *Titan:* the Sun, one of the Titans (children of Uranus and Gaea).

79–81 After losing Eurydice, Orpheus avoids erotic involvement with all women. Two possible explanations are offered: either his sad experience had turned him against the idea of marriage, or he had vowed to remain faithful to his wife even after her death.

80 *femineam Venerem = feminārum amorem. seu = sive;* parallel with the next clause. *quod =* "because." *cesserat:* "had turned out"; the subject is "the love of women" (i.e., his experience with marriage).

81 *sive [quod] fidem dederat [uxori]. multās [feminās]:* Orpheus remains the object of women's desire.

82 *iungere sē vatī:* depends on *ardor. doluēre = doluērunt.*

83 *auctor:* "precedent," followed by dative (*populīs*) and infinitives (*transferre, carpere*).

85 *aetatis breve ver et primōs carpere florēs:* The "springtime of their age" and "first flowers" refer to the youth of Orpheus' lovers.

17. Pygmalion: 10.243–97

Like most stories in Book 10, the story of Pygmalion is part of the song Orpheus composes to justify his rejection of women in favor of boys. Orpheus announces his topics as "boys beloved by gods, and girls afflicted with illegal passions." The tale of Pygmalion initially appears to be an offshoot of the latter topic, for he, too, has chosen a womanless lifestyle in response to the shocking behavior of his countrywomen, the Propoetides (10.238–42). The Propoetides had denied Venus' divinity and, as punishment, were made the first prostitutes; they eventually turned to stone, as evidence of their hardheartedness. Shocked by this depravity, Pygmalion, like Orpheus, renounces the company of women, but he crafts for himself an ideal woman out of ivory, whom he treats as if she were his real girlfriend. At a festival of Venus, Pygmalion prays for a wife "similar to" his ivory girl and, upon his return home, finds that the statue has become a real woman. Thus, through the favor of the goddess, Pygmalion finds happiness with a woman after all, although she originated as his fantasy.

The story of Pygmalion can be examined in two contexts. First, as part of Orpheus' song, it reveals something of Orpheus' thinking about the morality of women and the ideal type of woman. Second, as part of Ovid's own narrative, the story of Pygmalion is the story of an artist's relationship with his own creation. This theme is reflected in the story of Orpheus himself, the poet extraordinaire who cannot save his beloved, and of Daedalus, the artisan whose invention causes his son's death (*Met.* 8.183–235).

The relatively brief tale of Pygmalion is one of Ovid's most famous, known to English-speaking audiences as the inspiration for a George Bernard Shaw play (adapted as the musical *My Fair Lady*).

243   *quās . . . aevum per crimen agentīs:* the Propoetides, fellow Cypriots of Pygmalion; they were made by Venus to live as prostitutes in punishment for their denial of the goddess' power. We may wonder whether Pygmalion, a devout worshipper of Venus, was more shocked by the women's blasphemy or by their sexual depravity. *quās = illās;* the relative used as a demonstrative. *aevum . . . agentīs = vitam . . . agentīs.*

244   *plurima:* neuter plural with *quae;* translate as adverb: "abundantly."

244–45   *vitiīs, quae plurima mentī / femineae natura dedit:* The narrator here is the misogynistic Orpheus.

246   *consorte:* ablative after *carēbat.*

247   *mirā . . . arte:* ablative of manner.

248   *[cum] quā [formā].*

250   *credas:* "you would believe."

251   *si non obstet reverentia:* "if modesty were not an obstacle." The statue girl appears immobile not because she is inanimate, but because she is shy.

252   *adeō:* adverb.

253   *simulatī corporis:* objective genitive. *ignēs:* the proverbial "fires of love."

254   *an:* depends on *temptantēs.*

255   *corpus:* "flesh."

256   *reddique [oscula] putat.*

257   *credit tactīs digitōs insidere membrīs:* Pygmalion imagines that his fingers sink into the girl's limbs when he touches them; this belief explains his fear of bruising the statue, as noted in the following line. *tactīs . . . membrīs:* dative with *insidere.*

258   Rearrange: *nē livor veniat in pressōs artūs.*

259   *modo . . . modo:* "sometimes . . . , other times . . ."

260 *munera:* the next three lines list examples of these gifts, the sort of simple and sincere love tokens recommended by Ovid in the *Ars Amatoria* (in contrast to the expensive, crass gifts of a less sincere lover). *lapillōs:* diminutive form of *lapis.*

261 *parvās volucrēs:* Birds were popular pets in ancient Rome; remember the famous sparrow of Catullus' mistress Lesbia.

262–63 *ab arbore lapsās / Heliadum lacrimās:* the Heliades, daughters of the Sun, were transformed into trees and still wept in mourning for their brother Phaethon; their tears were said to be the origin of amber, drops of fossilized tree resin, and were used by the Romans in jewelery. Ovid tells their story at *Met.* 2.340–66.

263–66 Pygmalion dresses and adorns his statue with jewelry.

265 *aure levēs bacae [pendent]: bacae* are "pearls," here used in earrings. *aure* is poetic singular for plural.

267 *[in] stratīs. conchā Sidonide:* expensive purple dye made from seashells came from the Phoenician city of Sidon.

268 *appellat [eam] "torī sociam." colla:* poetic plural for singular.

269 *tamquam sensura:* "as if she can feel it." Pygmalion's concern for the statue's comfort (like his fear of bruising her, in line 258) is further evidence that he has lost touch with reality.

270 *totā . . . Cyprō: Cypros, -ī,* is feminine.

271 *pandīs inductae cornibus aurum:* the participle *inductae* should be taken in an active (or "middle") sense: "spreading gold on their curved horns," i.e., "with gold spread on their curved horns." Sacrificial victims often had their horns decoratively gilded.

272 *[in] niveā cervice.*

273 *cum:* an example of the *cum-inversum* construction, in which the circumstances are described in the main clause (*conciderant . . . iuvencae, turaque fumabant*), while the new action is described by an indicative *cum* clause. *munere:* ablative after *functus.*

275 *sit coniunx:* a subjunctive wish-clause dependent on *opto.* Pygmalion would have liked to pray, "*opto sit coniunx eburnea virgo,*" but instead prayed, "*opto sit coniunx similis mea eburnae [virgini].*"

277 *ut . . . aderat: ut* with the indicative here is "since." (*Oxford Latin Dictionary,* s.v. *ut* 21.) *suīs . . . festīs:* dative after the compound verb *aderat.*

278 *vota quid illa velint = quid vota illa velint:* indirect question dependent on *sensit* in line 277. *amicī:* adjective with *numinis.*

279 *flamma:* the fire on Venus' altar, before which Pygmalion was standing when he made his prayer. *āera:* accusative singular, Greek form, from *āēr.*

280 *ut rediit [domum]. ut:* "when."

281 *torō:* dative with *incumbens.*

282 *admovet os:* i.e., he kisses her, but this time to test whether she is actually growing warm (*tepēre*).

283   *positō rigore:* ablative absolute; *positō* here means "put aside or away."
284   *ut:* "as." *sole:* ablative of cause; from *sol, solis.*
285   *ipsōque fit utilis usū:* The similarity between the wax, which is softened by manipulation, and the statue-turned-girl is only implied; Pygmalion's handling of the ivory, meant originally to test its state, actually causes the softening and humanizing process. In this way, Pygmalion is in fact shaping the girl himself, still sculpting her.
284–85 *Hymettia . . . cera:* Mount Hymettus near Athens was inhabited by bees that produced famous honey and wax.
288   *sua vota: votum* can mean a prayer or, as in this case, the thing prayed for. *retractat:* echoes *tractata,* used of the handling of wax in the simile (line 285).
289   *corpus:* "flesh" (as in line 255). *temptatae pollice:* Pygmalion takes the girl's pulse.
290   *Paphius . . . heros:* Paphos, a city in Cyprus, took its name from the child of Pygmalion and the statue girl, as noted in line 297. The epithet "Paphian" for Pygmalion is technically an anachronism, since Paphos had not yet been born or named. Such a high-flown epic epithet is comically ill-suited to the unheroic Pygmalion.
291   *ora [virginis].*
293   *ad lumina lumen:* Ovid plays on the double meaning of *lumen,* "light" or "eye." The girl raises her eyes (*lumen*—poetic singular for plural) to the light of day— or else to her lover's eyes (*ad lumina*).
294   *erubuit:* Compare her apparent modesty even before her metamorphosis (line 251). *pariter cum caelo:* "along with the sky." The girl's first glimpse of the world is dominated by her lover's face; he is both her creator and her world, literally the center of her universe. Here again, the statue girl represents a perfect male fantasy.
295   *coniugiō:* dative with *adest. coniugiō, quod fēcit, adest dea:* Venus attends the wedding, which she herself had brought about.
295–96 *coactīs / cornibus in plenum noviens lunaribus orbem:* ablative absolute; an elaborate poetic way of saying "when nine months had passed." The crescent moon (*cornibus . . . lunaribus*) fills out into a full circle (*in plenum . . . orbem*) nine times.
297   *Paphon:* accusative singular, Greek form. The gender of this child is uncertain, since some manuscripts read *de quā* (as here), while others read *de quō.*

18. Midas: 11.100–145

This is the first and more famous of two stories about Midas. It tells of his Golden Touch, granted to him as a favor by Bacchus. Bacchus was grateful to Midas for providing the safe return of Bacchus' devotee Silenus, whom Midas had found and entertained for several days before sending him back to Bacchus

(11.85–99). Midas' choice of the Golden Touch as his reward is an example of the common folktale motif of the "foolish wish." Note that in Ovid's version, Midas' unhappiness culminates in his inability to eat and drink, not in the metamorphosis of his daughter, as in other versions. The story ends with the aetiology of the gold found in the river Pactolus, in which Midas bathed to be rid of his golden curse.

Although this story presents a fairly straightforward moral lesson, it also represents a superb example of Ovid's technique of brilliantly vivid, yet concise, narrative. Within forty-five lines, Midas' problem arises, comes to a head, and concludes. With just the right details, Ovid is able to convey the changes in Midas' psychological state, from excitement to frustration to repentance.

The second story of Midas, in which he is again punished for foolishness, is at *Metamorphoses* 11.146–93.

100 *Huic:* Midas. *deus:* Bacchus. *inutile:* because Midas does not gain anything from his gift.

101 *altore receptō:* ablative with *gaudens;* rejoicing "at the return of his foster-father" (literally, "at his returned foster-father"). The construction is similar to Livy's phrase *ab urbe condita.* The *altor* (from *alere,* "to nurture") is Silenus, a satyr who cared for the infant Bacchus.

102 *ille:* Midas. *effice [ut]:* "bring it about that . . ."

103 *aurum:* Note how often this word (or its related adjective, *aureus, -a, -um*) appears in this brief story (ten times in forty-five lines); like Midas' life, the story contains too much gold.

104 *optatīs:* dative with the compound *adnuit. munera solvit:* "granted the gift."

105 *Liber:* a name for Bacchus.

106 *Berecynthius heros:* Midas; Berecynthus is a mountain in Midas' kingdom of Phrygia.

107 *singula:* "individual things" or "things one at a time."

108 *non altā fronde:* take *non* closely with *altā.*

112 *arentīs Cereris . . . aristās:* Ceres is here used as a synonym for "grain." This contact with the grain and with the apple in line 113 foreshadows Midas' problem with food.

114 *Hesperidas:* The Hesperides, daughters of Atlas, guarded a tree that grew golden apples. *donasse = donavisse. putes:* "you would think."

116 Take *ubi* at the beginning of the line.

117 *Danaēn:* accusative singular, Greek form. Jupiter took the form of a shower of gold to impregnate Danaë, the mother of Perseus.

118 *animō capit:* "grasps." *fingens:* "imagining."

119 *[illī] gaudentī.* Here, as in line 106 above (*gaudet*), Midas foolishly rejoices in his gift. His joy contrasts with the real joy felt by Bacchus (*gaudens,* 101) at

the return of Silenus, the joy that inspired the ill-chosen reward. *posuēre* = *posuērunt.*

120   *nec . . . egentēs:* "not lacking" = "having in abundance." *tostae frugis:* "bread"; genitive after *egentēs.*

121–22   *Cerealia . . . munera, Cerealia dona:* the bread. Latin often shows possession by the use of an adjective formed from a name, rather than the genitive of the name. "Cereal gifts" = "the gifts of Ceres."

123–24   *avidō . . . dente, admotō dente:* poetic singular for plural.

124   *lammina fulva:* The food appears to grow a thin shell of gold on the outside, rather than turning solid gold. *premēbat:* "covered."

125   *auctorem muneris:* Bacchus, i.e., wine. *purīs . . . undīs:* The ancients almost always drank their wine diluted with water.

126   *fluitāre:* translate as a gerund.

127   *divesque miserque: -que . . . -que,* like *et . . . et,* means "both . . . and."

129   *copia [cibī].*

130   *meritus:* "deservedly."

132   *Lenaee:* vocative of *Lenaeus,* an epithet of Bacchus. *peccavimus* = *peccavi:* plural for singular.

133   *miserere:* imperative. *eripe [me].*

134   *mite deum numen [est]. deum* = *deōrum. peccasse* = *peccavisse.*

135   *munera solvit:* the same phrase used in line 104, but here meaning "removed [or released] the gift"—ironically, the opposite of its meaning the first time, when Bacchus "granted the gift" (or "paid off his debt").

136   *nēve:* negative purpose clause. *male optatō:* "foolishly desired." The phase contains echoes of the beginning of Midas' story (*optandi,* 100; *male usurus,* 102), to remind him of the foolishness of his choice.

137   *magnīs . . . Sardibus:* dative with *vicinum.* Sardis (here, in the plural, Sardes) was a city in Lydia.

138   *labentibus obvius undīs:* "moving against the flowing waters," i.e., going upstream.

140   *spumigerō . . . fontī:* dative with the compound verb *subde* in 141. *quā:* "where."

142   *iussae . . . aquae:* dative with *succedit.*

144–45   The river Pactolus, in which Midas was said to have washed off the golden touch, carried gold in its waters. Ovid imagines that when river water irrigated the land, "seeds" of gold were planted. The word *glaebīs* at the end of line 145 recalls the clumps of dirt that Midas turned to gold in lines 111–112 (*contigit et glaebam: contactu glaeba potenti / massa fit*); the earth around his homeland remains golden, even after the removal of the curse.

19. Aeneas and the Sibyl: 14.101–153

The following passage is Ovid's rendering of Aeneas' journey to the Underworld, an episode recounted by Vergil in *Aeneid* 6. The differences between Ovid's version and Vergil's are crucial to our understanding of their different perspectives on Aeneas' journey. Ovid's focus is not on the centrality of Aeneas' destiny, but on Aeneas' escort in the Underworld, the Sibyl, who tells Aeneas her personal history as they make their way back to the world of the living. Throughout his tales of Aeneas, Ovid generally downplays Aeneas' lofty mission of founding the Roman Empire, and instead concentrates on more personal concerns of less heroic figures. The Sibyl's history functions as an aetiology (telling how she came to be so incredibly old) and as one more variation on the theme of the gods' amatory adventures. Unlike many of the women whom the gods desired, the Sibyl successfully resisted the advances of Apollo, but she paid a high price for the retention of her virginity.

The geographic details in the opening lines of this passage describe Aeneas' arrival in the Bay of Naples (the Greek city of Parthenope).

101   *Hās:* Pithecusae, an island near the Bay of Naples. (Its name is grammatically plural, like many place-names, including the Sibyl's home of *Cumae,* which we see below in line 104.) The preceding story (14.88–100) told how the inhabitants of Pithecusae were changed into monkeys, as punishment for their treachery. *Parthenopeia:* "Neapolitan," adjective from *Parthenope,* the Greek name for Naples. *dextrā [de parte].*

102–103   *canorī / Aeolidae tumulum [deseruit]:* "Aeolides," the son of Aeolus, is Misenus, a Trojan trumpeter who sailed with Aeneas. In *Aeneid* 6.162–74, Vergil tells how Misenus foolishly challenged the gods and was drowned by Neptune's jealous trumpeter Triton. Immediately before entering the Underworld, Vergil's Aeneas must hold a funeral for Misenus; Ovid alludes to this episode by calling Misenus "Aeolides," the patronymic Vergil gives him in *Aeneid* 6.164.

105   *[ut] ad manēs veniat per Averna paternōs:* indirect command, dependent on *orat* in the following line. *manēs . . . paternōs = manēs patris:* Aeneas' purpose for visiting the Underworld was to see his father Anchises. The *manes* are spirits of the dead. *Averna [regna]:* Avernus is a lake, said to be one of the entrances to the Underworld.

106   *illa:* the Sibyl. *vultum:* "her gaze."

107   *deō . . . receptō:* When the Sibyl enters her prophetic frenzy, Apollo takes possession of her and speaks through her.

108   *factīs maxime:* address to Aeneas; "man of very great deeds" (literally, "very great in your deeds").

109   *dextera [manus spectata est] per ferrum, pietas spectata [est] per ignēs:* Aeneas' "right hand" refers to his strength in combat, proven during the Trojan War; he proved his *pietas* by saving his father, son, and household gods from the burning of Troy (*per ignēs*), as told in *Aeneid* 2.

110   *pone: pono* often means "put aside." *potiēre = potiēris;* from *potior,* which takes an ablative (*petitīs*).

111   *novissima:* "farthest, last."

112   *mē duce:* ablative absolute. *simulacra = umbram.*

113   *invia virtutī nulla est via:* one of Ovid's paradoxical (and usually untranslatable) wordplays. The meaning is that, since Aeneas has *virtus,* no place is inaccessible (*invia*) to him. "No path is pathless to [the man who has] courage."

113–15   In *Aeneid* 6.136ff., the Sibyl sends Aeneas out to seek the Golden Bough, a token required for safe entrance into the Underworld, and his mother Venus sends a dove as an omen to show him the way to the Bough. Ovid condenses this story (and removes much of its mysticism and *numen*) by having the Sibyl simply show Aeneas to the Bough and order him to pick it.

114   *[in] silvā. Iunonis Avernae = reginae Avernae.* Since Juno is the queen of the gods on Olympus, her name can be used of queens of other areas of the universe. Pluto's wife Proserpina, queen of the Underworld, is thus the "Juno" of her realm. Avernus here refers to the Underworld in general.

116   *Orcī:* Orcus is another name for the Underworld.

117   *atavōs:* The centerpiece of Vergil's account of Aeneas' journey to the Underworld is the vision of Aeneas' descendants, the great heroes of Roman history. In Ovid's account, Aeneas sees only his own ancestors; the prophecy of his offspring is omitted. Ovid's Aeneas has thus done a complete about-face from his Vergilian perspective: where Vergil's Aeneas looks forward, toward the goal of his mission and Roman generations to come, Ovid's Aeneas looks backward, at bygone generations of Trojans.

118   *iura locōrum:* As in *Aeneid* 6, Anchises explains the workings of the Underworld, notably the way in which souls are purified and then incorporated into new bodies.

119   *quaeque novīs essent adeunda pericula [in] bellīs:* "the dangers he would have to undergo in his new wars," i.e., the wars Aeneas fights against the Italians when he arrives at his destination in Latium. This revelation (*Aen.* 6.888–92; compare also 6.83–97) is a trivial part of Vergil's account of what Aeneas learns in the Underworld; by including it, Ovid calls attention to his omission of Vergil's centerpiece, the parade of Roman heroes.

120   *adversō tramite:* "on the way back."

121   *duce Cumaeā:* the Sibyl. *mollit . . . laborem:* The reference to the "work" of returning from the Underworld alludes to *Aeneid* 6.127–29, where Vergil's Sibyl warns Aeneas of this very *labor:* "the descent to the Underworld is easy, but retracing your steps and returning to the upper air, *that* is the task, *that* is the labor" (*hoc opus, hic labor est*). As we often see in the *Metamorphoses,* difficult times or tedious tasks can be lightened with storytelling (e.g., the daughters of Minyas, who tell stories while weaving, 4.38–41; or the river Achelous, who entertains Theseus' entourage with stories until a flood subsides, 8.547ff.).

122   *[Aeneas] carpit.*

123–28 While Vergil's Aeneas is a man of few words, Ovid's is almost silent; these six lines constitute his only direct speech in the *Metamorphoses*. This speech, mistaking the Sibyl for a goddess, recalls Aeneas' flattering speech to the disguised Venus at *Aeneid* 1.326–34, and Odysseus' speech to Nausicaa at *Odyssey* 6.149ff.

123 *seu dea tu praesens [es], seu dīs gratissima [es]*.

124–25 *mē . . . / muneris esse tuī:* "that I am [a result] of your favor," i.e., "that I owe my life to you."

125 *quae:* antecedent is the *tu* implied in *tuī. quae me loca mortis adīre [voluisti].*

127 *pro quibus . . . meritīs = pro hīs meritīs. aeriās . . . aurās:* "the upper air."

128 *templa tibi statuam, tribuam tibi turis honorēs:* note the mirror-image word order of the two halves of the line. The two gifts Aeneas promises thus appear prominently at the beginning and end of the line.

130–31 *nec sacrī turis honore / humanum dignāre caput: dignāre* is the imperative of the deponent *dignor, dignārī* ("to consider [something] worthy of" + abl.). In poetry, negative commands are often expressed with *non* (or *nec*) + imperative, where prose demands *noli(te)* + infinitive.

131 *neu = nēve.* Negative purpose clause.

132 *lux = vita. fine:* ablative after *caritura.*

132–33 *lux aeterna . . . dabatur, si mea virginitas . . . patuisset:* the indicative *dabatur* in the conclusion replaces the more normal pluperfect subjunctive (*data esset*) which we might expect in both clauses of a contrary-to-fact condition. The indicative suggests that the action very nearly took place, or began to take place. Apollo was in the process of granting the Sibyl eternal life, but never completed the gift.

136 *optatīs . . . potiēre:* for the form of *potiēre*, see note on line 110.

136–37 *ego pulveris haustī / ostendi cumulum:* an example of the use of the perfect participle to indicate the prior of two actions: "I showed a pile of scooped-up sand" is better translated "I scooped up a pile of sand and showed it."

137 *corpora:* "grains." *quot . . . habēret:* Subjunctive verb in a subordinate clause within an indirect statement (*tot mihi natalēs contingere*, 138).

138 *mihi . . . contingere:* "befall me." *natalēs [diēs]. vana:* Nominative adjectives modifying the subject can often best be translated as adverbs: "foolishly."

139 *excĭdit:* "It slipped my mind"; *excĭdo* is from *ex + cado* ("fall"), while *excīdo* is from *ex + caedo* ("cut"). *iuvenēs:* adjective.

140–41 *dabat . . . , si . . . paterer:* the same type of mixed contrary-to-fact conditional found in lines 132–33. *paterer* is from *patior. Venerem = amorem.*

143 *terga:* poetic plural for singular. *terga dedit:* The English idiom is "turned its back."

144 *saecula:* "centuries." The Sibyl has lived seven hundred years and has three hundred more to live, as she notes in lines 145–46.

145 *acta [esse]. superest:* The grammatical subject is *vidēre* in the next line; English renders such sentences best by inverting them: "All that remains is that I see . . ." *numerōs ut pulveris aequem:* purpose clause.

147–49   The Sibyl predicts that, with advancing old age, she will continue to shrink in size, until she is extremely small. (Compare the story of the goddess Aurora's mortal husband Tithonus, who was also given eternal life without eternal youth; after ages of shrinking, he became a grasshopper.) A character in Petronius' *Satyricon* (48.8) tells that the shrunken Sibyl was eventually housed in a bottle; asked what she wanted, she responded only, "I want to die." Ovid's Sibyl is more defiant in the end.

148   *dies = tempus. senectā:* ablative of means with *consumpta;* from the noun *senecta, -ae* (a synonym for the more common *senectus, senectutis*).

151   *vel non [mē] cognoscet, vel [sē] dilexisse [mē] negabit.*

152   *ferar = fiam. nullīque:* dative; prose would normally have *nec ullī. nullī videnda:* "visible to none."

153   Unlike many other victims of the gods' metamorphoses, the Sibyl retains her ability to speak. Having successfully fended off rape, the Sibyl also avoids the loss of her humanity. The loss of voice is often the most poignant evidence of the isolating, dehumanizing effects of metamorphosis: see the plights of the transformed Daphne, who can communicate only by nodding her branches, 1.566–67; Io, who cannot tell her family who she is, 1.647–48; and Actaeon, who cannot cry out "poor me," 3.200–203.

20. Diomedes: 14.454–511

Diomedes, son of Tydeus, is a familar figure from the *Iliad* and from other myths associated with Troy. Books 5 and 6 of the *Iliad* tell of his success in battle, when he is personally assisted by Athena, almost kills the Trojan Aeneas, and wounds Aphrodite. Diomedes is also often associated with the Trojan War exploits of Odysseus, such as the night raid of *Iliad* 10 and the theft of the Palladium. After the war, like many other Greek leaders, Diomedes encounters bad fortune on the way back to Greece and in his own home. Shipwrecked and separated from his companions, Diomedes finally returns home to find his wife and her lover plotting his murder. Fleeing abroad, he finally settles in Apulia, in southern Italy, where he marries the daughter of a local king. His adventures can thus be seen to parallel those of Agamemnon, Menelaus, Odysseus, and even Aeneas.

As the passage here begins, Aeneas and the Trojans have arrived in Italy and are engaged in a war with the local Italians, led by Turnus the Rutulian. Each side seeks allies; while Aeneas travels to visit King Evander, who occupies the site that will eventually become Rome (*Aeneid* 8), Turnus' men, led by Venulus, are sent south to solicit Diomedes' aid. They offer Diomedes another opportunity to fight Trojans, in a repetition of the Trojan War, but Diomedes declines (*Aeneid* 8.9–17, 11.225–95). As one of the few episodes from the *Aeneid* that Ovid repeats at any length, this story provides a source of direct comparison between the two works. Ovid's version contains clear echoes of Vergilian phrases and makes explicit the parallels between the journeys of Diomedes and those of Aeneas; Diomedes, like Aeneas, is homeless, suffers on land and sea, and is pursued by an angry goddess. Diomedes' enemy is Aeneas' own mother, Venus, who provides the excuse for the metamorphosis story. (During their wanderings, Diomedes' men became so discouraged that they spoke tauntingly of Venus; in punishment, the goddess transformed these men into white birds that sing a mournful song.) Unlike Aeneas, however, Ovid's Diomedes has no ambition or motivation to seek glory or empire.

454 *uterque:* "each side," i.e., the Trojans and the Rutulians, opponents in the Italian war narrated in the second half of the *Aeneid.*

455–56 *multī Rutulōs [tuentur], multī Troiana tuentur / castra:* Ovid does not always observe strict parallelism; the two objects of *tuentur* are "the Rutulians" and "the Trojan camp." But as readers of *Aeneid* 9 are aware, only the Trojans have built a full-scale *castra,* a Roman legionary-style fort.

456 *neque Aeneas Evandrī ad moenia frustra [venerat]: Aeneid* 8 tells of Aeneas' successful (*neque . . . frustra*) journey to Pallanteum, the city of king Evander, who becomes Aeneas' ally in the war against Turnus. The missions to Evander and to Diomedes leave at almost the same time at the beginning of *Aeneid* 8; Vergil follows Aeneas' mission exclusively for the remainder of that book and does not report the unsuccessful mission to Diomedes until Book 11.

457 *Venulus:* a companion of Turnus. Venulus' further adventures are recounted at *Met.* 14.512–26. *profugī Diomedis:* an echo of *fatō profugus,* used of Aeneas in *Aeneid* 1.2. *urbem:* the city of Arpi, in Apulia.

458 *sub Iapyge . . . Daunō:* Daunus is Diomedes' Italian father-in-law. The region of Apulia where Arpi was located was called "Daunia"; its inhabitants were also called "Iapygians."

459 *dotalia arva:* territory that was given to Diomedes as part of his wife's dowry.

460 *postquam:* take at the beginning of the line.

461 *Aetolius heros:* Diomedes, whose family originally came from the Greek region of Aetolia.

462–64 Indirect statements after the implied speech-action in *excusat:* "he gave the excuse that . . ." Diomedes explains that he cannot send the locals (*socerī . . . suī populōs*) as allies, and that he has no men of his own (*ē gente suōrum*).

462 *pugnae:* dative with *committere.*

464 *nēve haec commenta [esse] putētis:* negative purpose clause.

467 *Ilios:* (nom., fem.) "Troy." *Danaās:* "Greek." *Pergama:* (neu. pl.) "the citadel of Troy."

468 *Narycius heros:* the so-called lesser Ajax, son of Oileus. At the sack of Troy, he had raped Athena's virgin priestess Cassandra; in vengeance, Athena visited

her anger on the entire Greek fleet as they returned to Greece. *ā virgine:* "from Athena," a virgin goddess. *virgine raptā:* ablative absolute with causal force.

469   Rearrange: *poenam, quam meruit solus, digessit in omnēs:* although only Ajax had offended Athena, the entire army suffered the effects of her wrath.

472   *Capherea:* accusative singular, Greek form. Caphereus is a promontory on the coast of Greece, where the Greeks were shipwrecked on the return from Troy.

473   *ex ordine:* English says "in order."

474   *flenda:* "lamentable."

476   *patriīs . . . ab Argīs:* Diomedes' city of Argos, to which he returned after the war, only to find (like Agamemnon) that his wife had been unfaithful to him and was plotting his murder.

477   *antiquō memorēs de vulnere poenās:* note the interlocked word order. *antiquō . . . de vulnere:* Diomedes attributes Venus' hositility to the wound that he inflicted upon her hand in the battle in *Iliad* 5.

478   *alma Venus:* an ironic epithet; at the time of her injury, Venus was rescuing her son Aeneas from near-destruction by Diomedes. She was *alma* toward Aeneas, but certainly not toward Diomedes.

480   *mihi:* dative of agent.

480–82   Since Odysseus (*Od.* 5), shipwreck and drowning have been considered the most shameful outcomes of a hero's journey, for they bring death without conspicuous glory and without opportunity for a spectacular funeral. Diomedes' nemesis Aeneas, during his first appearance in the *Aeneid* (1.94–101), laments his own seemingly imminent death in a shipwreck and even wishes that he could have been killed in battle *by Diomedes.*

482   *vellem [ut] . . . fuissem.*

483–95   One of Diomedes' companions, Acmon, argues that, having suffered everything Venus can possibly inflict on them, they should have nothing more to fear. In essence, by arguing that their fortunes cannot get any worse, he challenges the angry goddess to prove him wrong.

483   *ultima:* neuter plural, object of *passī. bellōque fretōque:* "in war and at sea." These two words represent the spheres of the Homeric hero's adventures—fighting and wandering—and correspond to the *Iliad* and the *Odyssey.* Thus Diomedes' experiences parallel those of his ally Odysseus and of his adversary Aeneas.

484   *Acmon:* (nom.) one of Diomedes' men.

487   *Cytherea:* Venus.

487–88   *quid habet Cytherea, quod ultrā . . . faciat?* "What more does Venus have that she might do to us?" Acmon thinks Venus has exhausted her arsenal, but as readers of the *Iliad* and *Aeneid* know, goddesses are rarely without resources. (Consider Juno at *Aeneid* 7.312: *flectere si nequeo superos, Acheronta movebo.*)

488   *velle putā:* parenthetical and concessive; "imagine that she wishes to," i.e., "even if she wishes to."

489 *in vulnus:* "for a wound." *sors autem ubi pessima rērum = ubi sors rērum pessima [est].*

490 *securaque summa malōrum [est]:* "The height of misfortune is of no concern to us." *secura* has its etymological meaning *se-cura,* "without care."

491 *audiat ipse [Venus] licet: licet* is here used as as concessive conjunction ("although"), introducing *audiat* and *oderit.*

491–92 *quod facit, oderit omnēs / sub Diomede virōs:* "although she may hate all Diomedes' men—which she does . . ."

493 *magnō:* "at a high price." Acmon argues that although they have paid a high price, they now, as a result, have the power to scorn the goddess' anger.

494 *Pleuronius:* Pleuron is a town in Aetolia; like Diomedes (*Aetolius heros,* line 461), Acmon originally comes from Aetolia.

496 *dicta = verba. [nos] amicī.*

497 *Acmona:* accusative, Greek form. *cui:* dative of possession.

499 *colla:* poetic plural for singular.

502 *ora:* poetic plural for singular.

504–505 *Lycus, Idas, cum Rhexenore Nycteus, Abas:* names of Diomedes' companions. Each is to be taken as subject of *miratur* in 505.

504 *cum Rhexenore Nycteus = Nycteus et Rhexenor*

507 *remōs . . . circumvolat:* The transformation apparently takes place at sea, so that the newly formed white birds can fly around the ship's oars (*remōs*).

508 *volucrum quae sit dubiārum forma:* indirect question dependent on *requiris.*

509 *ut non . . . , sic:* "although not . . . , nevertheless . . ." *ut non [forma est] cygnōrum, sic albīs proxima [forma est] cygnīs.* Ovid cannot call these new white birds swans, because he has already narrated the origin of the swan at *Met.* 2.367–80, with the metamorphosis of Phaethon's friend Cygnus (there is also another Cygnus in 12.72–145). So Diomedes' companions become not exactly swans, but the closest thing to swans.

510 *Iapygis . . . Daunī:* Diomedes' Italian father-in-law; see note on line 458.

21. Caesar's Deification and the Epilogue: 15.843–879

When Julius Caesar was assassinated in March, 44 B.C., his heir Octavian (later called Augustus) employed some strategies of propaganda to increase his own status and to legitimize his assumption of Caesar's powers and prestige. One such strategy was the exploitation of the fortuitous appearance of a comet a few months after the assassination; the comet was declared to be the soul of Caesar ascending to the heavens, where he would live as a god. The officially deified Caesar was given the name *Divus Iulius,* and Octavian styled himself *Divi filius.*

In the lines just before this passage (15.807–42), Jupiter, in answer to Venus' complaints about Caesar's imminent assassination, has tried to calm her fears by explaining Caesar's death and deification as necessary conditions for the coming of Augustus, who will be an even greater ruler than his "father." At the moment of Caesar's death, Venus descends to earth to catch up his departing soul. The ascent of Caesar's soul in a blaze of glory creates the comet that is seen from the earth. Caesar's soul is not jealous of being eclipsed by his son, for many great heroes have sired even greater sons. Ovid then renews the analogy between Augustus and Jupiter, common in Augustan poetry and appearing throughout the *Metamorphoses* (see 1.163–208; compare, for example, the opening of Vergil's first *Georgic* and Horace, *Odes* 1.2 and 3.1).

In the final lines of the poem (15.871–79), Ovid predicts that his poem will outlast its author and will withstand the ravages of time, the elements, and history. Even the "wrath of Jupiter" will be unable to destroy it. In light of Ovid's ongoing analogy between Jupiter and Augustus, it is tempting to see in the phrase *Iovis ira* a reference to the poet's banishment to the Black Sea by the emperor in A.D. 8, about the time of the completion of the *Metamorphoses*.

843   *Vix ea [verba] fatus erat [Iuppiter]. medi[ī] [in] sede senatūs:* Caesar was killed in the midst of a meeting of the Senate.

843–44   *cum . . . constitit:* the *cum-inversum* construction, in which the main clause gives background circumstances (*vix ea fatus erat*), and the subordinate clause describes the new action (*constitit*) with an indicative verb.

844   *alma Venus:* a phrase used in the opening of Lucretius' *De Rerum Natura;* Venus is especially *alma* to the Julian family, which claimed descent from Iulus, son of Aeneas and hence grandson of Venus. Julius Caesar built a temple to Venus Genetrix. *nullī cernenda:* "visible to no one."

845   *eripuit [animam] membrīs. āera:* accusative singular, Greek form; from *āēr, āeris.*

846   *recentem animam:* object of the main verbs *eripuit* and *intulit,* as well as of the participle *passa.*

847   *[animam] lumen capere et ignescere sensit.*

848   *emisit [animam] sinū. lunā:* ablative of comparison with *altius. illa = anima.*

849   *flammiferum . . . crinem:* What we call a comet's "tail" was seen by the Romans as its "hair"; the word "comet," after all, comes from *coma.*

850   *natī:* Octavian, adopted as Caesar's son under the terms of Caesar's will. *bene facta:* "good deeds, accomplishments." Take as both object of *videns* and subject of the indirect statement after *fatētur.*

851   *suīs [factīs]:* ablative of comparison. *ab illō [natō].*

852   *hic:* Octavian. *quamquam:* take at the beginning of the line. *paternīs [actīs]:* dative with *praeferrī.*

853   *obnoxia:* "subject to," followed by the dative *nullīs . . . iussīs.*

854   *invitum:* "against his will." Thus Octavian is absolved of any charge that in outdoing his father's deeds, he has violated *pietas.* The eclipse of the father by

the son was simply the working of *fama*, not a result of any policy of Octavian's. *praefert [acta natī]. unā in parte:* "in this one respect." This was the only time *fama* refused to cooperate fully with Octavian's wishes. This entire argument, while not overtly critical of Octavian, strikes some readers as ironic.

855–56 A list of heroic sons who outshone their fathers. Atreus was the father of Agamemnon, Aegeus of Theseus, Peleus of Achilles.

855 *titulīs:* A *titulus* is a commemorative inscription listing a public figure's accomplishments, offices, and titles. As he often does, Ovid anachronistically inserts mythological figures into Roman cultural contexts.

856 *Aegea, Pelea:* accusative singular, Greek form.

857 *exemplīs:* ablative after *utar. ipsōs = Caesarem et Augustum.* The only father and son to whom Caesar and Augustus are really worthy to be compared are Saturn and Jupiter.

859 *mundī regna triformis:* The universe is divided into three kingdoms, ruled by Jupiter and his brothers Neptune and Pluto, with Jupiter as supreme ruler. The *terra* is ruled by Augustus in the same way that Jupiter rules the entire universe.

860 *uterque:* "each one," Jupiter and Augustus.

861 *dī . . . Aeneae comitēs:* the Trojan Penates, household gods brought by Aeneas from the ruins of Troy to Italy, to provide a divine link between Troy and Rome.

862 *Indigetēs:* After his death, Aeneas was deified under the name of *Indiges;* here, he is one of a group of "indigenous gods." *Quirine:* Quirinus is the name of the deified Romulus.

863 *Gradive:* Gradivus is a name for Mars, father of Romulus.

864 *Caesareōs inter . . . penatēs:* Like Julius Caesar, Augustus held the title of *pontifex maximus;* as such, he had to oversee the cult of Vesta. He built a shrine to Vesta in his house on the Palatine, so that Vesta was in fact "among Caesar's *penates.*"

865 *Phoebe domestice:* Augustus built a temple to Apollo (Phoebus) on the Palatine, so close by his own house that Apollo, like Vesta, could be considered a part of the emperor's household.

866 *altus . . . Iuppiter:* properly one of the vocatives, naming gods whom the poet invokes (*di, Quirine, Gradive, Vesta, Phoebe*); the name is here attracted inside the relative clause and hence is nominative. *Tarpeiās . . . arcēs:* The Tarpeian Rock, where traitors were executed, was on the Capitoline, where the temple of Jupiter was located.

867 *quōs aliōs = vōs aliī quōs.*

868 After the invocations in lines 861–867, Ovid finally reaches the actual prayer, asking that Augustus, although the equivalent of a god on earth, may go to join *Divus Iulius* in heaven only after a long terrestrial reign. Such a prayer echoes many such sentiments in the poems of Horace, e.g., *Odes* 1.2.45, 3.2.21.

869 *quā:* "on which," "when." The antecedent is *dies* in the previous line. *quem temperat:* Augustus' ruling of the world is described with the same verb used

to describe Jupiter's rule of the heavens (lines 858–859: *arcēs / temperat aetheriās*). *orbe relictō:* ablative absolute.

870   *caelō:* dative after *accedat.* *[nobis] precantibus. absens:* "in his absence."

871   *opus exēgī:* An echo of the opening line of Horace's famous Ode 3.30, the final poem in his first collection of odes: *exegi monumentum aere perennius.*

873   *cum volet:* Although Latin uses the future tense, English must translate as a present.

873–74   *quae nil nisi corporis huius / ius habet:* "which has no power [*ius*] except over this [my] body."

875   *parte . . . meliore:* ablative of specification or respect. *[ego] perennis.* The adjective is another echo of *Ode* 3.30; see note on line 871.

876   *ferar:* the first of a series of future tense verbs in the remaining lines which predict Ovid's own immortality: *ferar, erit, legar, vivam. nostrum = meum.*

877   *quā:* "wherever."

878   *famā:* ablative of respect.

879   *siquid = si aliquid. verī:* partitive genitive with *(ali)quid. vatum praesagia:* As he often does, Ovid wryly leaves room for a less reverent reading: *if* poets' predictions are worth anything, he will live on. Compare some of his other oblique doubts about poets' truth (e.g., 13.733–34).

Appendix

Latin Meter

CLASSICAL METER: BASIC CONCEPTS

While English poetic meter is made up of patterns of stressed and unstressed syllables ("Rough **winds** do **shake** the **dar**ling **buds** of **May**"), Classical Latin depends for its meter on patterns of long and short syllables. These patterns are distinct from the natural stress accent of Latin words. Our ears have trouble even hearing Latin meter, since we are accustomed to listening for stress to define meter. Our mouths also have trouble pronouncing Latin meter, since we are accustomed to lengthening the syllables we stress. In Latin, stress and length must be considered separately; sometimes they coincide, and sometimes they do not. However, with proper reading, Latin meter can become quite easy to hear and, with some practice, pleasant to read.

The two systems—stress accentuation and quantitative meter—at work in Latin poetry are a result of Latin poets' wholesale adoption of the meters and metrical systems of Greek poetry. Classical Greek seems to have employed a system of accents based on pitch—rising or falling tone—rather than on stress. Latin poetry replaces the "music" of this pitch accent with the interaction between the meter and the stress accent.

Dactylic hexameter, the meter of Greek and Latin epic, including the *Metamorphoses,* is based on the metrical unit called a **dactyl,** a long syllable followed by two short syllables: ¯ ˘ ˘ (Greek *dactylos,* "finger"; most people's fingers consist of one long joint and two short joints). Greek abounds in words containing two consecutive short syllables, but such sequences are rarer in Latin. Thus, Latin dactylic meter makes much more frequent substitution of a single long syllable for the two short syllables, so that the resulting metrical unit is comprised of two consecutive long syllables, called a **spondee:** ‾ ‾. This substitution can be understood by an analogy with musical notation: a short syllable is half the value of a long syllable, just as an eighth note is half the value of a quarter note. The number of syllables in a line of hexameter will vary, depending on the combination of dactyls and spondees.

QUANTITY

From the substitution of spondees for dactyls, we can see that "short" and "long" syllables are exactly what their names imply, syllables of different durations. The difference between short and long syllables is not necessarily one of quality, but of quantity. In English, long "a" and short "a" are completely different phonemes (or sounds). While Latin vowels of different quantities may also differ somewhat in quality, the difference is not nearly as dramatic as in English. Any basic Latin textbook or grammar will give you an introduction to the sounds of Latin vowels. For further technical details on Latin vowels, see W. Sidney Allen's *Vox Latina* (Cambridge, 1965).

One of the most important points to notice about a Latin word is the number of syllables; most mispronunciations occur because a syllable has been overlooked or discounted in the analysis of the word or meter. Remember: **a Latin word has as many syllables as it has vowels or diphthongs.** It is therefore essential to learn which vowel combinations constitute diphthongs and are thus pronounced as one syllable: *ae, au, oe, ei, eu,* and *ui.* (The combination *ui* is a diphthong only in words such as *cui,* not in verbs such as *fuit, habuit,* etc., where the *u* belongs to the stem and the *i* to the ending.) Do not confuse these combinations with their two-syllable opposites: *ea, ua, eo,* etc., are *not* diphthongs and count as two syllables (e.g., *me-a, omni-a, e-odem, su-a*). And of course the English speaker must remember that there are no silent vowels in Latin.

When counting syllables, the reader also needs to know how to divide a word into syllables. There are two basic rules: Latin words divide *before* a single consonant (*no-va, a-ni-mus*) and *between* two consonants (*for-mas, il-las*). In combinations of more than two consonants, the division occurs before the last (*sanc-tus*).

Rules of syllabic quantity: Note that we use the terms "long" and "short" for syllables as well as for individual vowels. In some circumstances, a syllable can be termed long even if its vowel is short. It is the pattern of long *syllables,* however, that defines a poetic meter.

A syllable is long:

1. **if it contains a long vowel or a diphthong.** Some noun and verb endings contain vowels that are long "by nature": in the words *formās, mundō,* and *exegī,* the final syllables are long because they contain endings that are regularly long. Other long vowels are part of the word's stem: in *nūbes* and *fēmina,* the first syllables are long because they contain long vowels.

or 2. **if it contains a vowel followed by two consonants.** In the rules of syllabification above, we said that word division occurs between two consonants. Such division results in a long first syllable, sometimes termed "long by position." In the word *cor-po-ra,* the first syllable is long because of the double consonant, although its vowel is short. (An exception to this rule: not all consonant combinations will lengthen the preceding syllable. In particular, a "mute" consonant [b, c, d, g, p, t] followed by a "liquid" consonant [l, m, n, r] may not result in a syllable that is long by position.)

These two rules apply equally to generate long syllables. Both syllables of the word *ter-rās* are long, the first because of the double consonant, and the second because of the long vowel.

ACCENTUATION

Once the rules of syllabification and quantity are understood, the rules of accentuation are easily grasped. (The main impediment is the terminology in which they are often explained.) Again, the basic rules are actually few and simple:

1. **Never accent the final syllable of a word.** Thus, in a two-syllable word, the first syllable always receives the accent, regardless of quantity: *nó-va, íl-las, cáe-lum.*
2. **In words of three or more syllables, accent the next-to-last syllable, if it is long by nature or position. If the next-to-last syllable is short, accent the syllable before it.**

Thus, the accent falls on the next-to-last syllable both in *adspiráte,* because that syllable is long by nature (contains a long vowel), and in *tepéscunt,* because that syllable is long by position (contains a vowel followed by two consonants). In the three-syllable *dícere,* the accent falls on the first syllable, while in the four-syllable *perpétuum,* the accent falls on the second syllable; in both cases, the next-to-last syllable is short. In traditional terminology, all these syllables have beautiful Latin names: *ultima* (last), *penultima (paene ultima,* next-to-last), and *antepenultima* (third-to-last).

All these rules of syllabification, quantity, and accentuation have a limited number of exceptions, which are detailed in any reference grammar.

READING DACTYLIC HEXAMETER ALOUD

Reading verse should really be no different from reading prose. The phonemes must be given their proper values, the accents must be placed correctly, and a distinction must be made between long and short vowels. If all these steps are followed, the meter should become apparent without any special effort. In practice, however, it often helps to have an idea of the metrical pattern before you begin to read. Again, a musical analogy is appropriate: some people can learn to play by ear, while others need a written score in front of them at all times. Some students will find it necessary to mark their text with longs, shorts, accents, and so forth, before beginning to read, while others will be able to express these features as they come upon them.

For most students, the first hurdle in reading Latin verse aloud is the proper pronunciation of the phonemes. However, since these are completely regular (unlike English phonemes), this step is relatively easy. Care must simply be taken to pronounce the vowels with their Latin, not English, values, and always to pronounce "c" and "g" hard.

Next, the accents must be placed properly. Remember that stress accent is distinct from length of vowel. As we saw in the rule of accentuation above, the stress accent can be placed on a syllable in which the vowel is actually short by nature. The challenge for the English-speaking reader is to pronounce an accented syllable with more stress without lengthening the vowel. The easiest solution is to remember that "short" syllables are, in fact, short; say them quickly and move on. Likewise, take your time pronouncing long vowels, double consonants, and long syllables.

A line of dactylic hexameter consists of six "feet" (metra), in a combination of dactyls (one long syllable and two shorts, - ˘ ˘) and spondees (two long syllables, - -). While a spondee is the metrical equivalent of a dactyl and may substitute for it, certain conventions limit this substitution. For example, the fifth foot of the line is almost always a dactyl, while the sixth is almost always a spondee. (Even when the last syllable of the line is short, it is treated as long in order to create a spondee.) Lines consisting of all dactyls or all spondees are extremely unusual; Latin poets prefer to mix the two patterns, to speed up or slow down a line for dramatic or emotional effect. Thus, while the last two feet almost always sound the same (- ˘ ˘ | - -), the first four feet can display any of several different patterns. Two consecutive lines will rarely have exactly the same pattern, but all are variations of the same meter.

Following are the first lines of the Metamorphoses with the syllables marked and divided into feet.

in nŏvă | fērt ănĭ- |mŭs mū- | tātās | dīcĕrĕ | fōrmās

cōrpŏră | dī cŏep- | tīs năm | vōs mū- |tāstĭs ĕt | īllās

ādspī- |rātĕ mĕ- | īs prĭ- | māquĕab ŏ- | rīgĭnĕ | mūndī

ād mĕă | pērpĕtŭ- | ŭm dē- | dūcĭtĕ | tēmpŏră | cārmĕn.

Note that when a final syllable ends in a vowel and precedes another word that begins with a vowel (as in *primaque ab*), the two words run together and count as one syllable for metrical purposes. Thus, the phrase *primaque ab* has only three syllables, as the final e blends with the initial a. This process is called **elision**. Elision also occurs when a final m precedes an initial vowel, as in *postquam evolvit* (1.24), which is scanned as four syllables, with the *-quam e-* elided into one.

One of the artistic features of Latin verse is the pattern of coincidence and noncoincidence of stress accent and the long syllable at the beginning of the metrical unit (the metrical "ictus"). The long syllable that forms the "downbeat" of a dactyl or spondee may or may not receive the stress accent; when it does, the accent and ictus are in harmony (as in *tempora,* in line 4 above), but otherwise a kind of tension is formed (as in *animus,* in line 1 above). Latin poets like to play with different patterns of these features. A verse in which stress accent and metrical ictus coincide is called "homodyne," and one in which they do not coincide is called "heterodyne." One of the most serious difficulties for the modern reader of Latin is the need to avoid stressing the syllable that receives the metrical ictus. (For example, in line 3 above, the second syllable of *meis* begins a foot—i.e., receives the ictus—but should not carry the stress-accent.)

RESOURCES

A book alone probably cannot teach anyone to read poetry aloud. Learning to hear and pronounce Latin poetry is an aural and oral process, which needs auditory support. One of the most useful aids for students learning to read Latin aloud is the set of cassette tapes by Stephen Daitz, *The Pronunciation and Reading of Classical Latin: A Practical Guide* (The Living Voice of Greek and Latin, Guilford, Conn.: Jeffrey Norton Publishers, 1984), which introduces the concepts of oral reading and some techniques for learning to read verse. Another set of cassettes, Robert Sonkowsky's *Selections from Vergil Read in Classical Latin* (The Living Voice of Greek and Latin, Guilford, Conn.: Jeffrey Norton Publishers, 1985), demonstrates the reading of extensive passages of dactylic hexameter and is excellent training in learning to *hear* Latin meter.

Some books with further details of Latin meter are:

James W. Halporn, Thomas G. Rosenmeyer, and Martin Ostwald, *The Meters of Greek and Latin Poetry,* rev. ed., Norman, Okla.: University of Oklahoma Press, 1980.

L. P. Wilkinson, *Golden Latin Artistry.* Cambridge University Press, 1963; reprinted by University of Oklahoma Press, 1985.

In addition, G. B. Nussbaum's book, *Vergil's Meter: A Practical Guide for Reading Latin Hexameter Poetry* (Bristol: Bristol Classical Press, 1986), offers a somewhat unorthodox but refreshing method of learning metrical reading.

Mythological Glossary

This glossary includes only mythological characters who appear in the text or notes. Geographical terms, historical figures, and obscure epithets are not included; for these, consult individual notes. Line numbers indicate the first occurence of the character in each story; characters whose names occur only in the notes are followed by the line number of the note in which they occur (e.g., 14.468n). The list includes some figures from stories not in the Latin passages included in the text, if these figures are relevant to stories that are included (e.g., Actaeon, Ino).

Achilles: Greek hero, son of Peleus and Thetis. The most outstanding Greek warrior at Troy, Achilles was offended by Agamemnon and refused to fight for some time; this incident forms the plot of Homer's *Iliad*. He was killed by Paris before the sack of Troy. (12, passim)

Acmon: companion of Diomedes. For speaking scornfully of Venus, Acmon and some of Diomedes' other men were transformed into white birds. (14.484)

Actaeon: grandson of Cadmus. Having accidentally seen Diana bathing, Actaeon was turned into a stag and devoured by his own hunting dogs. (3.138)

Adonis: son of Myrrha and her father Cinyras. As a beautiful young man, Adonis attracted the love of Venus, who warned him not to hunt dangerous wild beasts. Ignoring her advice, he was killed by a wild boar. (10.503–739)

Aegeus: king of Athens; father of Theseus. Mistakenly thinking his son dead, Aegeus threw himself into the sea, which came to be called the Aegean Sea after him. (15.856)

Aeneas: Trojan hero, son of Venus and Anchises. Aeneas survived the fall of Troy and sailed to Italy, where his son founded Alba Longa, the home of Romulus and Remus. (13–14, passim)

Aeolus: king of the winds. (1.262)

Agamemnon: king of Mycenae, leader of the Greek forces in the Trojan War. (15.855)

Agenor: king of Phoenicia; father of Europa and Cadmus. (2.858, 3.3)

Aglauros: Athenian princess turned to stone as punishment for blocking Mercury's way to the bedroom of her sister Herse. (2.833n)

Ajax: Greek warrior, son of Oileus; leader of the Locrian contingent in the Trojan War. Angry gods caused him to be shipwrecked and killed on the journey home from Troy. (Sometimes called the "Lesser Ajax," to distinguish him from Ajax, son of Telemon, who also fought in the Trojan War.) (14.468n)

Ammon: African god identified with Jupiter. (4.671)

Amphitrite: wife of Neptune. (1.14)

Anchises: Trojan prince; father of Aeneas. (14.118)

Andromeda: daughter of Cepheus and Cassiope, rulers of Ethiopia. Andromeda was to be sacrificed to a sea monster, but was rescued and married by Perseus. (4.671)

Aquilo: the North wind. (1.262)

Arachne: expert weaver who challenged Minerva. After their contest, Arachne was changed into a spider as punishment for her insolence. (6.5)

Argus: hundred-eyed monster assigned by Juno to keep watch over Io. Argus was eventually lulled to sleep and killed by Mercury. (1.624)

Astraea: goddess of Justice, who withdrew from earth during the Iron Age. (1.150)

Atlas: a Titan; father of Maia (mother of Mercury). He held up the sky, but was turned to stone by Perseus. (2.834)

Atreus: son of Pelops; father of Agamemnon and Menelaus. (15.855)

Aurora: goddess of the Dawn. (1.61)

Auster: the South wind. (1.66)

Boreas: the North wind. Denied permission to marry the Athenian princess Orithyia, Boreas abducted her and fathered the winged boys Zetes and Calais. (1.65, 6.682)

Cadmus: founder of Thebes. He was sent by his father Agenor to search for his sister Europa, who had been abducted by Jupiter. He married Harmonia, daughter of Mars and Venus, and became the father of Semele, Ino, Agave, and Autonoe. (3.3)

Calais and Zetes: winged sons of Boreas and Orithyia. They sailed on the *Argo* with Jason. (6.716)

Callisto: Arcadian nymph and follower of Diana. Raped by Jupiter, she was cast out of Diana's company when her pregnancy was discovered. After the birth of her son Arcas, Callisto was turned into a bear by Juno. (2.409, 3.356n)

Cassiope: (also spelled Cassiopeia) mother of Andromeda and wife of Cepheus. Her boasts of her beauty caused Jupiter Ammon to demand that her daughter be sacrificed to a sea monster. (4.738)

Cephalus: husband of Procris, daughter of the Athenian king Erechtheus. Cephalus tells the stories of his abduction by the goddess Aurora and of his tragic accidental killing of his wife. (6.681, 7.661–865)

Cepheus: Ethiopian king, father of Andromeda. (4.669)

Cephisos: river god who raped the nymph Liriope and fathered Narcissus. (3.343)

Cerberus: three-headed dog who guards the Underworld. He was temporarily abducted by Hercules in one of the Labors. (9.185, 10.64–71n)

Ceres: the goddess of grain and crops. (1.123)

Charon: boatman who ferries spirits of the dead across the river Styx in the Underworld. (10.73n)

Cicones: a people of Thrace. (6.710, 10.2)

Coeus: a Titan, father of Latona. (6.366)

Cupid: god of love, armed with bow and arrows; son of Venus. (1.453)

Daedalus: Athenian inventor and engineer. Exiled to Crete for the murder of his nephew Perdix, Daedalus worked for King Minos. Many of the clever devices in Cretan stories are attributed to him

(Pasiphaë's wooden cow, the Labyrinth, Ariadne's ball of string). He built wings to carry himself and his son Icarus away from Crete. (8.183)

Danaë: mother of Perseus; daughter of King Acrisius. Warned by a prophecy that he would be killed by Danaë's son, Acrisius imprisoned her, but Jupiter appeared in the form of a shower of gold and fathered Perseus. (4.698n, 11.117)

Danaids: (also called Belides) fifty daughters of Danaus. Forced to marry their cousins, the sons of Aegyptus, forty-nine of the women murdered their husbands on their wedding night. As punishment in the Underworld, the Danaids eternally attempt to carry water in leaky vessels. (4.463, 10.44)

Daphne: daughter of the river Peneus. Attempting to escape from Apollo's advances, she was turned into the laurel. (1.452)

Daunus: king in the southern Italian region of Apulia. The Greek hero Diomedes marries Daunus' daughter. (14.458)

Deucalion: sole male human survivor of the Flood, husband of Pyrrha; son of Prometheus. Along with his wife, Deucalion regenerates humans from stones. (1.318)

Diana: virgin goddess of hunting; daughter of Jupiter and Latona. (1.485, 3.254)

Dido: queen of Carthage who fell in love with the Trojan hero Aeneas when he visited her on his travels. Abandoned by him, Dido committed suicide. (10.49n)

Diomedes: Greek hero, son of Tydeus; companion of Odysseus in many exploits during the Trojan War. Driven into exile after the war, Diomedes eventually settled in southern Italy. (14.457)

Echion: one of the Spartoi, men who grew from the teeth of the serpent slain by Cadmus. Echion became the ancestor of one of the original families of Thebes. (3.126)

Echo: woodland nymph who loved and pursued Narcissus. For her incessant talk that delayed Juno's search for Jupiter, Echo was deprived of her ability to speak except by repeating other people's words. (3.559)

Epimetheus: son of the Titan Iapetus; brother of Prometheus; father of Pyrrha. (1.390)

Erechtheus: king of Athens, son of Pandion and father of Procris and Orithyia. (6.677, 701)

Eumenides: the three Furies, infernal avenging spirits who pursue and madden people who commit crimes. Their names are Allecto, Tisiphone, and Megaera. (10.46)

Europa: daughter of Agenor, king of Phoenicia; mother of King Minos. Jupiter, in the guise of a bull, carried her off to Crete. (2.844)

Eurus: the East wind. (1.61)

Eurydice: wife of Orpheus. When she died of a snakebite shortly after their wedding, Orpheus attempted to retrieve her from the Underworld but failed when he looked back at the last minute, in violation of Hades' rule. (10.1–85)

Evander: king of Pallanteum, a Greek city on the site that will become Rome. Evander sent his son Pallas to fight with Aeneas against the Italians. (14.456)

Faunus: god of agriculture and fertility. (6.329)

Heliades: daughters of the sun god and sisters of Phaethon. They were transformed into trees through their mourning for Phaethon. Their tears were said to be the resin that forms amber. (2.340–66, 10.262–63n)

Hercules: Greek hero who performed twelve Labors, plus many other feats. (9.1–320)

Herse: Athenian princess, loved by Mercury. (2.833n)

Hesperides: daughters of Atlas; guardians of a tree bearing golden apples. (11.114)

Hippolytus: son of Theseus and devotee of Diana. Falsely accused of assaulting his stepmother Phaedra, Hippolytus was killed in a chariot crash sent by Neptune in response to Theseus' curse. (3.356n)

Hyacinthus: young man beloved by Apollo. Hyacinthus was struck in the head by a discus thrown by Apollo and died, but became a purple flower which bears his name. (10.162–219)

Hymen, Hymenaeus: god of marriage. (1.480, 10.2)

Iapetus: a Titan, father of Prometheus. (1.82)

Icarus: son of Daedalus. Flying with his father away from Crete, Icarus flew so high that the sun's heat melted the wax binding the feathers of his wings. The sea into which Icarus fell was named the Icarian Sea. (8.195)

Inachus: river god of Argos; father of Io. (1.611, 4.720n)

Indiges: name of the deified Aeneas. (15.862)

Ino: daughter of Cadmus and sister of Semele. Incurring the hostility of Juno for nursing the infant Bacchus, Ino was driven mad and threw herself off a cliff into the sea. (3.313, 4.417)

Io: daughter of the river Inachus; object of Jupiter's desire. (1.588)

Iphis: girl who was secretly raised as a boy by her mother. When her father arranged for her wedding to a girl, the goddess Isis granted Iphis' wish to be changed into a male. (9.666–797)

Iris: goddess of the rainbow and messenger of Juno. (1.271)

Isis: Egyptian goddess of fertility whose worship was adopted in the Greek and Roman world. (9.773)

Ixion: king of Thessaly and famous sinner in the Underworld. Ixion attempted to rape Juno, but Jupiter tricked him by substituting a cloud in the shape of Juno, by whom Ixion fathered the Centaurs. After death, Ixion revolved constantly on a wheel. (10.42)

Latona: mother, by Jupiter, of Apollo and Diana; daughter of the Titan Coeus. When she was pregnant, she was pursued by the angry Juno and could find nowhere to give birth until the island of Delos accepted her. (6.313)

Lethaea: wife of Olenos. Along with her husband, she was turned to stone as punishment for excessive boasting of her beauty. (10.70)

Liber: alternative name of Bacchus. (11.105)

Liriope: water nymph, mother of Narcissus by Cephisos. (3.342)

Maia: daughter of Atlas; mother, by Jupiter, of Mercury. (2.834n)

Medusa: snake-haired monster, once a woman, whose countenance turned spectators to stone. She was killed by Perseus, but her head continued to petrify people. (4.772–803)

Mercury: son of Jupiter and Maia; messenger of Jupiter. (2.834)

Midas: king of Phrygia. After rescuing Bacchus' mentor Silenus, Midas was granted a wish and foolishly asked that all he touched become gold. Later, relieved of this gift, Midas incurred Apollo's anger by questioning Apollo's victory in a music contest with

Pan. To demonstrate the brutishness of Midas' ears, Apollo gave him the ears of a donkey. (11.100–145, 11.146–93)

Minos: king of Crete; father of Ariadne and husband of Pasiphaë; son of Jupiter and Europa. He made war on Athens, Aegina, and Megara. He took Megara by the treachery of the king's daughter Scylla, but rejected her love. After Theseus had killed the Minotaur, Minos imprisoned Daedalus on Crete. (7.453–89, 8.1–151, 8.187)

Minyae: term used of the Argonauts, many of whom were descendants of the Thessalian King Minyas. (6.720)

Misenus: son of Aeolus; Trojan trumpeter and companion of Aeneas. At Cumae, he challenged Triton, trumpeter of Neptune, to a contest and was drowned in punishment. His funeral was held immediately before Aeneas' journey to the Underworld. (14.102–103n)

Myrrha: daughter of Cinyras, king of Cyprus. Afflicted by an incestuous passion, Myrrha secretly became pregnant by her father. To escape his anger Myrrha prayed for metamorphosis and became a tree. Later, her son Adonis was born through the bark of the tree. (10.298–514)

Naiads: water nymphs. (6.329)

Narcissus: beautiful young man who fell in love with his own reflection and wasted away, becoming a white flower. (3.346)

Nemesis: a goddess of vengeance. (3.406n)

Nereids: sea nymphs. (1.302)

Niobe: daughter of Tantalus; mother, by Amphion, of fourteen children. After she boasted that she had more children than Latona, the mother of Apollo and Diana, those gods systematically killed all of her children. In her grief, Niobe turned to stone. (6.148)

Notus: the South wind. (1.264)

Odysseus: Greek hero of the Trojan War who spent ten years trying to return home after the war. His Latin name is Ulysses (or Ulixes). (10.58–59n)

Olenos: man metamorphosed to stone along with his wife Lethaea, who had boasted excessively of her beauty. Olenos was not guilty, but chose to share his wife's punishment. (10.69)

Orpheus: Thracian poet, son of the Muse Mnemosyne; husband of Eurydice. When Eurydice died, Orpheus charmed his way into the Underworld with his singing. He was allowed to lead her out, on the condition that he not look back at her until completely out of the Underworld, but he was unable to resist the temptation. After losing his wife again, Orpheus rejected all women, practicing pederasty instead, and was eventually killed by a band of Maenads. (10.1–85, 11.1–84)

Pallas: name of Athena. (3.102)

Pandion: king of Athens, father of Procne and Philomela. (6.676)

Peleus: son of Aeacus; father of Achilles. Peleus' wedding to the sea goddess Thetis was attended by all the gods. Peleus participated in the Calydonian Boar Hunt, the voyage of the *Argo,* and the battle with the Centaurs. (8.380, 11.221–65, 12.193, 15.856)

Peneus: river god, father of Daphne. (1.452)

Perdix: nephew and ward of Daedalus. Perdix aroused his uncle's jealousy by inventing the saw and the compass, so Daedalus threw him off a cliff to his death. Perdix was transformed into a partridge. (8.237)

Persephone: Greek name of Proserpina, Queen of the Underworld, wife of Hades, and daughter of Ceres. (10.15)

Perseus: son of Jupiter and Danaë. Perseus killed the Gorgon Medusa and rescued the maiden Andromeda from a sea-monster. (4.665, 4.753–5.249)

Phaethon: son of the sun god. Granted a favor as proof of his parentage, Phaethon foolishly chose to drive the sun's chariot. When he lost control and threatened to burn the world, Jupiter struck him down with a thunderbolt. (1.747–2.339)

Philomela: daughter of King Pandion of Athens; sister of Procne. Taken to Thrace to visit her sister, Philomela was raped by her brother-in-law Tereus, who then cut out her tongue and imprisoned her. After informing Procne by means of a tapestry depicting her misfortune, Philomela helped her sister get revenge on Tereus and was then metamorphosed into a bird. (6.412–674)

Phoebe: the Moon. (1.11)

Phoebus: the Sun; also, Apollo. (1.338, 4.715)

Priam: king of Troy during the Trojan War; father of Paris, Hector, Cassandra, and many others; husband of Hecuba. Priam was killed by Achilles' son Pyrrhus during the sack of Troy. (14.474)

Procne: daughter of King Pandion of Athens; sister of Philomela; wife of Tereus, king of Thrace. In revenge for her husband's rape and mutilation of her sister, Procne killed and cooked her son Itys and served him to Tereus for dinner. She was then metamorphosed into a bird, along with the rest of the family. (6.412–674)

Procris: daughter of Erechtheus and wife of Cephalus. Suspecting her husband of infidelity, Procris spied on him in the woods as he was hunting; mistaking her for a wild animal, Cephalus killed her with his infallible spear. (6.682, 7.661–865)

Prometheus: son of the Titan Iapetus; credited with creating humans from clay and with giving fire to humankind. Father of Deucalion. (1.82)

Propoetides: women of Cyprus, punished for denying the divinity of Venus. They were afflicted with sexual depravity and became the first prostitutes, but later turned to stones. (10.238–42)

Proserpina: Latin name for Persephone, queen of the Underworld, wife of Hades, and daughter of Ceres. (5.346–571)

Pygmalion: sculptor from Cyprus. Shocked by the depravity of the Propoetides, he rejected women and sculpted for himself an ivory statue of a woman. At his prayer, Venus brought the statue to life so it could be his wife. (10.243–97)

Pyramus: Babylonian youth who fell in love with his neighbor Thisbe. Finding her bloody scarf at their rendezvous, he committed suicide. (4.55)

Pyrrha: pious woman, sole female survivor of the Flood, wife of Deucalion and daughter of Epimetheus. With Deucalion, Pyrrha regenerated humans from stones. (1.350)

Python: huge snake defeated by Apollo. (1.460)

Quirinus: name of the deified Romulus, founder of Rome. (15.863)

Rutuli: Italian people who opposed Aeneas and the Trojans. Their leader was Turnus. (14.455)

Saturn: a Titan, father of Jupiter, Juno, Neptune, Ceres, Pluto, and Vesta. After his overthrow by Jupiter, Saturn is said to have retired to rule over the Golden Age in Italy. (1.113, 15.858)

Saturnia: epithet of Juno. (3.293, 365)

Scylla (1): daughter of King Nisus of Megara. When King Minos of Crete was besieging her city, Scylla fell in love with him and betrayed her father and city, in hopes of winning Minos' love. Rejected by him, Scylla became a bird. (8.1–151, 10.28n)

Scylla (2): monster—originally a nymph—who threatened travelers at the Straits of Messina. The goddess Circe considered Scylla a rival for the affections of the sea god Glaucus and so transformed her into a monster with fierce dogs sprouting from her waist. (13.730–14.74)

Semele: daughter of Cadmus and mother, by Jupiter, of Bacchus. She was killed by Jupiter's thunderbolt, after requesting to see his true form. (3.261)

Sibyl: prophetic priestess of Apollo at Cumae; escort of Aeneas to the Underworld. When wooed by Apollo, she had been given the gift of long life, but since she continued to refuse him, she was not granted lasting youth. (14.104)

Silenus: satyrlike creature, relative of Pan, and foster-father of Bacchus. (11.101n)

Sisyphus: one of the great sinners found in the Underworld. As his punishment, Sisyphus eternally rolled a huge stone to the top of a hill, where it always rolled back down. (10.44)

Tantalus: famous sinner of the Underworld, who was punished for having killed, cooked and served his son Pelops to the gods at a feast. Tantalus forever tried to taste food and drink that receded from his grasp. (10.41)

Tereus: king of Thrace, husband of Procne. Tereus raped Procne's sister Philomela and cut out her tongue to prevent her from reporting what he had done. He was changed into a bird. (6. 412–674, 6.682)

Themis: a prophetic goddess of the generation of the Titans; occupant of Delphi before Apollo. (1.321)

Theseus: hero and legendary king of Athens; son of Aegeus. Traveling to Crete with Athenian prisoners, Theseus killed the

Minotaur and escaped with Minos' daughter Ariadne. Theseus also participated in the Calydonian Boar Hunt and many other exploits. (7.404–452, 8.263, 15.856)

Tiresias: Theban prophet. He mediated a dispute between Jupiter and Juno, prophesied Narcissus' fate, and warned of Oedipus' doom. (3.323, 339)

Titan: the Sun; or, one of the generation of gods before that of Jupiter. (1.10, 10.79)

Tityos: famous sinner in the Underworld, whose liver is constantly eaten away by vultures. (10.41–44n)

Triton: son and trumpeter of Neptune. (1.333, 14.102–103n)

Turnus: Italian warrior, leader of the Rutulians. A suitor for the hand of the princess Lavinia, he went to war against the Trojans when she was promised to Aeneas. (14.460)

Typhoeus: a hundred-handed, fire-breathing Giant, son of Gaea (Earth). As punishment for his attack on Olympus, he was blasted by Jupiter's thunderbolt and buried beneath Mount Aetna. (3.303)

Ulysses: Latin name of Odysseus.

Venulus: Italian messenger, who travels to visit Diomedes with Turnus' request for help. (14.457)

Zephyrus: the West wind. (1.64)